The Joseph Communications:
Trance Mission

The Joseph Communications:
Trance Mission

Michael G. Reccia

with thanks to:
Jane, David and Tony
and
Maria Luisa

Band of Light
I N C .

First Paperback Printing November 2013
Third Paperback Printing August 2018

eBook edition December 2013

Published by The Band of Light Inc. © 2018

1930 Village Center Circle #3-6568
Las Vegas, NV 89134
USA

thejosephcommunications.us

ISBN: 978-1-906625-06-1

Printed and bound in the USA by LSC Communications Inc.
www.lsccom.com

Contents

'the Field' and 'the Fall' – a Brief Explanation

If you are new to *the Joseph Communications* and have not read *Revelation, Illumination, Your Life After Death* and *the Fall*, the first four books in this series, allow me to qualify the terms 'the Field' and 'the Fall', which Joseph refers to at points throughout this book.

The Field

When referring to 'the Field' Joseph is describing the conscious field of thought-energy we, as spirits on Earth, are surrounded by and live within. Every second of our lives we project our thoughts and beliefs as to the nature of reality into this energy field. The Field is actually created and maintained *by us*, but we have lost sight of this fact. As a result of us forgetting this, which is in itself as a result of 'the Fall' (see below), the Field is not operating as it was originally intended to. It was supposed to serve us, but at the moment we, in effect, serve it. It exhibits, and seeks to perpetuate in us, a negative charge and outlook, and, because of this and its disconnection with God-Light, is maintaining itself and us via a finite and dwindling amount of energy. The Field in its present state, and therefore also we as human beings existing within it, cannot last much longer. Joseph urges us to re-energise the Field with God-Light and, by doing so, to transform it and take control of it once again for the betterment and continuance of mankind and of the planet.

The Fall

...is a term that Joseph applies to a complex decision and action taken by human souls millions of years ago which resulted in a cataclysmic change in vibration that plunged the Earth into a darkness we and the planet are still suffering from and feeling the effects of. This change in vibration separated us in conscious thought from our God-heritage and resulted in the negative, violent, power-hungry world and society we currently live in.

Chapter One

Connections – The unseen journey that introduced Joseph to the world

...THEY CALL THEM 'POINTS' IN THE UK. 'SWITCHES' IN THE US. Defined as *'a position on a railway track where the rails (the metal bars over which trains travel) can be moved to facilitate the transfer of a train from one track to another'*. Via those points the rail companies and their employees know exactly how to manoeuvre their trains so that they end up precisely where they ultimately want them to be. And while all the track switching needed in order to relocate a train from point A to point B is taking place its passengers, comfortably seated at those panoramic windows and enjoying the view, usually remain totally unaware of having been transferred from one set of rails to another in order that they might arrive at the destination whose name is printed on their tickets. In the normal course of events that location is anticipated and is aimed for by those passengers. They might not understand the mechanics that allow them to reach it, but they are heading for their disembarkation point by choice... it's somewhere they have *consciously* elected to be. Along the route there might be stops at various stations, allowing the travellers time to alight for a meal or a magazine, or to take in the view and the local atmosphere, but their ultimate goal is never in doubt – all they have to do is to sit back and let the train take them to it.

Imagine now, if you will, a train station into which four separate trains are pulling in at four different times from four different embarkation points to four different platforms at four different speeds. Each train pulls just a single carriage and each carriage accommodates just one passenger... and the amazing thing is that each of these four passengers had absolutely no idea when they each set out on their journey that this station would be a major, life-changing destination for them; somewhere they spiritually – and subconsciously – desired to arrive at so that they could meet as physical and spiritual beings and so that, as a result of that connection, they could seek to accomplish momentous things on behalf of a higher consciousness.

The first traveller is myself... As a painfully shy, sensitive, awkward, private youth at odds with the ways of the world the prospect of salesmanship, with its prerequisite of meeting and influencing people, was my absolute *last choice* of career. Why, then, upon leaving college, did I constantly find myself in selling situations, first as a tele-sales operative hawking advertising space to individuals over the phone and working from the offices of a large, local newspaper (the only position I could find following six months of unemployment); then, later, as a reluctant trade advertising salesman 'on the road' and based in those same offices? Later still, when I had questioned the ethics of the manipulative sales techniques employed by the newspaper to the extent that I just couldn't live with or support them any longer, I moved across to the title's design department as an advertising copywriter, a far gentler and more creative and ethical way of selling, but selling nevertheless, and copywriting and public relations then became my means of earning a living for many years, working both full time and freelance for various advertising agencies.

Little did I then know that these occupations, seemingly thrust upon me by random circumstance, were vital 'stations' I was compelled to stop at along the journey of my life in order to learn how to sell with words, how to become eloquent when explaining concepts, and how to *ultimately* 'sell' the message that life continues after physical death, delivered through me as a medium as a precursor to Joseph's trance communications. I didn't even realise I was on any kind of journey as this process was taking place, and that my train was heading inexorably towards that all-important 'station' that would connect me with the other members of the Band of Light.

Independent of my train but running parallel to it, David was physically and mentally on a train of his own, carrying with him metaphoric 'suitcases' packed with the acquired knowledge he would need to make his all important contribution to *the Joseph Communications*. He was an accomplished artist, had studied computers and computer programming at university, and had become expert at creating and writing the complex code needed to construct and maintain websites. He had also worked as a computer-based graphic artist for various printing companies, an occupation that would ultimately lead to us meeting. In private he had for many years been a voracious collector, examiner and consumer of esoteric writings, with the effect that, when we first met (instantly appreciating each other's company and quickly discovering a shared sense of humour) to collaborate on a magazine project for a friend and I happened to confide in him that I was a medium his reaction was one of calm recognition and genuine interest rather than ridicule or disbelief.

On a third track Jane's train was slowly but surely bringing she and I together as life partners whilst delivering her to her own essential selection of 'stations' along the way. Twenty-five years earlier, on leaving university, she had migrated from Yorkshire to Lancashire, UK, to take up her first managerial position with a Courtaulds clothing manufacturer located in the north-west of England. In subsequent years she had been employed by several companies in various capacities – textile buyer, quality controller, work study engineer, stock controller, finance and credit management – honing, during those times, the meticulous organisational skills she today draws on to ensure *the Joseph Communications* are recorded, documented, publicised and made available worldwide via the Band of Light.

From an early age Jane had been fascinated by ghost stories and at junior school even formed a 'spirit society' (her whimsical society 'rulebook' from the time is included at the end of this title – I defy you to read it without smiling). By her mid-teens, whilst retaining her steadfast belief in the Divine, she had rejected the dictates of her religious upbringing with their promise of eternal punishment for some souls handed out by a loving God. Jane's life changed forever in her mid-twenties when she visited a medium and was amazed and overjoyed at the irrefutable evidence of an afterlife given; her confirmation of there being much more to this life than the surface illusion. From that day onwards she determined to share that knowledge with as many people as she possibly could.

Our fourth train is transporting Tony, a highly successful textile industry specialist and businessman who, some years ago, and at the point of having just sold one of his companies for a considerable sum of money, couldn't understand why, now having access to virtually anything he could desire *materially*, he felt so empty inside. The sale – long in planning and preparation – just hadn't brought him the satisfaction he'd expected it to, and from that time onwards his inner thoughts were increasingly at odds with his exterior approach to life. It was, he felt, as if he was only paying lip service to the outer state of contentment he tried so hard to project. So pressing was this out-of-step feeling with the rest of the world that he decided to embark on a journey of personal spiritual growth, one that would take him to 'stations' that were radically different than those he had visited in younger life, and which would help his spiritual yearnings bear fruit and ultimately evolve to the point where he would found, fund and create the Sanctuary Of Healing in Lancashire, UK, a centre whose doors are open to clients seeking to benefit from alternative, non-invasive methods of healing and also to souls hoping to address and advance their own spiritual awareness.

Four trains... Four people... Four very specific sets of acquired skills... Couple this with a pressing timetable from 'above', put together by an elevated group of discarnate spirits working in accordance with Divine Will in order to help souls on Earth *remember, realise and change* whilst there's still time, and you have the unfolding of a series of converging connections that would eventually lead to *the Joseph Communications*. The fine details of how we four inevitably met and harmonised (and how, prior to those events, I had made a vital connection at an earlier 'station' with Joan, my spiritual teacher and mentor), with those points along the tracks constantly being switched and fine-tuned by Higher Authority in order that we do so, are chronicled in the introductions to other books in this series – it is the sheer magnitude of the intricate spiritual planning and shepherding at work behind the scenes I wish to draw attention to here:

...The spiritual evidence that our 'mission' had been pre-destined long before David, Jane, Tony and myself had drawn our first breaths in our present physical bodies.

...The fact that negative situations and distractions in our lives – and in mine in particular – prior to our connecting – many of them major, and many so complex and entangling that they would seem, to the impartial observer, destined to completely engulf one or all of us and extinguish any hope of a successful spiritual mission were negotiated, avoided, transformed and rapidly moved away from.

...The realisation that we had each been outfitted by life with *exactly* the right skills necessary to get Joseph out into the world: myself with the mediumistic gift that would eventually develop further into an ability to enter a trance state and allow Joseph to make his voice heard, plus the acquired proficiency to write about and express those concepts and deliver them when needed to an audience face to face; Jane with her tenacity, her flair for organisation, her knack for negotiating advertising space that would stretch our tiny budget so that it worked harder than anyone would suspect it could ever do to get the message out; David, ready and able to format our books, visualise our advertising, construct and maintain our websites, design and send out our mailshots, and Tony with his unique vision, drive and energy, who would provide the physical platform from which Joseph could springboard into public consciousness via the Sanctuary's meeting rooms, and constantly give essential encouragement, support and advice that would enable the books to be published and our global advertising campaigns to be undertaken.

Because we were able, in microcosm, to do what huge publishing concerns could accomplish drawing, by comparison, on only a tiny fraction of their considerable funding and facilities, *we could keep the message pure.* An editor from a large publishing house looking for the next best seller would inevitably want to change words and alter concepts to make them appeal to the maximum audience. Joseph had cautioned us that his words should not be changed and, as 'keepers of the flame', and because of our in-house skill sets and single-mindedness, we could ensure that they weren't. A large-scale operation would also seek to launch a book just once, giving it a limited lifespan, whereas we wanted to ensure that *the Joseph Communications* would be made universally and constantly available for the rest of our lifetimes ...and beyond.

We did, however, having all disembarked at that 'central station' and having met, harmonised and agreed upon a plan of action, need to do one more thing in order to launch Joseph's message out into the world – and that was to introduce him to 'his public'.

It was therefore decided, with Joseph's approval, that we should organise a number of public trance demonstrations, many of which would take place at the Sanctuary of Healing, so that the source and authenticity of his message could be viewed and examined up close. This was not a decision that was taken lightly, as trance mediumship is a dangerous undertaking even in ideal conditions, and to submit myself to unknown audiences, a small percentage of whom might be aggressive or hostile or wish to see us fail, or who might break the link through forgetting to turn off their mobile phones or by unwrapping sweets whilst I was in trance (both these things happened – the latter regularly – but, fortunately, Joseph was always able to maintain the connection) was not a prospect I relished. Joseph, however, needed to be witnessed publicly so that the word could spread, and so that we would have the authenticity of his sessions on record to add weight to the book material which had been gathered by us as a result of us meeting regularly in private, controlled conditions.

...And so we took Joseph 'on the road', as it were.

Those evenings were daunting for me. If held at the Sanctuary I would wait alone and nervous in one of Tony's consulting rooms or in his office as everyone arrived. Invariably, and despite detailed instructions as to what was expected on the night being given to all attendees by Jane, some individuals would arrive late, prolonging my agony. Then, at last, the voices from the meeting room would become silent, Jane would come down the corridor to collect me and I would walk back with her into a now-hushed room, filled with people, sit down as Michael, and then...

...Joseph would stand up.

My legs would be locked into position and I would stay rooted to the spot, motionless from the waist down, for anything up to an hour and three quarters as I vacated my body and mind and Joseph moved in, opening with a little address, then inviting questions from the audience and answering them with his usual fact and information-packed eloquence and gentle humour.

At the end of each session Joseph, having invariably overrun my physical frame and mind to the point of complete exhaustion, would reluctantly vacate my body and I would be drawn back into it, my first returning sensation being that of extreme pain in both legs. I would subsequently, following a few seated moments to allow me to literally gather my senses and take a few sips of water, hobble off through the silent audience back to the consulting room, where a tray of sandwiches and a piece of chocolate cake would be waiting for me, courtesy of Tony. These I would devour like a man who hadn't seen food for a week, bolting everything down without really tasting it in a frantic, almost instinctive quest to reacquire some physical and mental energy. On one occasion I remember peering into the mirror in my post-trace state, unable to recognise what I was seeing. On another I simply wanted to crouch in a foetal position behind the examination table in the room, shut my eyes and hide until I felt better... I might have been back in my body but I was definitely not myself. Following each demonstration it would take me at least a week to fully recover my wits and my energies – but the ultimate outcome would be the same – Joseph would have filled in some further blanks in our spiritual knowledge and his presence whilst doing so would be on record.

We held a demonstration in Ireland, where a very dark conference room in a hotel, completely devoid of spiritual energy, was quickly transformed into a chamber of light and power for the duration of the communication by our guides; and also in various other UK locations, at one of which the overhead lights were extinguished in a burst of high-pitched noise by the Field, and the transformer on our camcorder was fried, cutting short our visual recording. Our final public demonstration, back at the Sanctuary, and whilst not affecting the communication, was the subject of attack by negative forces, the consequences of which had a debilitating effect on us all for some weeks – Joseph was, after all, making available liberating spiritual knowledge that the world as it is did not want to 'go public'. Such were the effects of that final demonstration that we decided the public communications were becoming too dangerous for us all and for me in particular, and that we would, from that point onwards, continue to bring through Joseph's observations in private only, lest my health suffer too much.

By that stage we did, however, have a comprehensive visual and aural record of Joseph's twelve public appearances, the transcriptions of which are the subject of this book. Each chapter is prefaced by details of the date and the place where that demonstration was held, plus a list of the topics discussed on that occasion. Inevitably, certain queries are raised more than once across the demonstrations, with members of the congregation at different locations and gatherings wanting in particular to understand more about 'the Field' and 'the Fall'. In addressing these questions Joseph, however, always weaves further enlightening information into his answers so that the transcripts offer the reader a view of his mission that expands and becomes more comprehensive with each successive communication. We, therefore, feel you will discover something new and deeply thought-provoking in each communication, even on those occasions where variations of questions that have been addressed in earlier communications have been asked again. Also included at the end of the book are a number of additional questions asked of Joseph in closed Band of Light circle conditions by its members and never before published.

This book, then, is offered as an essential companion to the Band of Light's other *Joseph Communications* titles, as a unique insight into the times when this highly-evolved spirit addressed an audience directly, and as a source of essential and life-changing spiritual perspectives at a time when this planet sorely needs such input.

As for myself, Jane, David and Tony, Joseph's input into our lives and, via us, the lives of countless souls across the planet is still unfolding, and our connected journey continues. At the time of writing we continue to regularly sit in closed circle conditions to bring through additional information from him, and a further collection of liberating, essential, *amazing* spiritual insights are assembling themselves, chapter by chapter, into a sixth book, due for publication as soon as energies and circumstance allow its remaining communications to be brought through and transcribed.

Many readers have expressed a desire for further information concerning myself and my life and the Band of Light's activities. My answer to those requests has always been that it is the communications that are of importance, not me. I am simply a human being who has found himself at the centre of extraordinary events. I receive no dispensation from the challenges of life that are common to the human race at this time, and am simply the 'instrument', as Joseph calls me; the means of transmitting the information into this area of 'reality'. However, as a thank you to all those who have expressed appreciation for our efforts and have encouraged and supported us over the years, we thought it might be appropriate to include a small photographic section with this book, enabling you to at least fit faces to the names.

Of course, it's also me on the cover of this title ...in a sense, that is. It's my body and my face, but not, at the moment the photograph was taken, my *consciousness*. You're looking at Joseph in that image... not his features, not his body, but his essence. Me – the spirit me... the *real* me, not the outer shell – is out of the picture at that point, allowing Joseph to take over and do what he does best: reacquaint people with their spiritual heritage and bring them knowledge that allows them to change themselves, and this world, for the better.

Forever.

Michael G. Reccia
November, 2013

Chapter Two

Joseph Trance Demonstration – 3rd June, 2009
The Sanctuary of Healing, Lancashire, UK

Spiritual topics discussed:

Life in Atlantis.

Spirit photography.

Crop circles.

What mankind can do to save the planet.

How to lift our vibrations.

The dangers of narrow religious beliefs.

The state of 'no-thing'.

Letting go of emotional baggage.

Negativity from past lives.

Combating negative thought-forms.

Reincarnation.

Joseph's work through Michael.

The role of workers for the Light.

God.

The nature of time.

Joseph: It doesn't take long – it is like Michael stepping out through a 'door' and me stepping in. He resists me at times and I find that amusing because we have worked together for a long, long time – longer than just *this* lifetime. He has seen me around today; he has seen me in silver and it is the silver vibration that I bring through to you first of all.

...Silver because it cleanses; silver because it takes away the negative aspects of this physical life that you pick up as a matter of course each day; silver because it uplifts; silver because it is noble; silver because I want to begin by *reminding* you that each of you is a travelling soul; that each of you is on a journey of exploration, of experience, of evolution; to bring back to you the nobility that your world cancels out day after day; to say to you that you are loved – **that you** *are* **Love**; to remind you of where you are going; to remind you that all you see around you is illusion – all you see around you is smoke and mirrors and dreams; to remind you that there are other planes that await you, other places waiting to welcome you, other people waiting to teach you, to be taught by you, other vistas that will open up to you.

I look at this world and I ...'despair' is the wrong word... but certainly I am saddened. I am saddened by the way things are going; I am saddened by the way that brother treats sister/treats brother; I am saddened by the pain that is inflicted on this world and on you *daily* through your thoughts, through your angers that needn't be there, through your politics, through people who wish to manipulate, through people who think that the world is an endless source of supply.

The 'shop' is about to shut, Ladies and Gentlemen! The 'offers' are about to be withdrawn, and *we have to make a difference whilst we still can* or that 'closed sign' will be up permanently.

I don't suppose you are interested in me – I am certainly not interested in me. I am interested in *doing* rather than in being; I am interested in what we can do, why we need to do it, how things work. And so I would like to put myself to one side – as Michael has done – and I would like to invite your questions. Who would like to speak to me?

Shirley Hayhurst: I would like to ask a question, Joseph, and thank you very much – it is a real pleasure to be able to talk to you. It is quite a frivolous question in a way: when you came here and you were an Atlantean did you have the same sort of a body then that we have now or was it…?

Joseph [*smiling*]: I had a far better body than you have now!

Forgive my sense of humour. We were basically the same but we had a more etheric quality than you have now. Over the centuries the world has added to your cares as you have reincarnated and reincarnated and you are denser in form than you used to be. It was far easier for us to slip into different levels of consciousness; it was far easier for us to communicate with the spiritual side of life; it was far easier for us to communicate telepathically (as you would understand it). So, in the respect of our *souls*, we had very different capabilities than you have now, but the shame and the upset is that **you** *still* **have those capabilities** – they are masked, they are surrounded by the dense matter of the thoughts on your plane of existence that *prevent* you from being so much more than you could be.

So, yes, I was similar to you in form but the atoms within my physical body were more rarefied than yours – as were they for all of us, for our society. And society was far different than it is for you because we took decisions as a *group*. And you might say: 'Well, we take decisions as a group – we have parliaments, we have governments.' That is not what I mean. We would, on a *psychic* level, decide upon the way forward – the call would go out to each of us. We were aware of our role as part of the group soul whilst we were on Earth, and so we operated very much like the group soul does on the higher planes of existence. So, there would be the individual part of ourselves – the part that you would recognise as 'you' and the part that I would recognise as 'me' – but we would have an overall consciousness that permeated this individual consciousness. And along that consciousness would be transmitted thoughts, and hopes, and dreams, and desires, and questions and we could... (you call it 'multi-tasking' now) ...we could multi-task quite easily. We could exist on this level of consciousness and we could also exist on a higher level of consciousness and make decisions on *both* levels.

So, anatomically similar, yes, but spiritually, no – we had a greater advantage than you have today and, as I have said, the framework of our physicality was less heavy than yours, but this is because of the effects of the Field of consciousness upon you. It is not an individual fault; it is simply a circumstance that has been brought on by centuries of thinking and of reacting in a certain manner.

Does that answer your question?

Shirley: Yes, it does. Do you think that we will ever get back to that situation?

Joseph: I would not be here this evening if I did not think ...and know ...and wish ...and pray ...and get down on my knees to ask that you get back to that position. You must remember that you are already at that position *within*. It is simply masked, it is simply 'trapped', as it were, by the all-pervading Field around you and what we are trying to do, by raising your consciousness and your awareness, is break that outer shell so that the 'butterfly' emerges once again.

Shirley: Thank you.

Joseph: Who is next, please?

Cameron Collinge: I would like to ask a question, Joseph. There is much debate at the moment regarding orbs and whether they are actually spiritual existence or whether they are just light reflected off dust particles picked up by modern digital cameras.

Do you have an opinion on this?

Joseph: Yes, I have a very strong opinion on that, and the answer is: you are creating technology with our help, with our inspiration – because all inspiration is filtered down from the higher levels, all your great creations, all your moments of saying, 'Eureka!' have been because you have connected with higher levels that are trying to steer your world – and you have technology at this point that is far more sensitive than it used to be. And were you to see the spirit life, were you to see the higher spheres than this one, you would be aware of brilliant colours. Were you to see the astral level that is very close to this one you would be aware of a million thought-forms, a million dreams given form by the thought-process of millions of human beings. From moment to moment, as *you* measure it, these things – these aspects of life – are all around you.

You have cameras now that can capture the beginnings – just the *beginnings* – of spiritual truth. We try to influence them but you must understand that you have thousands and thousands of people who are going out *trying to capture orbs!* What they should try to do is to pray before they take photographs, is to hold their cameras and infuse those cameras with Love and with peace, to talk to the cameras because the camera is a part of the matrix of Creation, the camera is sentient, the camera can be spoken to and can be conditioned.

If you want better orbs talk to your camera, love your camera and say: 'I'm not looking for orbs. I'm looking for evidence that I can give to others that will convince others – not myself.' You should not need evidence for yourself but pray for manifestations that will convince others, that will set them thinking, that will allow them to break out of their prison, that will allow them to think: 'There's something else! There's something I don't understand.'

We have recently begun to influence the lights that are picked up by **the Band of Light** [*reference to the group that helps*

21

Michael] to include images. It is a long job because in order for us to do this we have to love the camera too, we have to love the people who are taking the photographs and we have to love the people on the other side so that their images can be reproduced by digital media. It is a long process and you will always find the Field saying, 'It is *this*. It is t*hat*.' If a thousand spirits now were to tap-dance in front of you, there would be those looking through the windows who tomorrow would say, 'That did not happen – it was a trick of the light!' It is so sad that human beings are so willing to believe in everything they see on this level and yet give so little time to the possibilities *within* themselves.

There will be further breakthroughs in technology that will leave people in no doubt regarding spirit communication (because orbs are part of that movement of communication) that they are capturing images, colours and scenes from *somewhere else*. Our worry is that people will treat this as a novelty and it takes a great deal of power, a great deal of energy to influence the cameras and the machines that you have at the moment.

There are advances in digital clarity with regard to moving images too and you will see, over the next few years, reports on your news programmes of orbs that are moving, of colours that are moving, of things photographed that were not there when the person photographed them. And this is part of our subtle infiltration of this level of existence so that we can shake those who are not *at this time* spiritually aware and just open that consciousness by a crack so that we can get some truth in there.

Was that satisfactory?

Cameron: Thank you very much.

Mr. Arkwright: Joseph, what do you have to say about the significance of crop circles?

Joseph: I have to say that there are many phenomena around your world that people do not understand. I am not involved in such things ...neither am I involved in taking a piece of wood and a length of string and recreating crop circles for the amusement of the person with the piece of wood and the piece of string!

Are you being communicated with from other spheres of intelligence? **Always!** Always ...but I would advise you that some of these things are peripheral, some of these things are – not base, 'base' is the wrong word – are on the sidelines, are elemental, are not what you should be looking for.

In your dealings with the spiritual realms always look for the highest, always say to yourself: 'Why should a spirit not be able to contact me directly? Why?' and then ask, through God's Love, that that happen to you. If we wish to talk to you – we have not the time to talk to you through symbols, not the time to talk to you in a covert way – if we wish to talk to you we will talk to you *openly* and that is what you should always seek.

Remember that when you seek something, a vibration goes out from you to pull into you and around you a vibration of *similar* quality. Therefore, if you are seeking only at an entry level, only at a peripheral level, then you will see in those things great messages. We don't want you to look at us as 'Gods', as people who wish to lift you up through signs and miracles; we want you to look at us as human beings who have moved on and are quite capable of communicating with you **if *you* know how to communicate with us**.

...And you communicate with us by lifting that vibration of expectation, by saying: 'I expect the best. I expect high spirit communication and I will not settle for anything less!' And in doing so, yes, your crop circles are important and some of the other peripheral things are important – like the investigation into crystals and the need to see a medium on a regular basis – all these things are important but you can make them less important and raise your game, raise your expectations so that what comes to you is of a higher level ...**is food for your soul**.

Is that satisfactory?

Mr. Arkwright: Yes, thank you.

Mike Sly: I would like to ask a question about the condition of the planet and you made reference to that at the beginning. As individuals we may feel limited in our capacity to influence the continued damage that is being caused to the planet; what are your views on what mankind can or can't do collectively at this stage?

Joseph: If mankind was to recognise its God-inheritance the planet would change instantly!

It is unfortunate that the Field puts perceived limitations on you, 'I can do this perhaps. I can never do that!' And that in itself is creation. 'I can do this perhaps' means that you create your ability to do this *perhaps*, 'I can never do that' means that you create an ability *to never do that*.

You are God.

Each of you in here is God ...and at the core there is no 'each of you' – there is simply God experiencing His universe from different viewpoints. God creates. It is God's nature to create. It is your nature to create; you create daily. Unfortunately, because of the dominant thoughts in this matrix of thought – this Field that surrounds you – you create more of the same. You create more unrest; you create more disease; you create more poverty ...because you *expect* these things. You are told that these things are true, therefore, that is the way it must be and you perpetuate the myth.

You perpetuate the bad dream.

In order to change this world you have to change your outlook.

You have to believe in and see the world *you want*. And you have to be very strong and very brave, and you have to look at your news programmes and say, 'That is one point of view but it is not my point of view!' When the person in the street says that you are not looking well today, you say, 'That is one point of view but it is not my point of view!' And you begin to use the Light that you inherit to change things.

The world needs a makeover; the world needs the Love that Michael was talking about initially [*reference to Michael's opening remarks prior to going into trance, not included here*]. **The world needs Love!** And I look through Michael's eyes and I see his disgust when he sees people dropping cigarettes on the tarmac or throwing litter on the floor because the world is a spirit, the world is alive and — more to the point — the world is God and the world is part of *you*.

The world needs protecting and loving. When was the last time we said: 'Thank you, Earth, today for sustaining me, for sustaining my life, for giving me the oxygen I need to breath whilst I am alive on this level, for giving me beautiful vistas, for continuing to turn in space so that I can stand upright'? So few say these things, so few realise these things and it is your task — our task — to make the difference by *thinking differently*. We run around as human beings and say: 'I must do something. I must *do* something!' No, you must *be* something! You must be the person who thinks differently — before *doing* there is *being*.

You become the Light that changes the world through your meditations, through your thoughts and through what you say to others. And you change things where you can; you become brave enough to point out that there is another way; you become brave enough to say, 'The Earth is alive!' And many will laugh at you — it doesn't matter, some of that 'seed' will go in and in certain people it will begin to grow …that is how you change the world.

The world is in a very depleted state because mankind is in a very depleted state. Why? Because that is how mankind *thinks*. Someone has to think differently and it may as well be you ...and you ...and you ...and you.

It starts now! It starts here!

If you want to change your world ...change it ...see it ...dream it ...be it ...become it ...create it!

Forgive my soap-box attitude but this is a very passionate subject to me. Does that answer your question?

Mike: Yes, thank you.

Joseph [*pointing to the other side of the room*]: Someone over here, please!

Adam Bernard: I've got a question – when we talk about 'lifting vibrations' what does that mean? Does it mean being more positive about situations and things like that?

Joseph: The vibrations you give out as a soul are of a certain resonance; they are like a wave-form and you will know (as every human being does) that during the course of a day you can go from happy ...to sad ...to despairing ...to ecstatic ...to tired ...to in pain ...to healthy – all these things are going up and down the wave-form on a daily basis.

The problem is when the wave-form dips and you identify in your thoughts with something that is less than beneficial to you **then you draw more of it to yourself.** In other words when you are despairing, when you are despondent, when you are upset there are vibrations out there that are of a *similar* resonance and you pull them towards yourself so you become *more* upset. Isn't it so difficult when you are down to get up again?

When you lift your spirits, when you lift your mood, you operate on a totally different level. Your vibrations quicken and, because they quicken, they have access spiritually, psychically and intuitively to a **whole new world** – a world where people are happy, a world where you can tune into your intuition and can discover what to do next with ease, a world where you can bring joy to others because your vibrations have lifted. They are still your vibrations but they are operating at a *quicker* rate so you are at the top of the wave.

What we would ask of you is to try and keep those vibrations up for longer each day. If you feel despondent say: 'Well, this accomplishes nothing and it doesn't matter! What is the worst that could happen to me? I am letting go of this!' And by letting go of it and aiming for a higher vibration you lift your vibration, you bring in the sunshine and the Light that you want to feel better.

It is a little like hypnotising yourself at the beginning. It is a little like saying: 'No matter what is in front of my eyes – I am happy. No matter what is in front of my eyes – I know what to do next. No matter what is in front of my eyes – I know that my connection with God can never be broken so everything is alright. If I lose my physical life it doesn't matter – I cannot lose my soul; I cannot lose my connection to God. If I lose my job it doesn't matter – there is another one because God is taking care of me.' And by changing your attitude you change the rate of your vibrations and you bring to you that which you desire, and you bring to mankind that which you desire for mankind.

Do you see?

Adam: Yes, thanks.

Joseph: Thank you. Who else, please?

Phil Kubilius: Joseph, can I ask you a question? There is a Gnostic society that some of my family have got involved with called the C.E.A. and it was founded by a man called Samuel Aun Weor who lived in Venezuela and the current leader is called Ernesto Baron. I wondered if any of those names resonate with you and if you could tell me anything?

Joseph: They mean nothing to me.

If you have read the book, you will know that religion is one of the problems of today's society and that groups are one of the problems of today's society. People tend to want to label themselves, 'I belong to *this*. I belong to *that*.' ...and it is not always healthy because, in belonging to a group, you tend to want to operate within the parameters of that group and cut yourself off from possibilities *outside* the parameters of that group.

Labels at any level of life are dangerous. Labels cut off the ability to think outside of the box, to expand thought and to let concepts in that do not agree with the concepts you have by attaching yourself to a particular label. I would always in any group say: 'As your measure of what that group is doing, does that group enhance mankind? Does that group enhance its members? Is that group loving? Is that group patient? Is that group peaceful? Does that group love those who are not in the group or does that group become fearful when there are those around who do not believe what the group believe?'

There is truth, and Light, and creativity, and the ability to access God *within each of us* and at the basis of many religions and organisations there is truth, and Light, and the ability to contact and work with God. But then we see in macrocosm what happens outside. We see that people become polluted by the very rules that perhaps *once* were meaningful and perhaps *once* were helpful ...and the group becomes solidified as a consciousness and then it cannot move on and is useless to the cause of furthering the evolution of mankind.

My only concern with *any* group is – is that group capable of furthering the spiritual evolution of mankind?

And these are difficult questions, particularly for those who are attached to such groups. If you are worried by that association, you must put Light into the group. You must put Light into those members of the group that you are associated with. You must pray that the God within them talks to them – and sooner rather than later the God-within *shall* talk to them by bringing to them circumstances that will make them think, that will check them in their step and allow them to look at things with spiritual eyes. I do not wish to condemn religion – I wish to condemn that part of religion that imprisons people and that part of religion that stifles the soul.

Do you see?

Phil: Yes, good answer – thanks!

Joseph: Someone else, please!

[*Long pause*]

Someone else, please!

John O'Brien: Joseph, I would like you to speak about the 'no-thing' that you wrote about in your book [*reference to **Revelation***], about the field of energy that has no substance but can be shaped into substance and bring about form, as part of God's Creation and a gift to us to use.

Joseph [*laughing*]: Yes! Yes is the answer to that. Yes, yes, *yes* – that is exactly right!

Minute by minute, second by second, we are bringing things out of the no-thing *now*. Each of you is bringing things out of the no-thing and I, on my level, am bringing things out of the no-thing. But you see it as normal; you see it as a physical thing;

you see it as circumstances that you are at the mercy of ...when in fact you, individually and creatively, are contributing to those circumstances and are creating those circumstances from the no-thing.

It is refreshing at times to go back to the no-thing and live within that *potential*, to say: 'I will be back soon (and I am talking about my level and other levels). I need to go and contemplate my potential, other potentials, your potential, and to exist *without form* as energy (which itself is only a term for nothing – no-thing) and to contemplate and to be delighted in what could be, what might be, what will be – dependent on what I choose, what those around me choose, what the group souls choose and what God chooses through us as His will.'

The no-thing is a wonderful, peaceful experience and it would be of benefit to each of you in here to visit the no-thing in your imaginations ...to sit in God's Love and in God's Light and to slowly erase all of the things around you in your everyday lives until you are left just with you – not as a physical body – but you as a consciousness and you in the Light.

What a glorious thing to do!

What a *restorative* thing to do because – as you address the no-thing, as you rub out the physical concepts around you – you can rub out the illness; you can rub out the worry; you can rub out the animosity you feel for someone (and really know you shouldn't); you can rub out yesterday; you can rub out the effects of yesterday on today just for a little while and you can exist in the no-thing, and commune with yourself and with your God.

I would recommend that exercise for a few moments, for a few minutes or for as long as you feel comfortable with it *each day*, and in doing that you reset the clock, you reset the stopwatch. And when you come out of the no-thing you are starting again with opportunities that you have brought to yourself by being in that contemplative state: 'The illness belongs to *before* the nothing; the pain belongs to before the no-thing – they are gone. There is only what I choose to bring though now and when I am tired and when I am weary I can go into the no-thing with my God and simply *be*.'

Just simply *be*!

You have so much to do – so much to do every day of your lives that you do not seem to have the time to *be*. **When you simply *be* God speaks to you.** If you say, 'God speaks to me,' on this level, you will be locked up ...but God speaks to you constantly, communes with you and you are able to access that speech (either at a refined level through going into the no-thing or at a denser level through the things that happen around you) but God is constantly speaking. And the no-thing – that no-state – is the best way to commune with Him and also to ask that all important question ...not, 'How do I get rid of the pain?' ...not, 'Where is the new job or the new car?' ...not, 'Where is someone to love?' ...but that all important question, '**What would You like me to do?**'

Isn't that a turn round in praying? 'What would You like me to do? Is there anything I can do for You, Father? Is there anything I can say on Your behalf? Is there anyone You want me to visit? Is there anything I can do to help the people around me? What do You want me to do?'

And sometimes God will say *something,* and sometimes God will say *nothing,* and sometimes God will simply say, 'I love you' and you will come out of the no-thing refreshed and able to take up the mantel of the physical life once again.

Thank you. Another question, please!

Female member of the audience: Joseph, in the book you tell us about us manifesting stuff all the time but never un-manifesting, and so we just grow layer, after layer, after layer and get denser and denser. And, if I remember rightly, you recommend that we should spend time just letting go of things that we have manifested – is that what you were talking about just then or is it something else?

Joseph: It is an aspect of what we were talking about then. You begin to add layers to your physical existence from the moment you are born:

'Ouch that slap was upsetting – I will remember that in case it happens again; I will carry around a record of it with me in case it happens again.'

'Why does that person not like me in the playground? I will remember that and I will act accordingly in case I get hurt in the future by what I am carrying around with me from the past.'

As you add to your experiences – remember that you are in a negatively-charged Field that adds to the intensity of those experiences that makes them seem real to you *years after* they have actually happened because that is what the Field wants. The Field wants to remain as it is and anything that you can contribute to the negativity of the Field helps the Field and slows you down.

As you grow older your ability to exist on this level *effectively* is determined by the amount of baggage that you carry around with you within the physical Field. There is an exercise that you can do: you can sit and you can meditate and you can go back through the 'files' of your life. And you will know when you have hit a point of baggage because it will hurt you, because you will relive it, because you will say: 'How could that person have done this to me? How could that person have acted in that way? How could I have been hurt? How could I have been so afraid? How can I have been in so much pain?' And you will relive it.

At that point *let it go*.

Ask that someone come – a messenger from God come – and stand in front of you and to that messenger you can hand each of those painful points. But you have to *really* and *truly* want to let go, because another unfortunate effect of the Field is that we become used to the negative things in our life and they become a crutch: 'I am in pain but I am used to that pain – I am frightened of what *else* there might be out there. I am in sorrow; I am in poverty but I am used to those things – they have become my perverted friends.'

You do not need friends like that! You need to let go of those circumstances.

You will find that, as you do so, when you come back to a physical level you will stand straighter, you will stand tall, you will find that certain of the physical ailments that assail you will disappear faster than they ever could through physical treatment or through pills and potions. You will find that you feel younger, more alive, more alert, more able to take notice of what is happening around you at this moment.

And what is happening around you at this moment is vitally important because it determines, within your linear existence, what happens to you in the next moment ...and the next moment ...and the next moment.

Letting go is *very difficult* for a great many people but it is so vital and people often bury their pains and say: 'I couldn't get rid of that because I couldn't face it. I couldn't face seeing that pain or experiencing that pain again.' In those cases you have to be brave, in those cases you have to have to put your hand into God's hand and say, '*Father, off we go!*' And you will find that you can remove the baggage from your past and from your aura and from your dense vibrations without the pain that you expected to find there.

It sounded as you were talking to me like you were saying that things got heavier, and heavier, and heavier. Well, they do in the normal course of things, but in this room we are not experiencing the normal course of things – we are experiencing the *spiritual* course of things. We are experiencing liberation and it is liberation that I want and the people who work with me want. This is not 'I' in the sense of 'Joseph, the Great I' – this is Joseph in the sense of *Joseph the spokesperson* that wants you to be free, wants you to be happy, wants you to be peaceful and wants you, more than anything, **to come home.** We don't want you to be here – not for life ...after life ...after life ...after life. We want you to come home, and this is why I am speaking this evening and this is why I am using someone else's physical facilities to get through to you. Have I answered your question?

Questioner: Yes, thank you.

Tony Clarkson: Can I ask a question further to that question?

Joseph: Yes.

Tony: This denseness and heaviness that accumulates, can it come from before life or can it come also from external sources like the Astral Plane?

Joseph: That is an excellent question and it is a long answer. Consider this: if you drag with you baggage from one life and have not learned by the end of that life to let go of it, isn't it reasonable to assume that you will also drag *cumulative baggage* that relates to the physical with you so that when you reincarnate it is waiting for you as a 'nice present'? **...But not from anyone else – from yourself!** You have not yet decided that you have had enough of these circumstances and so you drag them around with you. It is inevitable if you come back into a physical body and you have not yet worked those things away from you that they come to visit you and to haunt you once again.

As I explained earlier, there is also a problem with low vibrations. When you become low, when you become upset, when you become disturbed or in pain then you resonate at a certain low level. And, unfortunately, there are existing *at a similar level* various thought-forms, various entities, various spirits who have not learned, who find you a very attractive 'snack' indeed, who regard the vibrations that you are putting out as something that will draw them closer to the physical; and so they try to anchor onto you, to attach themselves to you and to maintain – and this is important – **to maintain the low level of energy that you are putting out.** They cannot absorb higher levels of energy **but they *can* absorb your misery.** And so you have people, do you not, who say: 'I have been depressed for days and I don't know why. I can't seem to find any joy in life and I don't know why.'

There is *something* you can do …and the something you can do is to raise your vibrations above the level of those who would perpetuate your low-level vibrations. You can do it in several ways but meditation is the most effective way to go. You can see yourself travelling up an escalator, and at the bottom of the escalator you have grey, grey scenery and as you progress up the escalator it becomes increasingly light – increasingly light – until at the top you are stepping off that escalator into a land of perfect, brilliant, beautiful, loving, warm Light. Stay there as long as you can and then bring yourself out of your meditation by returning to this level of consciousness, and you will help to rid yourself of the things that you pick up on a daily basis.

It sounds terrible doesn't it? It sounds like the Earth is such a dangerous place.

Well, I have news for you – it is!

It is and, just as angels minister to you, there are darker aspects of mankind that would also communicate with you in a ruinous way if they got the opportunity. This is not a reason to be afraid; this is another reason to understand the mechanics of spirituality and the physics of spirituality. Once you understand something then it loses its power over you. And, please, if you wake up on a certain morning and think, 'I am depressed and I don't know why' – begin to separate yourself from that depression ...begin to say, 'This is not me!' ...begin to say, 'Where is this coming from?' ...begin to say, 'Thank you very much but I want no more of this – you can have back that gift!' ...begin to meditate and lift your vibrations and see how quickly you will be on top form again and how much better you will feel.

Have I answered your question?

Tony: Absolutely excellent, thank you.

Joseph: I will just say a little bit about some of the people who work with me. You would not imagine, would you, that we, as spirits, grow anxious? But we do grow anxious for mankind and we grow impatient, and we have to take ourselves away and we have to meditate and we have to say: 'Enough of this, *Joseph*, this is not the way to do it! You have to become calm or you will be of no use to the people on Earth.'

We are anxious because we can see what you cannot see because we can see the other layers of consciousness that operate around you that try to influence you and we can see the Field. Oh, dear me, the Field! Oh, dear me, the thickness, the heaviness, the stickiness of the Field of mankind that always expects the worst ...and so creates the worst! And so we become anxious and so we try to imprint orbs onto photographs, we try to make a difference to make you aware wherever we can. And it is a privilege to be able to talk to you this evening and it is a privilege we want to expand. It is a privilege that we want to see operating all over the place – not with me as a speaker – but with similar speakers, a similar group-consciousness bringing these points of Light around the globe so that they network, so that they join up and give us less anxiety and give you the lives that you *deserve*.

You *deserve*!

I want to get *that* through to you tonight: you deserve a good life; you deserve to be healthy; you deserve to create and be happy in your creativity. You deserve all of these things because you are an outpouring of God and God deserves to create; God deserves to have Love. You deserve these things and, unfortunately, the Field ingrains you with a sense of being inadequate from the time that you are born: 'You don't really deserve this. You don't really deserve the riches. You don't really deserve the health. You don't really deserve the Love. You don't really deserve the peace.'

Of course you do!

This is one of the things that you must take away and let go of, 'I am not worthy!' Yes, *you are*! Whilst you say, 'I am not worthy' you are not worthy because *you create the unworthiness*. You have to say, 'I deserve the best!' Remember that your religions often tell you that you do not and it is good to be poor. Is God poor? Does God at the end of the week have to look for loose change to make ends meet? Of course not! You do not have to be poor! There is nothing worthy about being poor and being poor comes from being poor in spirit – from not understanding the mechanics of the physical universe that you are a part of for a short time.

Is there another question, please?

John Hill: Can I ask a question? A little while ago you mentioned reincarnation. Well, if we have reincarnated several times from a distant past to where we are today, we must be higher up the ladder from where we started, presumably. And, if it is so, if we are in a kind of trouble before we arrive on this Earth and if all the people we meet at that point [*are too*] surely we must be *having to* meet people because of lessons we have not learned. So, all this going forward can only be done if you have met people that add to those problems, which have met you on the way back. If you cannot advance further on this ladder without having problems – I hear you talking about how to get rid of your problems – but if it is a logical progression from a long time ago to where we are today, and if it is a structural ladder surely we *need* the knocks, we need the experiences from all these people? And someone might come for about two minutes to say, 'Good morning' and you feel wonderful but it doesn't mean to say you have spend twelve weeks with them or anything. Everyone who is a partner – you are spending some time with someone and you are actually spending a lifetime but somebody you meet on the bus you are spending half an hour with and so for that person to get to meet you, if you get a lesson from that meeting and if it is a bad lesson you have to meet it so someone is helping you – is it an intricate way of going up the ladder that is leading towards a spiritual solution?

Joseph: Gosh, that's a *busy* question!

[*Audience laughter*]

There is a spiritual ladder but for a number of people they keep revolving around the same rung, and we have to bring into the answer to your question, the question of free will. If you do not as a soul – and remember only *part* of your consciousness is on the surface, as it were – if you do not as a soul *wish* to leave this plane, I cannot make you leave, God cannot make you leave, the people who are part of your spiritual family on that side cannot make you leave because you are exercising your free will.

The only way that you can *eventually* decide to stop spinning around that rung and take a step up is through God speaking to you (as I mentioned before) via the things, as you rightly say, that happen to you in life. And the things that happen to you in life, if you consider your life, are a series of letting-goes, of saying: 'I have had that experience – I don't need it. I have touched the fire – I don't want to do that again. I have sat for a thousand years on a rock contemplating mankind – I don't need to do that again.' ...until eventually, through your own volition and no one else's (because God has given you ultimate free will), you decide that you have had enough of the physical existence and want to explore elsewhere.

Of course there are good spirits (there are no other kinds of spirit), of course the people that you meet on the bus or at work or wherever you meet them... of course they are good spirits. It is only a degree: you have a good spirit or a positive spirit or an evolving spirit and you have a spirit that is also evolving that is mired in the stickiness of the Field – we talk about 'good' and 'evil' in the book [*reference to **Revelation***] and about how those are misnomers.

But your reincarnations do not have to be nose-to-tail; they do not have to be this helter-skelter of coming back ...and coming back ...and coming back ...and coming back because [*smiling*], like everything else in your world, there is some queuing involved. And so you do return to a very pleasant place and are allowed to live in that place and are allowed to look at your options, but ultimately there are still many spirits who feel that they have unfinished business on Earth and that unfinished business needs to be taken care of in one lifetime or in a dozen lifetimes. And so given the option (I know this sounds strange to you on a physical level) of moving on or returning to address what *they* see – not what God sees, not what the advisors who sit around them and try to help them see – what *they* see as being imperative in the growth of their soul, they come back *mistakenly* to repeat what has happened before or to terminate, as they see it, unfinished business by bringing it, as they see it, to a conclusion.

There is no 'unfinished' business – there is only experience and the results and consequences of that experience ...but [*smiling*] as they say, you try telling that to the kids these days! People want to come back until they don't and so, yes, the experience is there to teach you and, yes, it is beneficial but it is a long-cut. It is a painful way round when the quick journey, when the short-cut is to go within and experience the truths within and apply those truths to your life because they transform your life. And you look at things that before were so important to you and say, 'They don't matter anymore.' Or you look at them and say, 'I was tied to this situation, now I choose not to be.'

So, yes, of course mankind is evolving but not quickly enough! The Earth is finite on a physical level; the Earth is tied into the Field and the two are in a worrying state at the moment, so we are trying to bring Light into individual consciousness to light up their existence so that they know from the heart, *from within*, why they are here, how long they should be here and where they want to go to next. And we are trying to bring Light to the globe too, to disperse the Field as it is and to return this world to the Utopia it once was.

Have I answered that very complex question?

John: Yes, thank you.

Joseph: Thank you. God bless!

OK. [*Pause*] Three more questions, please!

Gale Sagar: I have a question. When Michael started talking [*reference to his introduction*] he said that you had worked with him a long time in other lives – have you done this kind of work with him before in another life, and when Michael's life ends on this Earth plane what will you do then?

Joseph: I will be joyous and also very sorry in equal measure. We have touched the group soul that Michael is a part of before, but 'before' is a relative term because time does not unfold itself quite for us as it does for you. And there has been preparation for people like Michael and groups of people who are working through this world now for a long time, because there first has to be the volition to return on behalf of the spirit – in this case Michael – who seeks to bring through the information. Remember what we have just been talking about – there comes a time when the spirit wants to move on and says, 'Oh, gosh, do

I really have to go back?' And so there has to be a preparation process; there has to be a cutting-off process where the speaker does not have access to the layers of his (in this case) soul that would make this journey something that he would not undertake. Had he full knowledge of who he was on a soul level he would seek to step aside from this work and not go through his own personal evolution as a soul – because you have to remember that Michael is also evolving as a soul and Michael has trials and tribulations to go through.

But the answer to your question is *I have known him for a long time*. He cannot remember that – he believes that I made contact with him around five years ago but that is not the case. I made *physical* contact with him then, with his physical mind and physical body, but I have been in contact with him since his moment of incarnation. It had to be so. The other guides that work with him are also connected to him in this way.

I have my separate existence. I have my life which is rich and full and I enjoy it, and there are times when I need to retreat but I am always linked to Michael so that communication can take place when it is asked for. Mine is not the function of a guide who will speak to him through his intuition to help him through those creaky, difficult moments of his life. My function is to bring through communication. I am aware to a lesser or a greater degree, depending on how close to Michael's sphere of influence I am at any given time, as to what is happening in his life but I am not allowed to interfere with anything that is happening in his life. Certain of his guides are allowed to advise him through his intuition (as your guides advise you through your intuition) but I am not allowed to do that (which is upsetting to me at times) because my sole function is *purely* to act as a communicator.

Is that a suitable response?

Gale: Yes, thank you.

Joseph: Another question, please!

Mary: Can I ask a question, Joseph? A lot of people have come forward to work for the Light – is that helping the Field and is that helping to lighten the load?

Joseph: Any worker for the Light lightens the load. What you have to remember is that you have a global Field, you have a Field that is influenced by millions of souls and, as I am sure each of you in this room realises, whenever you work for the Light there is an equal pull to try and take you away from that work, and the harder you seem to work for the Light, the harder and tougher it seems to be to reach that Light.

I do not want to discourage you (I have no business to discourage you) because every act of Light and Love *does* lift people up, but you are not yet at the stage where there is enough of a change of mind globally for there to be a *permanent* difference in the Field. Having said that, there are miracles on a daily basis and they are brought about through communication and through manipulation of people who are working for the Light – so do not be discouraged.

Also understand that there is a plan to all this; that, as you say, there are many people now who are being born who are ready to work for the Light who have certain of their soul memories intact so that they can sweep aside the physicality of this world more quickly than most people can and start to make a difference... and it is the 'ripples in a pond' effect. Ripples in a pond – there is a ripple over there ...there is a ripple here ...there is a ripple in front of you ...there is a ripple behind you ...there is a ripple that *you* have caused ...ripples of Light going out into the Field. And the more ripples of Light, the more the Field becomes charged with Light and begins to change, which is the plan for it ...but it is a long job in terms of physical time.

It is a long job because the world is rooted in adoring materiality. It believes that happiness exists in the next car, or the next house, or the next DVD, or the next object... and when do those objects ever bring happiness? And those objects are being worshipped. God does not require your worship – He requires your attention so that His plan can work through you.

You solidify the objects around you by adoring them, by giving them power. So, you see on a physical level a representation of what is happening on a soul level to your world – you see the fridges and the televisions piling up, you see the rubbish, you see the junk, and this is again God speaking to you and saying: 'This is what is happening within the Field that you are a part of.' Take your eyes off the materiality, withdraw from it. Use it, yes, but do not become a part of it. Do not buy into it to the extent that your soul suffers.

...A big job but many people are being born to change things. Within a couple of generations (please God, Father above and within, please God!) things will change more rapidly, more quickly. There have to be pioneers and you are a pioneer. Keep on!

Have I answered your question?

Mary: Yes, thank you.

Joseph: I am going to have to give this body back in a moment.

Joe Hellak: You mentioned the word 'God' many times, Joseph, which is a word that doesn't sit comfortably with a lot of people. How should we conceive God or is that purely an individual thing?

Joseph: You come from Divine Consciousness. You *are* Divine Consciousness. On a God-level there is nothing else but Divine Consciousness.

It hurts us to realise that people are uncomfortable with the term 'God' but they are uncomfortable with the term 'God' either because they have approached God through religion and found Him wanting or because they look at the world with physical eyes and say: 'There cannot be a God – if there was a God such things would not exist.'

Well, such things would not exist if we all changed our minds – *nothing* to do with God. Not God's fault! *Not God's fault!*

And many religions build, around their image of God, rules:

Do this or God will be upset! ...Don't do this and God will reward you! ...Do not talk to these people! ...Do not embrace those people! ...Do not think outside of our rules!

And those who are brainwashed by such religions look at God and think: 'What a terrible God! How can God be like this?' *God is not like this.*

GOD IS. YOU ARE. That is all there is to Creation.

That is all there is to everything:

GOD IS.

YOU ARE.

You exist to experience on behalf of yourself and on behalf of God. Everything else is where it gets muddy; everything else is where it goes wrong. We have to bring back to mankind the concept of there being an 'Issuer' – a Father that brought us forth but a Father *that is also us*. We have to bring that concept back because with Godlessness you have the society that you see in front of you. But it is a difficult task because, in connecting people with God in the *right way*, you have to strip away their misconceptions, their preconceptions and their disbeliefs.

'I cannot see God!' say the atheists ...and they see nothing but God in front of them and within themselves, and they will continue to exist when they pass from this life *despite* themselves.

What a shock – and so much work that needs to be done in order to bring them around to the concept that:

1) They are still alive.

2) God exists and is part of them ... *is* them.

When we deny God we deny ourselves, we deny what we are and there is so much fear of being more than the individual on this level of consciousness, of being anything more than one point. As I stand talking to you, I am also viewing myself talking to you through your eyes. As I stand talking to you I also sit at home in my level – on my illusion that I can collapse at any time and go into the 'no-thing'. I cannot hurt you. I cannot call you. I cannot judge you because *I am you* and *I am God* and *you are God*.

God is not the property of priests. God is not the property of elite religions. **God is you and you are part of each other for ever and ever and ever and ever. Amen.**

Have I answered your question?

Joe: Yes, thank you.

Joseph: I am reminded of cars with boosters on them where you can just boost to get a little more fuel out and, with Michael's permission, that is what I intend to do because there is still energy for communication. I may have to exit at some point and, if I do so, thank you in advance for listening to me but does anyone else have anything they would like to ask?

Male member of the audience: I have a question... you talk about time and that time is different for you. Is time set linearly or can you go forwards and backwards as you wish?

Joseph: You experience your outside world, your physical world on this level as a linear existence ...point ...to point ...to point ...to point moving forwards, but isn't it also true that *within yourself* you experience movements in time backwards and forwards? You relive things that happened to you seemingly years ago. You go forwards and extrapolate as to what will happen to you in the future. The nature of time can be dismissed by presenting good mediumship as an argument because, through your good mediums, the future (as you see it) can be seen. What is actually been revealed to the medium, through communication with higher levels of being, are the consequences of what happens to a person extrapolated into their future experiences...

Sorry let me re-group that – I am losing the communication. I am sorry but I will try to answer the question.

Yes, we can re-experience, on our level, things that have happened to us 'before' (as you would understand it) – we can revisit those lives and relive those lives. And at a certain point in your future you will do the same thing because you will revisit the life that you are living now, and not just revisit it and review it, but **relive parts of it so that you can understand the experiences that you have gone through.**

Time does not exist but in order for you to experience a physical existence it has to have an order; it has to have a linearity. But that linearity, if you step back from it, is a circle, and your experience of your life is a point at any given time within and upon a circle that leads you back to the spirit world so that you can start out on another cycle of experience.

So, your perception of time is, in reality, a cycle of experience and not time at all.

You experience decay on a physical level and you measure time through decay – someone is getting older, that building is falling apart. Decay and time are two different things. You attribute something to decay that does not actually exist. And have you noticed how you can travel backwards and forwards in time dependent on how you are enjoying or being upset by an experience? If you are in a bubble of delight over something that you love doing the available time seems to go very quickly. If you are sad or upset or bored through something that you are having to experience – that time seems to go very slowly. An hour of joyous time goes quickly; an hour of sad time goes slowly …but in both cases, *isn't it an hour?*

You have the ability to travel backwards and forwards in time *now*. You do so at night because at night you leave your physical body and you reunite with the people that you know on the spirit level – with your guides, with your spiritual family, with your group soul – and you are outside of time. You may see – or mediums see – spirits who come to them at different points in their incarnations so the same spirit can visit a medium once and [*the medium can*] see him as a child and another time see him as an old person or even a different person because it is all to do with the internal clock – with the clock of experience.

I am sorry, I am going to have to terminate the communication because I have tired the instrument beyond the point that I should do so. I should know better, *I do know better …but I will do it again*!

[*Audience laughter*]

47

Chapter Three

Joseph Trance Demonstration – 19th June, 2009
The Sanctuary of Healing, Lancashire, UK

Spiritual topics discussed:

How to raise the collective consciousness of the planet.

Global pandemics.

Jesus.

Balancing masculine and feminine energies.

The Field and the Fall.

Sending out the Light to help save the world.

2012.

Living spiritually and tuning into the heart-centre.

God and spiritual hierarchy.

Who meets us when we pass over into the spiritual realms?

The contribution of animals to the Field.

Infant mortality.

The significance of seeing spiritual lights.

Joseph: Some of you have come a long way this evening and I thank you for doing so. I have come a *slightly longer* way but it is a delight to be here and to be able to serve you.

Michael often feels he can second-guess how I am going to open proceedings but he can't and that frustrates him. He likes to be in control, and what a strange life he lives as control is taken away from him at times like this and he has no conscious memory of what he has done or what he is going to say.

My reason for coming back – my reason for contacting the Earth plane again – is a simple one: **I CARE.** Hundreds, thousands, *millions* like me care and we are worried. We are worried about the state of the planet; we are worried about the state of the human condition; we are worried about people's minds, people's actions; we are worried about the 'thick tar' of physical reality that surrounds people, that prevents them from seeing through to their spiritual core and acting always from that spiritual core.

Ladies and Gentlemen, things are bad!

Things are getting worse!

There are pinpoints of Light around your globe but we need to *nourish* those pinpoints of Light. We need to expand those pinpoints of Light into earthly reality to banish the darkness, to banish the violence, to banish the upset, the pain, the lack of understanding ...and *this* is why I return.

Communication is difficult; it is difficult at best because you are surrounded by the thoughts of millions who do not want to believe or accept or look at the things that you are looking at this evening. Nevertheless they are true, which is why I come back. As I said at the last demonstration this is not about me; it is about the information that I – and the millions on the spirit side of life in the spirit spheres – can offer you at times like this, for which we are incredibly, wonderfully grateful. Thank you so much.

I would like to invite your questions... who wants to talk to me?

Debra: I would, please. I am Debra. If you were to advise us of the one thing that would have the biggest impact on raising consciousness on this planet, what would it be?

Joseph: Light! The one thing that will raise consciousness on this planet is Light – to see the Light that you have within yourself but, not only that, to see the Light that *everyone else* has within themselves, to recognise the Light, to ignore the darkness. In doing that you draw the Light out of others; you remind them of who they are; you set alight that soul-path that is constantly calling to them but they cannot usually hear it.

You might say that the one factor that is missing from this world is Love. The two are interchangeable; the two are the same thing: **Light is Love – Love is Light.**

For you to wake up in a morning and have a day of Light – to project Light into your workday, to project Light into your dealings with your friends, with your family, with your workmates, and also – and *particularly* – with those you do not like... to project Light to those you do not like; to project Light to those you see on your news programmes that cause you so much pain. Ignore the surface! Ignore the darkness! Reach in and project the Light from yourself to the Light within them. Ignite that Light and the planet will begin to reassert itself as the Eden it once was; you as souls will begin to reassert yourselves as God's children in full knowledge of that fact.

And the incredible, the wonderful, the joyful thing about Light is that Light changes *now*!

People say: 'What can *I* do?' **Everything!** You can do *everything* by wielding, by using, by directing Light. You may not see the results of your actions instantly but they are there. You are nurturing the seed within the people that you direct the Light to, when at the moment you nurture the darkness. You say: 'What a terrible person! What a terrible act! I would lock them away and throw away the key. I despise what they are doing – therefore, I despise *them*.' ...And in doing that you add not Light, but darkness, confusion, heaviness... the 'tar' that I spoke of earlier.

Forgive me becoming agitated but you asked the question, Debra. Does that answer the question?

Debra: Yes, thank you.

Joseph: Who is next, please?

Cameron Collinge: I would like to ask a question, Joseph. I am Cameron. It's about something that we are all under threat of at the moment – a global pandemic [*reference to the bird flu scare in 2009*]. Is there any spiritual reason why we are going to be experiencing something like that?

Joseph: I do not believe in global pandemics! I want you to examine that sentence: 'I do not believe in global pandemics' – and there is your answer. If you were not to believe in a global pandemic there would be no global pandemic.

You are told what to believe and what to think. You are manipulated by the Field – the Field of energy that you exist within on this physical level, and the Field is always trying to maintain itself as a negative state. So, the Field – which is sentient because you contribute to this as a race, as a species around the globe, second by second – the Field *wishes* you to be upset, *wishes* you to rely on it, *wishes* you to be enveloped in it as it is. And so those who are susceptible to the Field (more susceptible than the spiritually-minded) are prompted by the Field to deliver false information, to make you believe that black is white and white is black: 'You are going to die from this ...You should be worried about that ...Everything is terrible...You are reliant on those around you.'

You are reliant on the God-within.

You are a perfect being, a perfect *human* being. It is only the pressure of the Field and your lack of resistance to it – because you become worn down by it – that allows in the beliefs and the misdirection of the Field, and so you are told there is a pandemic *…and there is.*

What if you were told that today is going to be a perfect spiritual day when everyone gets on with everyone else and where there is only love, and harmony, and peace and health? But you are not told these things. Were you told these things by those in authority – those that you look to for answers – and *believed* that today would be a perfect day …then today would indeed be a perfect day.

The best barrier, the best defence you have against the suggestions of the Field, is laughter: 'It doesn't exist. I am not worried about that. That's nonsense. It's nothing to do with me. You believe what you want to believe – I know I cannot be harmed.'

Remember that you are a child of God, that you are part of God. Is God worried about 'flu? Is God worried about hair-loss, or growing old or lack of funds? Of course not! God has everything that He needs *now* and, therefore, so do you. It is just a matter of turning your belief around, ignoring the Field and saying: 'Go away you *silly Field*, you make me laugh! You don't make me angry (because that is what the Field wants), you make me laugh. You are a nonsense. Away with you! I am healthy. I am happy. I have sufficient each day – *more than sufficient* – I have abundance because I am part of God and God knows nothing of lack, of illness, or of upset.'

It is a matter of changing your thinking, which of course is part of the reason that I come back – to say to people, 'You can do whatever you want to do.' Unfortunately, on a subconscious level, many of you want to be ill, want to believe in these things, want to be upset, want to be in pain, want someone else to say to you, 'I will make it better.' No – *you* make it better. Make it better now! Believe in who you are and you cannot be touched by illness or lack.

[*Smiling*] I am shouting again. Has your question been answered?

Cameron: It has, thank you.

Joseph: Another question, please!

Russell Evans: Joseph, if I may? My name is Russ... I would just like to ask one. Jesus was perhaps our greatest healer and the one talked and written about the most... what is your take on his skills ...and did he have any siblings?

Joseph: His skills – as he said – **are your skills**. Jesus came to say: 'I do all this because you can do all this. I do all this to prove to you that it is possible,' and to say: 'What I do you can do better than I.'

Jesus was a great healer because of his belief in God, because of his belief in a matrix of thought that was stronger than the Field and a belief and a connection to God that was stronger than the Field. Again – *silly Field!* 'This is not the way it is ...but this *is* the way it is: ...you are healed ...you are well ...you have abundance.' This was Jesus's message and it is a message that is misunderstood by the religions that have formed around his teachings *not understanding his teachings*. His teachings are simple:

You are God. You can do all this. You can heal yourself. You can heal others. You can put right the Field.

Two thousand years ago: *you can put right the Field!*

Have we put the Field right?

Two thousand years ago!

It is such a simple message and books have been written to explain the complexity of what Jesus said. ...What complexity? The message was simple, it is the same message, it is *my* message, it is the message of those who work with me, it *should be* your message to each other: 'We are part of God – there is nothing to fear.'

Jesus overlaid, in the case of someone who was diseased – considered themselves to be diseased – Jesus overlaid over that image of the person's disease an image of the person's perfection. In other words, he recognised within them the God, the Light within them, and such was his faith, such was his connection to God, that that image was stronger than the person's belief in disease. And at that point that image became the person's image of themselves and that person was healed.

But remember that 'dis-ease' is a product of the Field. If you were to die of cancer today would your *soul* have cancer? Would you, as a spirit, have cancer? No, it is only your belief in the way that society presents things to you – your belief in dis-ease, your belief in the illness being stronger than health, your belief that illness has to be cured *outside* of yourself ...when, if you went *inside* yourself and looked at the sources of your disease, you would remove them. It is only your belief that stops you being healthy *now* because I tell you: **you *are* healthy now; you *are* perfect now.**

Regarding siblings... there are questions I am asked and I have to ask if they are relevant? I could go now, if you like, and look at the records but it is not important. The *message* was important. You see, again the Field presents you with another angle: 'Was Jesus married? Did he have a sister or a brother? Did he have children?'

...Is it important?

...What *is* important is what he said, and we surround ourselves with complexities – needless complexities. Keep it simple:

You are healthy. You are part of God. Everything that Jesus did you can do *now*.

You have to believe that then, I tell you, *then* the spirit, the *Christos*, will rest. Can you imagine what it is like seeing an Earth that you came to, to give a specific message to, that *two thousand years after you gave it* is not recognising that message?

And yet thousands and thousands of people are saying: 'Help me, Jesus! ...Help me to do this! ...Help me to win over this person! ...Help me to win over this disease! ...Help me to convert this person into my way of thinking.'

And all those thoughts go up into the spirit realms – not very high – but they pull at the consciousness of the Christos. Such bravery to incarnate knowing that that might be the outcome, that years later people may still not be following the message.

Is that a sufficient answer?

Russell: Yes, thank you Joseph.

Joseph: Thank you.

Ron: Could I just ask about the 'Divine Feminine' and the impact it will have on the Field?

Joseph: In what respect?

Ron: What impact the Divine Feminine energies returning to the Earth plane will have on the negative Field.

Joseph: Are you talking about the imbalance at the moment?

Ron: Absolutely!

Joseph: Each of you is – and I am – a blend of masculine and feminine energies. Throughout my long existence, as you would measure it, I have sought to balance those two energies so that one is not dominant over the other. Those two energies – the masculine and the feminine, or the positive and the negative – are there as tools to enable me to become more God-like and to operate on higher spheres of consciousness ...to *create,* in effect. Because that is your destiny, each of you. Your destiny is not to 'sit at the right hand of God' – your destiny is to become more God-like as you travel back towards Divinity, and masculine and feminine are the tools that will allow you to do that... your *mastery* over those two tools.

At the moment there is a predominance of the feminine energy around the world but it is distorted. It is distorted, unfortunately, through many females. Many females (again, being affected by the Field into which they are pouring this dominant feminine energy) believe that they should be feminine but also should be masculine; believe that the way that they were born is wrong for them; believe that they should be dominant at all costs; believe that they should control at all costs ...yet still give into their urge to bring through the next generation, and then all but abandon that generation within the parental home because they seek to be masculine.

This is a corruption of the feminine side, but the corruption of the feminine side is also leading to a corruption of the masculine side because the masculine side is saying: 'I agree, I will succumb to your wishes. If that is what you want, that is what I will give to you.' And the masculine side, ironically, is becoming more feminine, having exhibited more feminine traits because there is a confusion here.

Many of the females at the moment think that it is wrong to be feminine and confuse being feminine with being subservient. And many of the males are saying: 'Well, it is wrong to be masculine' because they confuse being masculine with being dominant, not realising that they have been born into a specific body – either male or female – for a specific purpose and that the people that they will meet during their lifetime (either friends or family or eventual relationship partners) are an *opposite charge* to theirs so that when they come together in a relationship or in a friendship then the two people involved (or maybe more – the group of people involved) will work to balance masculine and feminine energies through the experiences that are brought to them as a result of coming together. That is part of the karmic plan – the karmic plan for the individual and the karmic plan for mankind as a whole ...and [*smiling*] I hope you will not be upset because I have said 'mankind' and not as you say today: 'person-kind'.

The family unit is not being embraced. ...The family unit is not being embraced because the feminine side seeks also to be masculine and, therefore, abandons part of its purpose in being feminine: to nurture the next generation and to do the most important job of all – to instil in that generation moral responsibility and spiritual knowledge. And so you have the knock-on effect of generation to generation you see now, where there is an increasing abandonment of values, an abandonment of the ability to stay together and to work with each other. The moment there is friction the feminine side (or many females) say, 'That's it – I move on!' And then they repeat the same process, the same pattern because, built into their feminine side, is the lesson that they are to embrace that feminine side.

This is nothing to do with intelligence or ability or work capability; it is to do with their purpose in incarnating as a spirit. If you are masculine then there are certain challenges during this life that you have to face that rely for their outcome upon you being in a masculine body and having a masculine perspective. The same is true of the feminine aspect of creation.

This is why there is great concern about the future. I can make the analogy of one half of the Earth being too heavy and the Earth tilting on its axis. It is only an analogy, but things are skewed and the Earth reacts by presenting back to you an image of what is happening and what is wrong around the globe. So, your natural disasters, your earthquakes, your floods, are an expression from the Earth of what is wrong with the input from the masculine and feminine side.

Remember you are linked to the Earth – **the Earth is part of you.** If you were to say this to many people outside of this room, they would laugh or the words would slide off their minds but, nevertheless, the words are true. The concept is true and we are back to focussing Light at people, blessing them, not condemning them, not saying, 'You are skewed; you should be acting in a different way,' but sending Light to them and asking only that God remind them, as that Light envelops them, of who they are.

It is a slow process. As I said earlier there are pinpoints of Light around the globe ...there need to be pinpoints and pinpoints and pinpoints that become brighter and brighter and brighter but that does not mean you give up.

The power of one person thinking and sending out Light to another is more powerful than a thousand thinking their dark thoughts.

You have to rectify and restore the balance – that is your duty as spiritually-minded people. You will not do it in church. You do it as you meet people, you do it by praying for people in the *right* way and you do it by sending out the Light.

Is that sufficient?

Ron: Yes.

Joseph: Who would like to speak to me, please?

Sergio Solazzo: Joseph, can you explain about 'the Field' that you have been referring to – what is the Field?

Joseph: To explain the Field we have to explain what you are and why, originally, you were here.

What are you?

You are Light. Also you are angelic, if you understand that? You talk of angels and have books about angels, you revere angels, you pray to angels ...**you *are* angels.**

Originally as angelic beings you were given an 'area' (and that is an approximation in words for something that I cannot build in words) – you were given an area in which to experience yourself, in which to experience other aspects of yourself. At that time you were totally aware of who you were, totally aware of your connection to God and totally aware of your ability – as part of God, as God's issuing, as God's children, if you like – **you were totally aware of your ability to create.**

And into this sphere, this *realm of potential*, you came ready to create, ready to have your 'games', ready to be actors and actresses in a 'play', ready to work out a million-and-one different scenarios that would bring you experience that you could take back to the Godhead. And if, for example, you thought that you needed a stick, that stick would manifest in front of you because *you created...* because you were an angelic being.

Because of the Fall – which is something I have mentioned in the books thus far and which will be covered in greater detail at a later date ...if I can hold on to Michael and he doesn't drop dead at my feet [*Reference to the book on the Fall that was subsequently published in 2012*] – because of the Field, because of the shift in judgment, you as angelic beings masked your connection to God. You forgot who you were, you forgot what you were capable of and yet – because you are God, part of God, a child of God – you *still* created. You *still* create, but you chose to put into this matrix of potential around you from that time onwards ...creations of fear ...creations of mistrust ...creations of violence ...creations of lack.

And so all you see around you is *your* creation ultimately as a mass, as a group of souls inhabiting an area of reality. The Field is that matrix of potential and the Field is what needs to change in order for the Earth to become the wonderful, glorious, living playground that it once was.

Every day you contribute, *each of you*, to the Field via your thoughts, second by second. What are your thoughts? If you review today, what have your thoughts been? Have they been thoughts of anxiety? ...They go out into the Field. Have they been thoughts of fear? ...They go out into the Field. Have they been thoughts of irritation? ...They go out into the Field and help to maintain that Field at its negative setting.

Your mission, the reason (whether you are aware of it or not) that you are here tonight, is to reset yourself and the Field, to remember that you are part of God, to remember that you are angelic in origins and to remember *most importantly* that **as you think, as you believe, so you create.** You pour into the Field that which you believe to be true, and you have millions of souls who believe the Field – i.e. the 'reality' that you perceive around you – to be a terrible place. Minute by minute you say, 'It's a terrible place!' ...and you *maintain it as a terrible place.*

So, the Field is your – 'plaything' is the wrong word – the Field is yours to manipulate, it's an extension of what you are; it is a Field of perceived 'reality' that is anything but, because that reality comes from *within* each of you. And that Field needs to change, and you and others like you are the ones who will change it. Is that sufficient?

Sergio: Yes, thank you.

Debra: Joseph, can I just follow up on one of those points that you just made there – that one person can overshadow the darkness of a thousand people by projecting Light? How many people would it take on the planet projecting Light to counteract the darkness?

Joseph: Until there is a balance. There is a lot that you have to consider here (and I welcome this question, thank you) – because you are sending out Light to those souls who are already here you are affecting those souls with your Light *who are already here*, who have already incarnated. As part of your daily spiritual practice you should also send out Light to those souls who are *about to incarnate*.

What a wonderful meditation, to take yourself into a quiet room and to see babies, who are about to be born, floating in the most glorious Light. And then to see yourself encapsulating each of those children in a bubble of Light that is impervious to anything less than its vibration: that cannot be touched by illness, that cannot be touched by the negativity of the Field, that cannot be touched by the upset that will be projected *inevitably* towards those children during their lives on Earth by other people. Then you begin to affect the future generation, you begin to prepare *within the Field* the conditions within which they can blossom, because the spirits come here with the greatest of intentions in many cases, but the Field has a dragging effect, has a treacly effect, has a slowing-down effect on their purpose. So you have to tend, yes, to the people who are here now but also to those who are to come.

[*Smiling*] I would love on an exercise [*book*] page to be able to say: 'You need one million, two hundred thousand and sixteen and a half souls in order to change the world!' ...But I will say that the more people who do this, the positive energies that are poured into the Field begin to quicken and you network (there's a modern word); you network – you link, when you are praying in this way, when you are sending out Light to people – you *network* with others who are also sending out the Light, and your Light becomes doubled ...trebled ...quadrupled. The power of that Light becomes so unstoppable that anything that is put in its path cannot help but change.

It is difficult. (I should not say that!) It is difficult. No one after all these years – thousands and thousands of years – can tell you that it is easy. It is not. **But you have to start now because the planet is preparing itself for cataclysm** – so negative is the Field, so weighted is the Field towards negativity.

Is this repairable? Yes – or I would not be here! [*Smiling*] I would put my feet up at home and I would enjoy the equivalent of a cold drink, and I would say: 'Well, they've done it again – maybe next time!'

Not *maybe next time* – THIS TIME!

Certainly *this time* we are going to change things, and you see within the fabric of the Field that things are, despite holding people on some levels, not entertaining them on others. They are seeking (as you are seeking tonight) because conventional religions do not provide the answer. They are looking at their governments and saying: 'This is wrong! I want to do something about it.' They are looking at the world and saying that the world is suffering. Those people are points of Light (the pinpricks that I talked about earlier). It doesn't matter whether you can see them working spiritually *openly*. They may not say, 'God bless you!' but in their actions they are blessing you, in their actions they are blessing the planet, in their actions they are changing things.

Do not despair! Be delighted, be joyous – you have an opportunity to put things right. And you who have come here tonight have reached a point where you have popped your head and shoulders above the Field and looked out on a sunny day and said, 'Boy! I never thought that was there.' Now your task is to grab everyone else and pull them up above the dark clouds and say, 'Look what is here! Look what you are capable of! Let's change and let's change *now*!'

I am sorry I have not provided an exact number but you are also looking at possibilities, probabilities. This meeting tonight sends out Light, so the very fact that you have come together to listen to me *changes things* because you are producing Light ...Light-energy that allows me to work, Light-energy that is going out and is being used by those that are around this circle of friends on the spirit side of life and is being used to help where help is needed most. Jesus again said, 'Join together! Wherever there are two or three of you, there I am.' *There* is the Christos, *there* is the Light.'

Join together like this, produce the Light, send it out, ask that it be used (if you do not know *where* to send it or *how* to send it) **and you *will* change things.** And then, from a probability of success, it will become a 'positivity' of success, a *certainty* of success ...and then a **success**. Then the Field, immediately *at that point*, will change from negative to positive and you will think: 'Oh, *that's* who I am! I remember now – *that's* how it was. Yes, I remember now – everything before then was just a bad dream.' Does that answer your question?

Debra: Thank you.

Joseph: Thank you.

Adrian Incledon-Webber: May I ask a question, if that is possible? As human beings we always seem to impose deadlines on ourselves i.e. 1984, 2000 (when the computers were all going to go crash and 'the end of the world was nigh') and 2012 is a question on a lot of people's lips these days. Many people fearfully think that the end of the world is on its way but others seem to think it is the beginning of a rise in human consciousness.

Joseph: If you do not change the end of the world *is* on its way – this is how serious things are!

2012 – very modern! 2012 signifies a *spiritual* change – it was foreseen by the ancient civilisations. But if you were to go out on the 1st of January, 2012 and look up into the sky you would see the same sky; if you were to look at the workforce you would see the same people going to work – busying themselves, being happy, being depressed. It is a *gradual* change and it is a time when there will be many endings but these endings will be subtle. [*Smiling*] I am often amused and I have in the past stood unseen by people with billboards: 'The end of the world is tomorrow at ten o'clock!' ...and I prod them at one minute past and say, 'Well, where is it?'

Again the human mind (as you have rightly said) does love to work to deadlines, does love to say, 'Well, I will be rich by the time I am 34.2' ...or, 'I will be dead by the time I am 76.' It tries, confined within the limitations of human perception, to box everything and to say *this has to happen by this date* – and that is very dangerous because you project on a personal level and on a global level into the ether, into the Field, 'I am going to die by the time I am 76.' And you believe that more than you believe, 'I am going to be rich by the time I am 34.2.' Very dangerous!

But, having said that, within you there is the ability to *perceive* the patterns of Creation, to receive information about the patterns of Creation, and you will know when you manage to put your busy minds to one side that there are times when you can feel change personally or globally without any evidence *physically* of that change looming. Would you agree with that?

Adrian: Yes.

Joseph: What you are experiencing at the moment is the underlying pattern that is bringing to an end certain crystalline structures that *need* to go. You will see in the next few decades the overthrowing of many conventional ways of looking at the world. You will see the overthrowing of many conventional ways of government. You will see the dying out, unfortunately in violence, of certain religions. You will see certain religions as it were 'going up in their own flame' because if certain aspects of reality, certain formations of vibrations, do not have God-Light within them they may last for a hundred years or two hundred years but eventually they burn out. It is like putting one firelighter in a fire and expecting that fire to burn for days and weeks – it cannot because it does not have fuel, it does not have energy.

So, many of the constructs of the Field – such as certain religious beliefs, such as certain political beliefs – are in a state of 'dying embers', and those are the things that you will see change. And if you are spiritually perceptive you will begin to see the pattern and think, 'Ah, there is another one. Yes, I expected that to happen.' But do not mourn for any of these things dying out; they could not exist for much longer because they did not contain within them God-Light. And any construct that does not have within it God-Light is *doomed to failure* – either failure this evening, failure tomorrow or failure in a thousand years – but it cannot maintain itself unless it is coming from within and unless it has Light within it.

This is one of the reasons why your Earth is edging closer to *oblivion*, because there is only so much energy within the Field. And where does the individual go for energy but to the Field? 'Doctor, give me something to give me energy!'... 'Father, give me something that enables me to do what I want to do!' – that prayer has no power. You are not feeding the Field with Light so the constructs within the Field are dying. We need to feed, as I have said (I must sound like one of my parakeets), **we need to feed the Field with Light.** If you put constructs into the Field that are nurtured by God-energy, that are sound *spiritually*, they will last ...and last ...and last ...and blossom.

But, to return to your question, yes, there is a change *around* that date and *from* that date, but you will not open your door on the 1st of January, 2012, to see stars and a burnt cinder. Thank God! Does that answer?

Adrian: It does – thank you, yes.

Joseph: Are you sure?

Adrian: It does. It depends very much on our thought-patterns; I think we are all here to transmit as much Light as we possibly can. It seems to be working but obviously very, very slowly with many people.

Joseph: Impatience is part of the Field. There are so many ways that the Field can get *to* you and can get *at* you – 'It's not working!' …'It's not working fast enough!' …'Is it working?' …'I can't see it!' – and all the time the Field is chipping away at you.

And don't forget that roaming the Field (and this is something that we have not touched on) are those thought-forms that men and women of violence or perversion have placed there. You create – remember you are angelic – *you create*, and so you put into the Field (not you, personally) but certain key people put into the Field thought-forms. They give sentience to thought (thought has sentience anyway) but they coalesce thought into irritations, into 'creatures', if you like, that will drain your energy. They maintain them and the Field maintains them. They are 'smoke and mirrors' and can be gone in an instant but, because of the weeping and wailing that goes into the Field they are maintained by that energy. The voice in your head... *sometimes* does it not say to you, 'Why don't you do this?' and you say, 'I don't want to do this!' **Does that not prove to you that there are two things going on?** You are not mad – you are being influenced by something outside of your personal God-experience.

So, you have to combat things such as impatience. Yes, it is so difficult. I grow impatient at times and then I have to correct myself – have to be corrected – and the huge 'Finger of Divinity' says, 'Joseph, no! Don't be impatient!' And I have to remind myself of my purpose to work within God's plan in *His* time and *His* scale, and to be absolutely grateful for opportunities to talk to you because each opportunity is created by God, and God is saying: 'Go there, Joseph! Talk to them! Reinforce what they already believe so that they go out with more Light than they came in with. Go, do it now!' And then on certain days I have to sit there and wait because I have to wait for instruction from Higher Authority.

Thank you. Who else please?

Tony Clarkson: Joseph, could I ask a question – it's Tony. You've been explaining tonight about right thinking and about how, with right thinking, we can project the Light, and that that Light is what's going to change everything. Can you say something about Light-practice that we can do on a day-to-day basis that will help us increase our Light, help us get through that Field? ...And I am thinking in terms of: should we be vegetarians or should we eat meat? I am thinking in terms of: do we chant or do we meditate? I am thinking in terms of: is it a good thing to drink alcohol or not to drink alcohol ...in terms of increasing our own spiritual energy in order to do this.

Joseph: I will never say to you, 'Do not!' – I *will* say to you as a friend, as a brother, 'It is a good idea *if...*'

I say to Michael before a demonstration that he should not drink alcohol, that he should eat more green, leafy vegetables, and the reason that I say this is that I do not want any trace of the Field polluting him – so that I can use him for the maximum amount of time during a demonstration. So, the alcohol is out ...but tomorrow he will have some. [*Audience laughter*] The leafy green vegetables have absorbed more light than certain foods; therefore, they stimulate Michael's higher atoms and allow me to connect with him more easily.

My own personal preference – *personal preference* because I am one point of view (you have asked me, so I will respond) – **my personal preference is that you should be vegetarian.** The meat that you eat absorbs the Field; the terror that you wreak on your animals is absorbed by the meat that was once the flesh of those animals. Meat is heavy, dense matter and contained within it are the heavy attributes of the Field. Therefore it makes sense, does it not, if you are seeking to connect with the God-within on a daily basis to use your body as the 'temple' that certain religions say it is (and it is) to try to stimulate those higher atoms. But that is not Joseph dictating – that is Joseph *suggesting*.

And Joseph suggests *more than anything* – more than the vegetarianism (until you are ready for it), more than setting aside the alcohol and the cigarettes – suggests that daily you go within yourself and shift your consciousness from the head-centre to the heart-centre. You take that journey down the body in consciousness to here [*pointing to the heart-centre*] and then, when you are viewing your life from the heart-centre, you ask: 'Is there anything you want me to do, Father, today?' And you will receive the message – not via your physical mind but via the heart-centre – either 'yes' or 'no'. If it is 'yes' you ask to be directed to the circumstances where you can make a difference and you ask to be given the words and actions to make that difference.

You also can ask *anything* of the heart-centre with regard to how your life is going – 'Am I certain I want this job?' The mind will say 'yes' ...but then 'no' ...but then 'yes' ...but then 'no' – round, and round, and round. And you will be exhausted and will probably go to someone else and say, 'Should I have this job?' And one person will say 'yes' and one person will say 'no' and you are no further along the road.

The heart *knows*!

Your heart connects you to God. Your heart-chakra, your heart-centre, knows the answer to every aspect of your life – from the job, to the relationship, to the religion, to the health. 'Do I want this job?' Go into the heart-centre; what does the heart-centre say to you? How are *you* speaking to *yourself*? Go to the heart-centre and say: 'I am God. We are both here, God – You and the 'I AM' that I am – what do we know about this? What is the answer to this?' Then listen for the still, small voice or the physical sensation that brings you either a 'yes' or a 'no' or brings you insight in visions.

Go to the heart – that is the greatest and *first* thing you must do. Learn to live from the heart and not from the mind then everything else is added; then you make your decision about the cigarettes, or the alcohol, or the vegetarianism, or the hundred and one other things that might perplex you spiritually. Go to the heart first – in other words **go to God first and all else will be added.**

Be patient. Don't let the Field say to you, 'I'm not hearing anything. I'm not seeing anything.' Don't believe that! Listen, be good to yourself, be loving to yourself and know that you within yourself have the answer to everything that arrives in front of you along life's path. You come equipped – *perfectly* equipped. You are not born into this world at the mercy of this world and at the mercy of other people – you just believe that because that is what the Field tells you.

Daily at any time – three, or four, or five, or six times a day – you can go within to see the heart's perspective and, if you follow that perspective, you will never go wrong. **Never go wrong – it is something *so* worth cultivating.** Does that answer?

Tony: Thank you, Joseph.

Gordon Bagshaw: Could I ask you a question, please? A few moments ago you spoke referring to 'Higher Authority' – could you comment, please, on spiritual hierarchy such as the Higher Authority? Is it intellectual, spiritual, evolutionary achievement or creative ability?

Joseph: It is never intellectual – not in the sense that the earthly mind means. It is never intellectual because when viewing something and saying *it is intellectual* you are viewing it from the point of the Field, and the Field seeks to rationalise everything within its own *small* viewpoint. Michael has been told – and I will add to that this evening – that *we* do not know everything about God. The discovery and the wonder is part of Creation; discovering more about Divinity and about the Divine plan is part of Creation as though, in a very real sense, God unfolds His wonders little by little to make the journey back to Him ever more interesting. To define God in words is *impossible* but I will give some angles that you might find interesting.

In this room, outside of yourselves, seemingly, there is no lack of God. No lack of God! There is nothing in this room outside of yourself that is not God. 'Yes,' you would say: 'Well, the other people in this room are part of God, I'll accept that, but what about the chairs, and the carpet, and the walls, and the windows, and the roof, and the lights?' ...All God. **All God!** All part of God-energy, God-creative energy – albeit manipulated by you as individualisations of God.

And yet that individualisation is also an illusion. You only perceive yourselves as individuals in order to experience this realm, and the realm is skewed so your *perception* of the realm is also skewed. This is where your scientists, for the most part, amuse me when they say: 'It does not fit within my world-view.' *Your* world-view... How small! How boxed in, how blinkered, how blind! The world-view is the view of the Field.

To experience something of God, you need again to go within – *outside* the Field, away from the Field – to contact the God-within and to feel that eternal connection that can never be severed, to feel that flow of Love and energy that is yours by inheritance and to feel that everything is alright, everything is as it should be – it simply requires adjusting on this level.

God talks to you daily. People clasp their hands together and kneel down and say, 'Talk to me, Father! Talk to me, Father!' ...and then, 'You still haven't spoken to me, Father!' God has to penetrate this Field in order to talk to you. If you will not talk to him from *within*, then He has to talk to you from *without* – He has to manipulate the Field. So, the chance conversation that you have that solves a problem is not by chance, the challenges that you find yourselves in are not by chance because they teach you something and bring you closer to God-consciousness. God will talk to you from the television set; God will talk to you in the garden through the plants; God will talk to you as the neighbour next door who says something profound; God will talk to you as the book that you find unexpectedly in a book shop that answers your questions; God will talk to you by that sudden flash of inspiration you get when you understand one aspect of this world as you have never understood it before.

God constantly talks to you. If you would learn of God, forget the intellect. Allow the experience of God to flow into you, connect with God on a daily basis and start to talk to God. Start to say, 'Father, this is upsetting to me' ...or 'This I don't understand' ...or 'I would like illumination on this, please' ...or 'I am seeking You.' And then be patient – don't allow the Field to say, 'This is not happening!' ...**because it *is* and it *does* all the time.** We have to look beyond the physical reality.

We – as we evolve through spheres of creative ability and spheres of creation (they are the same thing) – become more God-like. We gravitate towards each other. We are still individuals but we are linked in a way that also applies now but you cannot feel. And our ability to create increases so that we influence directly the 'spheres' (for want of a better word) in which we live. We create by believing, by imagining and if you are looking for the mechanism of God you can see it in the way that we operate. You can see it in the way that *you* operate on a soul-level ...those feelings of compassion that you have, those insights that you can pass onto people that change their lives. That is God speaking to you and through you, and that is – in the tiniest amount – a view of how God is.

There is a lot spoken about hierarchy and how many levels. Are there seven levels ...or seventy-seven levels ...or seven hundred and seventy-seven levels?

How many levels, Ladies and Gentlemen, do *you* have within yourself? How many levels of mood, for example? How many levels of sensation?

And for me there is no barrier or edge between one level of existence and another other than the vibrational capability of the soul trying to enter that level versus the vibrational resonance of that level itself. In other words, a soul cannot enter a certain level until it vibrates at a similar vibrational resonance. I do not see hard edges, I do not see ladders and then a floor ...and then we are on level three ...and then we are on level four.

The people who work with you and with me are not all at the same point of evolution *spiritually*. Michael has seen people who appear to him as Light (you all appear to me as Light – I am seeing you as Light now) but there are people who are so used to emanating as Light that they appear as Light itself and not as human. There are levels; there are experiences *beyond that*. Wipe out the word 'level' and substitute the word 'experience' and we then get back to the original point of Creation here – which was to allow souls to experience a set of experiences to know themselves through a certain physical realm. God's possibilities for evolving souls are endless ...endless ...and endless ...and endless. As far as we are aware – because we haven't reached there yet – the ability to experience is infinite. **Infinite!** And that is part of God's mind that He wants His children – and therefore *Himself* – to experience infinitely and to experience universes from within His children and universes that His children create around themselves. Have I given you some insight?

Gordon: Yes, thank you. I realise that resonating at a certain level of wisdom and creativity is the key to being able to progress higher.

Joseph: Those are the only barriers. There are no 'locked doors' except within the heart of the souls who are trying to open those doors to get into those spheres. And they are instructed, they are educated once they have reached the spiritual realms – but this is also a *spiritual* realm – once they have reached the *non-corporeal* realms, they are shown how they can obtain that level of harmony and how they can increase their vibration so they can inhabit those spheres. But then, once they inhabit a certain sphere, there is another sphere beckoning, because God is always pulling, through infinite experience, His children homewards.

And for none of us is there the experience of putting our feet up and saying: 'I want to stay in this house or in this realm forever.' Change is an aspect of God because it brings experience that enriches our souls. And on Earth you dig your heels in and say: 'I will not change! I hate change. Change is not for me – it frightens me, it terrifies me, it angers me.' And yet change is experience and change *will come* to you. If you dig your heels in for a lifetime ...at the end of that lifetime a change comes to you doesn't it?

Welcome change and see it as God talking to you, an expression of God saying: 'Here is something else to experience. Here is a means of growing. Here is a means of reaching those spheres that you want to live in on a soul level. Remember, because of the effects of the Field, you are parted from your soul memory. It was not always so but your soul, your subconscious, your spirit knows what it wants and indeed cries out to God for what it wants, and God rewards it by the experience of *change* to allow that soul to elevate itself into different spheres of experience.

I am beginning to tire Michael's body [*smiling*] but that has never stopped me before. Yes, please, another question!

Susan Leach: Could I ask a question, Joseph, please – it's Susan. When our body dies and our soul passes on to the other side, are there other souls that come to greet us and welcome us?

Joseph: No soul is ever alone – ever! Were you to see your Lights, as I can see them this evening, you would see that there are people standing around you. Some of those people have been relatives in previous lives, some of those people have been relatives in *this* life, but you also have guides who love you and see in you, perhaps, a challenge! Isn't that wonderful, that a guide does not always link to you because they think: 'Oh, they're just like me'? Sometimes they link to you because they think: 'I like a challenge. I like the spark in this one and I will try to stimulate that spark whenever I can – whenever I can get in a thought or influence them through their intuition.'

So, it is always known in advance. You must understand that you are here for a certain amount of time – *generally speaking* you are here for a certain amount of time. It is written; there is a 'book', and in that book (or the equivalent of a book) there is a date, and there is a minute, and there is a second. And we, at a certain level, a certain degree of evolution, have access to that book, and when it is known that you are coming 'home' – not dying, not leaving this *terrible world* that you grumble about (but hang onto its coat-tails and don't want to leave) – when it is known that you are coming home that knowledge is made 'public' (as you would understand it) on the various levels.

So, you will have people who are close to the Earth (relatively speaking) who know that you are about to pass over and make your transition. There are people who have regained their soul memory and have moved onto a higher sphere but were also once connected with you (and still are) and they will know that you are about to make that transition. And there are friends who will know that you are about to make that transition. And it depends on the manner of your coming over and your physical mind's awareness of a spiritual reality as to who comes for you and how you progress to that side.

You will be taken over sometimes via a 'collection point', via a personality who will say, 'Come with me – step on this plane,' or 'Go up the gang-plank to this boat,' or 'Sit in this bus and off we go!' And you will be taken via this illusion (for that is what it is – it is something that you are familiar with and feel happy and feel comfortable with) to a higher state of vibration. And waiting in that higher state of vibration – on that shore, perhaps, because that, maybe, is how it manifests to you – will be those people that you have loved and have known.

If you are spiritually aware to a degree you will say, 'Oh, there's my wife,' or 'Oh, there's my husband,' and they will come directly for you *if* they are of sufficient vibration themselves.

So, no one is ever left alone. It is so sad that the Field says to you, 'You are alone.' *You are never alone.* How, if you are a part of everything – *everything* – can you be ever alone? You are never alone here and you are never alone when you pass over. Is that sufficient?

Susan: That's fantastic – thank you.

Paul Kalus: Could I ask a question please – my name is Paul Kalus. Do animals contribute to the positivity of the Field?

Joseph: Poor, poor, poor animals! Poor animals ...and yet *blessed* animals because they do not have the complexities of the human mind to deal with. It is far easier for animals to pass over than it is for many human souls to pass over.

Animals – *any thing* – contributes to the Field. ...A blade of grass can contribute to the Field if it evokes a feeling of Love in you, and will also respond to that Love, as animals respond to that Love, and give it out. So, yes, they contribute to the Field, but it is a contribution that is of such a pure vibration that it cannot be picked up by most of mankind.

And they find themselves in a world that is violent towards them, that does not recognise them as *equals*. Consider what I said earlier: everything in this room is God, so, in God's eyes, are you more or less important than the chair in front of you? Are you more or less important than the carpet under your feet? If you are all the same thing, how can you divide that *same thing* into degrees of importance? You cannot!

God loves the whole of His Creation *equally*. Unfortunately, the attitude of many people towards animals is that they are lesser beings ...*they* can see angels, *they* can see elementals, *they* know when you are ill and need comfort, *they* know when you are lonely, *they* know when you need that companionship ....and they are *lesser* beings?

Again, this is personal (because we have our personal views – as we progress we retain our personal views. That is one of the joys of meeting other people and sharing different aspects of how you view Creation) – my *personal* view is that we should be kinder to animals, we should respond to them with Love. And you may say: 'Well, animals attack each other – one animal attacks another for food.' This is correct but it is to do with the Field. They *also* are influenced by the Field and there is an illusion in the Field that power is needed, that an intake of heavy matter is needed, so the animals to some extent are polluted by the Field as you are. But they are blameless, they cannot go back to the spirit world and say, 'I did this and I did that and I am sorry for it.' All they can say is, 'What a relief I am back! I have been influenced by the Field and I no longer am.'

We need to be kinder to all aspects of Creation, and if you are – and not just to animals but the chair I mentioned and the carpet I mentioned – those things will respond back to you because they are alive, they are part of God. Pray when you get in the car, pray when you turn on the television – mundane things – pray over the food, respond to the Love within those objects and they will bring Love back to you. Is that a sufficient response?

Paul: Yes, thank you.

Joseph: Thank you

We are tiring now, I think ...if I go during this question, forgive me. Who would like to ask a final question?

Sheila Clarkson: I have just got one final question if that's alright? I would like to ask, Joseph, about children who are born ill, who die early, and you spoke about 'coming homeward' and I wondered about the going homeward in this very primary state and what that means.

Joseph: You must remember that none of you is who you appear to be. You look at yourselves in the mirror and say: 'I am young ...I am middle-aged ...I am old ...I am a child ...I ...I ...I ...This is how I see myself.' But you are wearing a 'suit of clothes'.

You are an angel. You are an angelic being. You have been coming here for some time and you come here repeatedly with different sets of 'clothes' in order to experience. And the amount of time you are here is dependent on the amount of challenges you can face *versus* the effects of the Field in being detrimental to your body.

Sometimes souls from a high level decide that they need to visit the Earth for a short time only. Sometimes that is because they need to observe something from physicality again for perhaps only a few moments. Sometimes it is because they have something to teach those whose lives are touched by their short life on Earth. Believe me, when you attain a level where you retain enough soul memory to know that you do not need to be here any *longer* than you have to be, then – once you have set yourself a challenge that has been agreed by your advisors and that challenge has been met – **you go**. You do not *want* to stay here.

So, remember the child that may have gone young, the child that came with a disease, is not who they appear to be. They are far older and, when they return to the spirit world, they regain their soul memories. If they have been polluted by the Field for a number of years (because that *does* happen) then they are gently eased back into their soul memories and are initially brought up as a child but then more rapidly – much more rapidly than you would see on Earth – they regain their soul memories, they regain their spiritual stature and they move away from that 'suit of clothes' that at that point must be discarded.

There is always purpose to the life of *every* soul and that purpose may seem like suffering from an earthly point of view but in *reality* is not. It is either to gain further personal individual experience or bring that experience to the lives that that life touches. Do you understand that?

Sheila: Yes.

Joseph: Does that answer your question?

Sheila: Yes, it does, thank you.

[*Pause*]

Joseph: At this point there may be one more question. One more question, please!

Nicola: Joseph, it's Nicola. If I see blue lights – which I do very, very regularly – what is it I am actually seeing?

Joseph: You are seeing what is around you. What you *usually* see is illusion; what you are seeing is an aspect of spiritual reality. The colour may be significant or it may not be significant. You can see the *spiritual* field at times and react to the blue vibration; you can see the chakra of a soul who is around you and see the blue from that chakra ...but you are always seeing *through* this earthly illusion.

And the *reason* for seeing lights in many cases, until you are used to seeing them, is to say: *there is something more*. Trust yourself. Trust that you have seen that light. Ask to see more in order that you can re-educate yourself as a spirit and educate the world by bringing spiritual knowledge into it. It is almost as though the lights are teasing you and are saying, 'We are here!'

Seek out through meditation, through asking for a teacher, ways in which you can coalesce that light into a message, into somebody talking to you, into somebody standing in front of you, into an unfolding scenario via your heart-centre that is away from the illusion that means so much to you.

The lights are an invitation, and they are an invitation to work and they will continue to appear until you have said: 'Yes, I will work. Yes, I am going to work. What's next?'

With all spiritual evolution do not get caught up in one aspect of it. If you see a light at some stage say, 'Thank you, I have seen a light, what's the next stage?' Often – because there is a perceived glamour to spiritual work – often there is such an elation when you see something at first that you do not get any further. If someone stands in front of you and you see them (having progressed from the lights), say, 'Hello' (which is good) but also say, 'Why are you standing in front of me?' Spiritual power is never wasted. If someone has punched a hole through the illusion of this Earth to reach out to you – *why*? What do they want to say? Be demanding. Don't be in awe. Always move on and develop your *true* mediumistic skills.

We are moving out of an age now where mediums exist to give messages for family members. With the cataclysmic potential ('*potential*' only) of this planet, should we waste mediumship in this way?

Seek the highest. Seek information. Seek points of view that will change your life for the better (but try them out thoroughly) and change the lives of others for the better. That is the *new* mediumship. That is what we are also introducing at this time. Pray, see Light around the children who are mediumistic, send out Light to those who are struggling to be more than clairvoyant – who are struggling to say: 'I am clairvoyant but I need *more*. On behalf of mankind, I need and want and demand more. I want spiritual truth, I want spiritual perspective, I want to be able to answer questions' ...and that Light is the beginning of that process.

Chapter Four

Joseph Trance Demonstration – 12th August, 2009
The Sanctuary of Healing, Lancashire, UK

Spiritual topics discussed:

Suicide and assisted suicide.

The causes of illness.

The best way to send out healing.

Healing the Earth's magnetic grids.

Ascension and the spiritual realms.

Discovering spirituality on this level.

Tuning into the God-within.

Effective meditation.

Hypnosis as a route to meditation.

Your angelic heritage.

Balancing spirituality and materiality.

Missing DNA strands theory.

Dealing with dark energies.

Assessing the truth of spiritual literature.

Using intuition. ~ The Fall.

Accessing the heart-centre when busy.

Joseph: What colour are you this evening?

I am purple this evening because that is the colour I feel most like expressing from within. But as I look around this room I can see many colours and the *blending* of colours – which is as it *should* be. As you give out, you create energy; you create all the time, second by second. And I wish I could open your eyes (as mine have been opened) to show you the colours of the place where I reside, and to show you the colours *here*... the colours that are possible, the colours that are always here but you cannot, unfortunately, see them because of the density and heaviness of the Field; the density, the heaviness of the Earth plane.

So, I reach out to you in *colour* this evening, because in colour I am saying, 'I am open to you' and you should be open to each other, and open to possibilities and open to the intelligence that we call God – the Divinity, the all-pervading Divinity that shapes us minute by minute **according to *our* wishes**.

I have not come this evening to talk about colour, principally – I have come this evening to, hopefully, talk to you but I need *your* input. I need your questions. Who would like to talk to me, please?

Cameron Collinge: I would like to ask a question, please. There's a lot of interest in the media at the moment about assisted suicide and I was wondering about the spiritual side of that – whether it was a good thing or a bad thing for somebody to end their own life or be assisted to end their own life?

Joseph: A very delicate question from your point of view and a very delicate question from the mind's point of view ...but not a delicate question from the *heart's* point of view.

In all areas such as this one you have to engage the heart; you have to see what your heart-mind is saying to you. When you incarnate upon the Earth plane you have a set number of days that are allocated to you with your permission, with your agreement, *if everything goes according to plan*. And there is a set number of days because, within that set number of days, you have the opportunity to learn the most *versus* being 'attacked' by the Field. In other words, there is a rich and deep calculation that goes on to ensure **that you are here *not a moment longer* than you should be here** ...and yet you are given the opportunity, day by day, to learn to get the most out of that time.

Suicide, of course, ends the *physical* – it terminates the 'voyage' or journey on this level, but unfortunately (and this is what people do not understand) it does not terminate the karma; it does not terminate the journey on a *spiritual* level. And so you find that spirits are moving onwards ...but with nowhere to go because the Earth plane is still pulling at them. They are still encapsulated by the rays from the Earth plane, by the rays from the Field that are supposed to hold them here for a certain amount of time. So, you have stories in religion of people who have committed suicide finding themselves in 'limbo' and, yes, for some of them, they *do*. It is only the stronger spirits, it is only the more evolved spirits that learn to disentangle themselves from the Earth plane and return to a 'waiting station' where they can review the effects of having terminated the physical existence early.

For those who are not so evolved (and by 'evolved' I mean mentally aware from the spirit-heart) there are problems. They find themselves pulled by the Earth plane; they find themselves pulled by the spiritual plane and they need a great deal of counselling – counselling without judgment – to get them away from that 'parcel' of energy that they agreed to be encapsulated by before they incarnated.

My personal view on suicide is that it should not take place.

Indeed, one of Michael's other guides committed suicide [*reference to Silver Star*]. Being an evolved spirit, he managed to escape the pull of the Earth plane but still has to visit the Earth plane at times – not to 'make amends' but to reconcile with his heart, with his spirit, the fact that he should have been here longer.

You see, you only see the physical – you see the suffering, you see the pain and you say: 'I have to terminate that pain. I am being compassionate.'

Are you?

No! Because that pain, that end, is *meant* to be, is a result of choices by the spirit and those who have interacted with the spirit in order that the spirit may learn. And it seems cruel; it seems 'heart-less' that a spirit can be damaged in this way. But the spirit *itself* is not damaged; it is only the material form that is damaged; it is only the material form that is undergoing certain cause-and-effect circumstances so that the spirit within it, linked to it, may learn.

So, in my opinion, suicide should not take place because of the after-effects, because of the problems that occur as a result of a soul taking its own life. And I want to tell you all something: eventually you each 'take your own life' but within the prescribed time. Your spirit knows that it has to leave – the physical does not but the spirit knows! And so you take your own life (just as you took your own life *into* the Earth plane) but at the end of a prescribed period of time, and this is the important thing when considering suicides – **within a prescribed period of time that *you* agreed to.**

How do you know the effects of your suffering on someone else? How do you not know that because of that suffering someone else is learning, someone else is evolving? How do you know that, as a result of your suffering, you are elevating yourself as a spirit? And the suffering is illusion – the nerve endings tell you otherwise but the nerve endings are illusion.

We have to rearrange our means of healing people, our means of making people comfortable, so that even the terminally ill and those who are suffering to a great extent can be bathed in Light, can be bathed in peace, so that their suffering ends but their existence continues until the date when they are due, according to the 'covenant' they have made with God, to return to the spirit worlds from whence they came. Does that answer your question?

Cameron: Yes, thank you very much.

Joseph: Who else, please?

Shirley Hayhurst: Could I ask then, Joseph, is some illness due to karmic reasons and some illness we bring upon ourselves?

Joseph: You cannot separate the outside karma and the inner karma because you create your path minute by minute and second by second by the way that you think, by the way that you react to people, by the way that you observe and consider yourself. So, illness or 'dis-ease' is a breaking down of communication between your spirit and your outer-flesh or your illusion of flesh. And that breakdown of communication is **what is *really wrong* with you** and, in conjunction with the doctors and the nurses on your level, there have to be people who can identify and pinpoint what is *actually* wrong with you before the illness can be removed.

The illness is *never* the cause – the illness is *always* the effect.

And what is it the effect of? ...So many things. It can be the effect of sadness, the effect of insecurity, the effect of anger, the effect of bitterness, the effect of so many different things but *always* it is the effect. And you are right to treat the effect, you are right to alleviate the symptoms, but you have to also alleviate the cause or the illness will return.

Are you responsible for the illnesses that come to you? To a degree, yes, because you are part of the Field; you make decisions based on what you expect from the Field. How many of you in an epidemic situation expect to be ill? ...Expect to be tired at the end of a day? ...Expect an old wound to hurt you? And so, the healing process – the natural healing process as your body is lifted up in prayer to God, to White Light – is slowed down by your own thoughts and by the thoughts of the Field around you ...those thoughts that expect you to wake up tomorrow morning with the same symptoms that you have tonight.

Is that a sufficient answer?

Shirley: Yes, thank you, Joseph.

Joseph: Thank you.

Helen: Can I ask about what you were just talking about in terms of healing people in general? There are a lot of diseases in society at the moment – increasing depression, stress and related illnesses. How can we, as people, get the message out there to get more people to buy into a more holistic way of healing themselves?

Joseph: The message is a universal Light-giving, Light-spreading. You have to remember that when you are talking to someone, unless they understand what you understand *consciously* on an earthly level, you will never be able to affect them. But *within* each person you meet there is a core of Love, a core of Light, and that Light responds to the Light that *you* send out. In other words, a person may be ill and you can talk to them and say nothing about their illness ...and yet you can heal them because they are off *physical* guard when you are praying for them, when you are sending the Light out to them.

You are one organism and that organism changes according to your collective thoughts. The work that we are doing is so important, so vital. And [*smiling*] it is an *undercover* operation; it is a *spy* operation; it is a *secret* mission because you can sit next to the person who is arguing in a queue or on a bus and **you** can change them without them ever knowing – by sending out the Light from your heart, from your solar plexus, to their heart, to their solar plexus.

You can use the *immense* capacity for imaginative creativeness that you have got to see Light going out into every corner of the world, to see Light going out into every heart, to see Light going out into every mind, to send Light out into the places where other people would not consider Light *should* go because they make judgments: 'The Light is conditional.'

The Light is *not* conditional!

The Light should go into prisons. The Light should go into death-row. The Light should go to those who are leaving this world in intensive care units. The Light should go to those who are being born, to babies. **And *in particular* the Light should go to those you do not like** – the person in the same street you do not like, the person in government you do not like, the person in a dictatorship you do not like. **Send them the Light!**

When you send Light – when there is enough Light – the world changes.

You will never change the world by arguing on a physical level with someone: 'There is a spirit world! There is a God! You should change!'

No! The change comes from *within* and the heart reacts to Light. Imagine yourself being a cell in a vast organism, able to irradiate that organism with Light. And, you *are* that cell! And you *do* have that capability! And, that is what you can do every morning, every night, with everyone you meet – send out the Light to them.

And the physical mind will say: 'You haven't made a scrap of difference. Nothing has changed. Why are you doing this?' Remember that the physical mind is under the control to a great extent of the physical Field, the Earth's Field – *mental* Field. Ignore the mind! Do not be pulled into the trap of feeling that you have done nothing and accomplished nothing.

Every time you send the Light out – *the Light goes out*!

Every time you send the Light out the Light 'goes on' in someone – you switch the Light *on*. Then collectively, when we have sent out enough Light, there is enough Light to overpower the Field because the Field will have to retreat into a corner. The Field will be like a little dog that you have turned on that realises it cannot frighten you. And at that point the Field becomes Light, at that point the Field resets itself and at that point you have 'Heaven' on Earth. So, you don't worry about illness because there is no illness. You don't worry about karma because your karma is positive karma. You don't worry about dying because you know you will never die. You will have changed things.

I come at this point in time because this is a *dangerous* point in time. This is a time when the 'see-saw' could go in either direction dependent on you – not dependent on the politicians or the religious ministers – **dependent on you because *you* know the difference.** Therefore, you have to make a difference. You have to tip that see-saw, weight it down in the direction of the Light and then all things follow, all things change, all things become as they once were – as I remember them – without the conflict that you have and, to a large extent, without the pain that you have. The pain that we had was just a mechanism to say: 'You have cut your hand on a thorn – be careful,' not the mental pain that you have, not the lasting suffering that you have. The Light changes these things forever.

Is that a sufficient answer?

Helen: Yes, thank you, Joseph.

Joseph: Thank you.

Denis Barnes: Could you tell us about the magnetic grids around the Earth, and what ascension means to you where you are at the present time?

Joseph: The magnetic grids?

Denis: ...Around the Earth.

Joseph: Yes. The Earth is polluted. The lines around the Earth – the energy lines, the veins, the arteries of the Earth – were once crystal clear, and the Earth was more crystalline in structure than it is today. The heavier rocks, the uglier rocks that you see, are a result of pollution being held by them.

Where does the pollution come from?

The pollution comes from the minds of men and women and, unfortunately, children because we feed them with our expectations of life from an early age. So, when you are encountering a grid, you are encountering a lack, a blockage, a pollution of a Light-stream. And, the Earth was far more 'generous' in its energies than it now is before the accumulative effect of the mental debris of the Field polluted many of its energy lines. So, a grid is not a natural occurrence; **a grid is a pollution of a natural line of positive... of God-energy.**

The way to clean grids, of course, goes back to what I was saying before; it goes back to the way that you think, the way that you influence the Field because when the Field is cleansed the grids will be cleansed. If you find a grid, if you find a line of seemingly negative energy, you need to put your hands onto it and pray and see Light going into it, and pray that it be restored to the condition it was in before we – you and I – polluted it. And you can, for a time, clear those lines by doing this.

Grids, because they are pockets of *intense* Earth pollution, are terrible places for the unaware to live; are terrible places for the unaware to sit on in an office chair; are terrible places for the unaware to build a hospital on because the energy goes into the grid. The grid pulls more of the Field's energy into itself, and the grid is powerful enough to pollute those who are on it or in its proximity.

There should be psychics, there should be mediums, testing for grids now, but only in certain parts of the world does that happen. It should happen as a matter of course. And, initially these places should be avoided. But then, later when they are recognised and have been avoided, they should be changed; they should be prayed over; they should be lifted from their polluted state. And one of the quickest ways that you can change a grid is by kneeling on it, putting your hands on the centre of the line and saying: 'Forgive me, I am sorry. Forgive us, we are sorry. We love you as you love us.' And you will clear the grid and will heal the line.

With ascension are you talking about the evolution of souls or the changing of souls' consciousness on *this* level?

Denis: Changing of souls' consciousness on this level.

Joseph [*sighing*]: It is again the see-saw, it is a game, it is almost like a game of tennis where you bat Light to one end and the Field bats back pollution – mental pollution, spiritual pollution – to you.

There is a plan to all this, you know, and the plan involves every soul – *every* soul – lifting itself into a new consciousness. And you stand at a great crossroads; you stand, as I have said, on one half of the see-saw ...**and things could go either way.** There is *so much* that depends on what you do over the next few decades.

We cannot get out, either, until each of you has got out of the pollution of the Field. *You* cannot get out *totally* until each person has got out of the pollution of the Field because you are all one being. This does not mean that you will necessarily be drawn back into an earthly incarnation again, but it does mean that the spiritual levels are also cleansing areas. I want you to think of the spiritual levels that you have read so much about. The various levels (and people quote different numbers of levels and different looks to levels) are cleansing stations. Those levels are designed to get you, as a spirit, back to the point you once were at.

Do you see the implications of that?

You were once as evolved, as a spirit, as the angels that you see.

The problem occurred because of the Fall that placed you within the illusion of a negative Field. So, I want you to look at the spiritual planes and to understand that these are not the 'be-all and end-all' to your existence. They are, if you like, the 'spiral staircase' that slowly, slowly, slowly takes you through a number of healing 'washes' and 'baths' until you are back where you once stood.

Or are you? Because when *you* are back where you once stood ...what about the others? You will find a pull from your heart – a sadness; you will find upset because you cannot lift each person up, and you will want to. And you will realise, at that point, that you cannot move on *beyond* the spiritual realms that surround and interpenetrate the Earth until each soul is out of the negativity of the Field. So, you will, even at the highest level – not be *forced* to come back in some degree of consciousness – but will *want* to come back in some degree of consciousness because you will be so sad for those souls, your brothers and sisters who are still immersed in the illusion, who still believe that your way of life on Earth is the way of life that they should live here, and you will work to reach a 'hand' down towards those souls ...And that is what is happening tonight because there is a circle above me and a circle above them – hands reaching down to bring Light into the darkness.

Ascension is dependent *here* on the changing of the corruption, on the banishing of the pollution, on a percentage of souls – an ever-greater percentage of souls – realising what we realise here tonight. There then comes a point where there is more Light than darkness and you have ascension on Earth. You have a rediscovery by souls who are incarnate of who they are, of their spiritual heritage, and then decisions can be made on this Earth as to what you want the Earth to be *in goodness*.

What do you want the Earth to be in goodness? Because the Earth is a 'playground', a *willing* playground, a participant in your worlds – your inner and your outer worlds. And once the Light has been restored you can work with the Earth to make this playground somewhere where you can have physical experience that enhances your spiritual understanding and evolution. But it is dependent always – not on a person here ascending or a person there ascending – **but on us all ascending** both on the Earth plane and in the successive layers that lead to ...and the word I have to use is... 'escape'.

Is that sufficient?

Denis: Perfectly, thank you.

Joseph: Thank you.

Please?

[*Audience silence*]

Denis: I will continue, then, if I may? Would you say that it is a change of mankind's consciousness, this ascension?

Joseph: It is a rediscovery of the spiritual consciousness. The spiritual consciousness has to influence the physical consciousness, and at present it is totally the other way round: the physical consciousness is imprisoning and is masking the spiritual consciousness. It is in the interests of the Field – the collective consciousness – to keep you ill; to keep you unhappy; to keep you insecure; to keep you irritated; to keep you bored; to keep you biting your fingernails; to keep you with that strange feeling in the pit of your stomach ...because *that* feeds the Field. **As long as the Field can keep you like that it can maintain itself.**

And I want to tell you something else: **the Field is not evil.**

The Field has been given consciousness. The Field *is* consciousness – it is an extension of the collective consciousness of men, women and children around the world. It is not evil! It has programmed itself to survive and it believes that the only way it can survive is by feeding itself with more of the things that keep it in the state that it is in – in a state of negativity.

So, we have to not only re-educate people, but – as a result of teaching them to send out the Light – we have to re-educate the Field. We have to show the Field that it will continue to exist; that it does not have to feed simply on earthly energies; that it can be powered by spiritual energies for ever, and ever, and ever, Amen! ...but working with the people of the Earth, working with the spirits who visit this world to create, to give experience, to enjoy bliss and Love rather than the darkness it has plunged itself into. And so the Field you should consider as a 'frightened child' who only wants to exist, only knows one way of life and wants to cling on to that one way of life forever. We have to educate ourselves; we have to educate the Field.

Is that a sufficient answer?

Denis: Thank you very much.

Joseph: Thank you.

Who would like to talk to Joseph? Who has a question?

Pat Jackson: Joseph, can I ask... I'm relatively new to the field of spirituality and of having my spirit there and talking to my spirit and listening to my spirit. It's taken me quite a lot of years to get there – is that quite natural, is it something that will carry on growing now and have more 'positive-ness' than hitherto?

Joseph: Once you have rediscovered – not *discovered* but *rediscovered* – your origins and your potential you can *never* go back. **You can never go back!** That is not to say that the Earth will not pull at you, will not make *even more* demands on you because, when you become a 'light', there is a danger ...**and the danger is you have become a *light*.** You are a light that the Field can see, a light that the Field can concentrate on, a light that the Field can surround and say: 'I'm not having this! I will take this soul back to the state where this soul is feeding me, not being fed by the Light.'

So, you will find on the spiritual path that, as you progress along the spiritual path of understanding, it will seem as though the world has turned against you for a while. And every time you take a further step up the staircase of spiritual evolution, the Field will seem to want to trip you, to put its hands in front of your face so you cannot see the way ahead and to convince once again that your old way of life was correct.

Don't let it!

...And the way not to let it is to recognise what it is trying to do. I have said in here before in this very room: 'Silly Field! Go away silly Field, you cannot return me to the ignorance that I had.' And you will find that even if you do go down the path of the Field masking what you have discovered spiritually there are other forces at play. There are *stronger* forces at play because within you there is Light that will say to you: 'I'm still here. I will show you that there is a different way. I will bring to you wonders. I will bring to you guides. I will bring to you inspiration. I will bring to you love.' You will sit alone in your chair and you will feel such love and wonder where it has come from. You will find that concepts come into your mind that you have not considered before and which you now understand. And remember that as you progress along the spiritual path it is not a matter of believing or having faith – it is a matter of *knowing* from within.

That which you *know*, you know eternally.

That which you know can never be taken away from you.

You mentioned a number of years before you discovered (or felt that you had discovered) your spirituality. Well done! Well done ...because there are so many for whom the years pass and they *never* discover that hidden treasure within themselves. And they pass from this life and they incarnate again and again and again and they do not come to the point that you have come to. So rejoice! It cannot be taken away from you.

And, remember that you came here to discover things about yourself and you will have discovered this point in time – this blossoming of spirituality – because of the things that you have gone through. So they have not been your enemy – they have brought you to *this* point. But having brought you to this point you now have to recognise them as a tool that you no longer need: 'I have used the seemingly negative aspects of the Earth to get to this point, but from this point onwards I can approach the challenges in my life in a new way. I can be dispassionate, I can remove myself from them, and I can see only Light and Love in everything that comes to me and in everything that comes to those that mean the world to me – and I will not be shaken in that.'

The second half of this equation is that once you have said, 'I want to advance spiritually,' you are really saying, 'I want *everyone else* to advance spiritually,' and so you have to ask God. ...Where *is* God?

...Where *is* God?

...Here [*pointing to the heart-centre*] ...right here: '**I am right here!**'

You have to ask God and say: 'What do You want me to do? What on Earth do You want me to do now, Father? How can I pass on a little – or a lot – of what I have learned thus far?'

And then you listen very carefully. You look very carefully. And you wait for the people and the circumstances that God will place around you to come to you. And those circumstances will bear in mind *always* that, no matter what you do during your daily life, there is another aspect. You will work to put bread on the table, yes, but you will also work to put Light into people's hearts and you will be shown the way. It does not come from a book, it does not come from a teaching, it comes from *within* and that connection to God and God saying: 'Go here! Don't go there! Talk to this person! Don't talk to that person! Rest today! Work today!' and a complete surrender to the Divinity-within, which is *you*.

Does that make sense?

Pat: Yes, thank you.

Joseph: Thank you.

Tony Clarkson: Joseph, could I ask a question that follows on from the last question, and that is: in our own personal practice we all talk to God in our own way and we all have thoughts, but what is the best way to actually tune into God and know that the link is the strongest link that is possible?

Joseph: We have to go back to the principle, to the *reality*, of you having two minds. You have a mind in your head that is influenced by the Field. You have a mind in your heart that is influenced by your soul and your connection to God. Therefore, in praying to God and requiring a result – requiring *guidance* – you need to think not from the head but from the heart.

You need to make an agreement with yourself that each day you will spend a few minutes thinking from the heart-mind.

How do you do that? You do that by retreating from the head-mind, by switching off the effects of the head-mind. You will sit, you will become quiet, you will ask for protection from God and your mind will be crowded with a million-and-one things and sights and sounds and sensations. And you will then see yourself retreating from those sights and sounds and sensations and taking a path – perhaps taking a path through a golden cornfield that leads you gently down to an oasis, or a well that is perfectly still. And behind you, as you have walked down that field, is your physical mind getting fainter and fainter – you cannot hear the sounds, you cannot see the sights, you cannot feel the sensations or the demands. You can only, *only* see this beautiful, still pool of Light, and, under a perfect blue sky and surrounded by the golden corn, you sit down at the edge of this perfect, vast, deep, still water.

And you look into it and you *know* that you are now contacting God from your heart. And then you ask, 'Father, am I right?' and look into the pool and see the reflection of yourself and look into your eyes and the answer will be there: **yes** or **no**.

'Do I need to modify my plan – yes or no?'

'Do I need to work with You today – yes or no?'

'Are the feelings that I have while I am not operating from the heart-mind true or false? Are they there or not? Are they illusion or heart-truth?'

And do not expect instant answers but expect to have to go to that well, to that pond, on a daily basis whenever there is something troubling you, whenever you need an answer, because you will always get an answer once you are used to tuning-in. And you will either see that answer in your reflection or you will sit there on the edge of that pond with your eyes closed in your imagination and you will hear your own voice say *yes* or *no*, or you will feel yourself say *yes* or *no*. You will feel it – not just say it, not just think it – **but *feel* it!**

And, you will become used to contacting *you*; to making friends with you; to operating from the centre, from the source. And the promptings of the heart-mind apply in *all* areas of life: in business, in relationships, in healing, in having peace of mind, in knowing how to work spiritually.

The heart-mind answers all.

Do you feel, do you think that God would leave you here without a connection back to Him?

Ah, the men and women over the years have said: 'This way lies God! I will connect on your behalf. I will connect through the physical mind and through praying for you on your behalf to God.' Avoid those ladies and gentlemen! *You* **will connect with the God-within because you *are* the God-within,** and therefore, as the God-within, you have access to all knowledge. You know in every situation what to do – it is just that the head-mind masks the promptings of the heart-mind.

And so, having sat by your still, wonderful, deep, peaceful pool for as long as you wish, you can retreat back – and back up through the cornfield and bring out into the physical mind the gold light of that cornfield, the blue of the perfect sky and the peace that you have discovered from your heart. And then, because you are operating again from a combination of heart and mind, *trust* what you have been given. **Trust what you have been given!** Put it into practice; try it out. And you will see that time and again *you* are right because you cannot be wrong. Only your mind can be wrong. The 'you' that is *you* can only be right in the circumstances that come to you for you and the good of others.

The heart-mind… we are coming to a time when people must trust, must consult the heart-mind because the heart-mind gives access to the greater self, and the greater self can see and hear; the greater self knows what to do on a God-level, knows how to put things right, knows how to comfort, knows how to counsel, knows what to do in *every* situation and also how to repair you. When you are depressed, when you are down, when you are ill – the energies from the heart-mind can repair you, *will* repair you, time and time and time again – a limitless and endless source of comfort.

Is that sufficient?

Tony: Thank you, Joseph.

Joseph: Another question, please!

Frank Marr: Joseph, I've been told that you can read all the books you like and they will not bring you to spirit and the only route to spirit is meditation, which presumably is the heart-mind: Would you agree with that?

Joseph: I would agree that meditation is the track to the heart-mind and I would agree entirely – including my book [*reference to **Revelation**, which was the only book of the series published at that time*] and I have said in the past that the message in my book is *underneath* the words because the words are taken in by the physical mind but the message, the blessing of the group that I work for, is underneath the words and that is taken in by the heart-mind.

There are many types of meditation and you have to be careful because the physical mind will seek to trick you along the road to meditation. The physical mind will say: 'I can't have this person moving in this direction away from the Field, away from my source of perceived energy. I will, therefore, have to engage them in a mind-play, in a game. I will have to make sure that during the time they feel they are meditating they are looking for signs and symbols; they are trying to listen to this guide or that guide; they are trying to perceive something clairvoyantly about someone else.' And the mind will engage you, if you are not careful, in a loop.

The true way of meditation is to go *in love* to God and the heart-mind and let go, knowing that you are perfectly safe. The true meditation is to let go because, only in letting go of the physical thought-process, can you allow other thoughts – your true thoughts, the thoughts of God, the thoughts of those who try to guide you, the thoughts of angels – in. You cannot fill a vessel that is already full; you first have to empty it, and there again there is an illusion from the Earth plane: 'I cannot make my mind go blank.'

...Yes, you can, by turning away from it, by moving towards the heart-mind, by entering into love and Light and peace and trusting as a child would do. A child does not have all the complexities that you as adults have. A child trusts. A child trusts its parents. You have to unlearn. You have to take yourself away from the physical mind and enter into the God-mind and see then where, unbidden, those streams of energy take you. Then the things that emerge from here [*pointing to the heart*] and not from here [*pointing to the head*] will be the ones that you can trust, will give you guidance, will accelerate your perception of spirituality, your spiritual evolution. Do not allow the mind to take you captive once again. You can see how dangerous a place the Earth plane is, not only out there, but in here [*pointing to the head again*].

With regard to the written word, with regard to anything that you read regarding spirituality and spiritual evolution, take the words into your physical mind, test them out with your spiritual heart, and if you feel in sitting by that pool, if you feel in letting go in your comfortable chair, that what you have read *offends* you, that what you have read is a smoke screen, that what you have read irritates you or doesn't feel right in some way ...**then go with that feeling.**

Do not make the mistake of thinking: 'If I reject the book, I reject my spirituality.' That is wrong! If you reject the book it is because the things in the book are not right for you and you are using your soul as a barometer, as a Geiger counter, as a gauge, to let you know whether your soul *truly* links to what you are reading. If it doesn't, move on to something else.

If you do not get your satisfaction out of books then ask God to show you another way, and maybe the conversation that you will have with someone – a stranger – will put you on the right path. Or you will find a book that someone has left in a train station and it will be just what you need, not necessarily a spiritual book, but one sentence or one paragraph will make you think in a different way. Or it will be as though the television set is speaking to you and someone is saying something within a play or a documentary that is *exactly* what you need to hear.

God talks to you all the time. All the time there is a constant message, a constant dialogue between Father and child, but we have to know how to pick it up. And we pick it up by not being complicated but by being simple – simple of the mental field, simple of the heart – and then being observant, and then recognising what God is saying to us, and trusting in that message that can help us time and time and time again, and will guide us to the right things to read, the right things to see, the right things to feel in order to evolve spiritually.

Is that a sufficient answer?

Frank: Thank you.

Joseph: Thank you.

Frank: Can I just follow up by asking: meditation is very difficult to get into – would you accept hypnosis as a route to meditation, as a route to spirit?

Joseph: Hypnosis... They say in hypnosis that you can never be made to do what you don't want to do. However, you have to consider that the hypnosis applies to the physical mind. So you are programming the physical mind and, true, you cannot make a soul *at core* do what it does not want to do, but remember that that soul is living within a multi-layered existence that also has, as one of its facets, the physical mind. So you have to be extremely careful.

Hypnosis has to be used extremely carefully and has to be blessed! The person who is doing the hypnotising should bless the person who is going to be hypnotised and should bless the tool of hypnosis before applying it, and should say: 'Father, I wish to reach into this mind, but only as far as You will allow me to; only in the measure that You will allow me to; only to talk in free will to this soul to perhaps get them to see something in a slightly different way – not to control, not to mask.'

And, hypnosis also has the effect of masking at times. 'Yes, I'm fine!' Are you, at core? Have you removed the problem at core or is it masked by the physical mind saying that everything is alright when that situation is still there within the person? All these aspects of help for others have to be used as tools of Love. Nothing more! **Tools of Love!** 'I pick up the tool of hypnosis. I put Love into it. I ask God to put Love into it. I ask God to put Love into me to guide me and then I apply it as I feel' – not from the physical mind but from the heart-mind it should be applied. Then, and only then, are you safe to apply a technique that can alter someone's *physical* will.

Does that answer the question?

Frank: Thank you.

Joseph: Thank you.

Another question, please!

Shirley Hayhurst: Could I ask, Joseph?

Joseph: Of course!

Shirley: You mentioned the angels previously – do you actually work with the angels in the spirit world?

Joseph: I am working with the angels now!

I am working with the angels *now* – I am not flattering you. **I am not flattering you!** I am not looking for a compliment; I am stating something that is *factual*.

There is information that we are working to bring forwards within the next few years [*reference to the fourth book in the Joseph Communications series that was subsequently published in 2012*]. That information concerns something that you will have heard me talk about before called 'the Fall' – the Fall that altered physical perception on this level; the Fall that eventually led to the Field being as it is at this time.

I want to share a secret with you. Can you keep a secret?

[*Audience laughter*]

...Before the Fall you were all angels.

Can you keep another secret?

...You still are!

You are compressed, you are battered by the effects of the Field. You are used to thinking in 'less' terms rather than 'more' ...'I couldn't possibly be an angel. I couldn't possibly be worthy. I couldn't possibly talk to God.' These are all the effects of the Field and the effects of the Fall.

You were originally angels who, in full volition, came to this level of physicality *to experience* – much as you might enter a beautiful garden, much as you might enter a beautiful manor house to see what that manor house could bring to your senses, to see what perfumes there were in that beautiful garden.

Things went wrong. You became trapped by the illusion and, in being trapped by the illusion, you lost your memory. You forgot that you *were* an angel and *are* an angel. You forgot your link to God. You forgot that all this is an illusion.

Yes! The answer is, yes, I commune with angels. We see angels who visit us from their sphere; we see angels who assist and advise us and souls on Earth. But I tell you this when I see an angel I see a shining being, but I also see a reflection of myself as I *will be* when I have finally evolved through the cleansing spheres and take my place *again* with my brothers and sisters. That is what I see. When I look at you, looking at you with spiritual eyes, I see colours and I see within those colours the core, your spirit, and I see – within the various shells of physicality and physical and spiritual atoms – I see the angel that you are.

It amuses me that so many books are about at the moment where you can call on angels to do everything for you. Everything for you!

…You need to park your car – call on an angel!

[*Laughter from the audience*]

…You need to change your job – call on an angel!

…You need help with your relationship – call on an angel!

…You need to do the ironing – there is an angel of ironing!

[*More laughter*]

They have got one thing right, and the one thing that they've got right is that you *can* call on an angel...

...You can call on the angel-within.

There has been for many years, for many decades, an 'us and them' situation in literature, in spiritual teaching, to say that the angels are *apart* from us, that we are one line of evolution and the angels are a different line of evolution. In fact, this is what Michael believed many years ago when he started out as a medium and he saw angels and said: 'How wonderful to see angels! They are completely different from us; they are taller; they have glowing colours; they have booming voices; they are beautiful.' And all these things are true, but the time has come now to reveal the truth — globally to reveal the truth — to lift Man's mind, to lift Man's heart and to say: 'You were an angel. You are an angel. You just took a wrong turn in that 'garden' — that beautiful garden — and found yourself in a maze. But it is time to come out of the maze, and there is no quicker way to come out of the maze than to recognise what you were, what you are, where you are going and what lies ahead of you.'

God's first born — angels!

God's first born — highest expression as a child of God, as a spark of God — is the angel ...is you!

You fell out of the 'Heavens' ...you fell to Earth. You are disguised, you are undercover, but the secret mission is now revealed ...the secret mission is to remember who you are **and reveal it to other people.** Do you see angels? All the time! Look in the mirror — you see an angel. Sit on the bus — you see angels. At a football match — you see angels. **You cannot see anything other than angels in the human form because that is what the human form really contains.**

Is that a sufficient answer?

Shirley Hayhurst: More than enough!

Joseph [*smiling*]: I am delighted when I can give more than enough.

[*Audience laughter*]

Next question, please!

Jill: Joseph, I'd like to ask should we be living a more simple life not surrounded by material things and so on and so forth? Should we be looking to live more simply?

Joseph: The material things... you see, even within the Field set to negative, *messages* surface and the material things you have around you are a cry for help because the material things are almost as though the human race is saying: 'If I can raise the level of technology things will be alright; if I can invent a better car things will be alright; if I can build a bigger building things will be alright because all these things will elevate me *somehow*. All these things will make me feel better,' ...**for five minutes.**

The message that you are giving yourselves is that you are trying to get back to that connection with God. So, you invent better, bigger, faster 'things' in the subconscious *hope* that those things will lead you to a better life. And, it is the better life that you want that is in the subconscious, but not the better life that is the yacht and the pool – the better life that comes from knowing who you are and reacting to other people in a God-like manner ...and they to you.

The material things that you have around you are not evil. The material things are only 'evil'... (but that is the wrong word)... are only a smoke screen when you allow them to be. And there is nothing wrong with enjoying your technology, enjoying your cars, enjoying your buildings, enjoying your music but at the same time you have to remember two things:

...The first is that they are not yours. **They are not yours!**

...And the second is that one day you must leave them behind for someone else. **You must leave them behind!**

Again, there is a subliminal message, there is a subconscious message, in so many people saying: 'This is mine! This car is mine! This house is mine! This holiday is mine! This money is mine! These people are mine!' because you are trying to draw to yourself that which constantly slips away on a subconscious level – the need to be part of each other and to be part of God. But you misplace your quest; you place your quest into materiality when you should be placing your quest in the search for God within and within each other. *Then* you enjoy the materiality but it does not dominate you; you enjoy the materiality but it does not imprison you, and you can work just as spiritually as you could have done in ages past without the technology.

The technology can be good. The materiality can be good. It is knowing how to use it and it is recognising yourself that point at which the material is taking over. Then you have to withdraw and say: 'Yes, it is a nice car ...for the amount of time that I have got it – *thank you, Father.* Yes, it is a wonderful television ...for the amount of time that I have it; it is a privilege to have it – *thank you, Father.* But, yes, it is also a nice world; it is a spiritual world; it is God's world and that is forever – *thank you, Father!*' And no-one can take that away from you. Do you see the distinction I am making?

Jill: Yes.

Joseph: Does that make sense?

Jill: Yes.

Joseph [*smiling*]: I always want to make sense. I always want to make sense. One of my colleagues is giving me a lemon and he is saying that the lemon looks wonderful – *looks* wonderful with such beautiful yellow skin ...and then you bite into it and it is bitter! And then you think there might be a lemon further up the tree that is sweeter because it has been in the sunshine. That too is bitter and you take another lemon ...and another ...and another ...**and they are all the same.**

And that in effect is what materiality is like: 'That is a beautiful lemon – I'll just bite into it. Not so good! I'll try for another one ...and another one ...and another one,' when the tree – the actual lemon tree – just stands there and allows the power of God to flow through it and is blissfully happy.

You don't need the fruit – you need to be like the tree. You need to say: 'Father, I am happy and, whatever else you send to me, I thank You for. At the core I am One with You, I always will be One with You, and I am going 'home' and that makes me happy.'

Who else please?

[*Silent pause*]

Or should Joseph go home?

[*Audience laughter*]

Denis Barnes: I have a question but I don't want to take the space up when others could ask a question. What is the benefit of having the twelve-strand DNA reconnected that basically disconnected thousands of years ago? What is the benefit of having it reconnected now?

Joseph: I am sorry but I don't understand that question.

Denis: OK.

Joseph: I do not understand the question – can you explain that more to me?

Denis: I was told by my teachers that we have DNA – we all have DNA – but twelve strands of it were disconnected many, many thousands of years ago by ETs. Is this correct?

Joseph: According to *my* knowledge it isn't, according to *my* viewpoint. You must understand that there are many viewpoints on my level, on the levels above and on the levels below.

What I have to say to you is that the Fall – *as I see it* because I was part of that shift in consciousness – was caused by certain factions on Earth believing that, *in goodness,* they could second-guess and accelerate God's plan for this part of the universe. And as a result of that they caused an imbalance in the speed of vibration on this level. And because of that imbalance the souls then became locked into, if you like, an 'angry' world. If you apply heat to something you agitate the molecules. They become hot, they become angry, they scurry around, they hit each other and the result is pain if you touch that heat. A similar thing, according to *my* background, happened at the time of the Fall.

It is a complex matter and it took place over many, many years as you would understand it but the effect of that speeding up, of second-guessing God, of saying, 'We know a better way' was to create conflict ...'heat' is the easiest word I can think of. We agitated the molecules of this world and created anger, created need and cut ourselves off from God – not the other way round; cut ourselves off in physical consciousness, not in spiritual consciousness. This is why we always talk about the heart-mind to reconnect yourself to God on a daily basis. We cut ourselves off from God.

And instead of this area of space, this area of illusion, being fed by God-energy channelled through His angels – YOU – the aggravated energy was contained within a closed Field of consciousness and then *began* the troubles that you perceive now. Then began the illness, the disharmony, the war, the anger, the seeking for power, the lust which are all symptoms of the original 'experiment', if you like, that went wrong – **of the speeding up of the vibrationary process on a physical level.**

Things happen in this world too quickly – *too quickly* – because the molecules are set at a rate in which they cannot decay completely, neither can they be recreated completely via the souls of men, women and children on Earth. So, the Field is a finite cloud or area of energy. Finite! This is why our message is so important at this time – **the energy is running out.**

You have to begin feeding the Field from outside of itself, as it were, from the God-power outside of itself. You have to begin feeding yourselves with God-energy, not with energy from the Field, which is polluted like the grid lines we talked about earlier. Then you begin to change the effects of the Fall.

We have talked about simplicity tonight. I am a simple man. I studied many times – I studied in great cathedrals; I studied in great temples; I studied military history during one lifetime, but my mission is simple and I become worried sometimes by the complexities of *spiritual* literature on this level of consciousness, and also (forgive me, Father) by the promptings of some of my fellow workers but that is *my* point of view.

My view of the Earth is that the Earth is simple, that the Earth Field went wrong because of the souls within it choosing a way that divorced them physically, materially, from God and that we are here to put things right.

You may well be correct about DNA – I do not know. I can only say from my point of view and from my group's point of view that our way of rectifying everything – *everything* that is wrong in this world is to bring Light into it; is to restore the 'connection' if you like (you are talking about connections), is to put the 'plug' in between the human being and God once more so that the energy flows, so that the energy flows into the Field, so that the Field is not a allowed to destroy itself, to implode and it is replaced, replenished, by positive energies and the world changes and, Ladies and Gentlemen, is saved! ...**Is saved!**

Is that a sufficient answer?

Denis: Very much so!

Joseph: Thank you.

Josephine: Joseph, good evening.

Joseph: Good evening.

Josephine: Could I ask – something you said earlier about always sending Love to people that perhaps we don't like. But is there ever an occasion where someone perhaps has such negative, dark energies that you should just walk away or should we always try and send Love and Light out...?

Joseph: If the person has ...thank you for that question... if the person has terrible, dark energies you should always walk away. But you walk away *physically*, you do not have to walk away mentally, and you should not be afraid of someone who seems to exhibit dark energy. You should send the Light out to them 'in the dark' as it were, without them knowing. You do not have to tell them. You should send out Light to them and surround them with Light almost as a subconscious exercise, so that person is being fed by Light – the correct type of Light – from some source. Otherwise if that person is truly steeped in the darkness of the world and the darkness and negativity of the Field then they are being fed *only* by the Field and how can they ever change?

How can they ever change?

If you will not be a champion for them, who will?

It begins by one person recognising the Light within each soul, by saying: 'I do not agree with what you are doing. I do not agree with how you are. I do not agree with how you treat me, and I will not, on a conscious level, allow you to treat me that way. But on a spiritual level I will send you my unconditional love because I know that there is a seed of God within you that wants, that longs to grow out into the Light and can only grow if I, and others like me, send out Light to you.'

It seems frightening on this level; it seems that there are certain people who can crush you, who can damage you, who can cause you pain, who are greater than the Light-within. They are *never* greater than the Light-within. If they kill you they don't kill you – they take away the physical illusion but you are still there as a spirit. They have accomplished nothing; they cannot harm you. So, you should never in any circumstances be afraid if you have God and Light within you on your side, *which you do.*

That is not to say that you are foolish and confront people physically. In confronting people physically you can come to harm. And you are not 'confronting' them *spiritually*, you are simply sending out the Light to them, a ray which will feed them. That is what you are doing – you are feeding them. And you must not be afraid that, back along that ray that you are emanating, will come their lack of positivity, their 'evil' – for want of a better word. It cannot – your protection is the Light that you are sending out.

Remember, too, that you may be sending out the Light to that person but, if they are not well-liked, there may be a hundred, a thousand people sending out anger to them. It has to stop! We have to make a stand, and we do not make a stand with the people that we love. We do not pick up the little puppy and say, 'I am sending Light out to you and it is terribly difficult!' Of course you send out Light to the little puppy, but you also send out Light to those that it is difficult, *most difficult*, to love because they need it most. And they are trapped – just as you are trapped; they have simply lost their way and are struggling on a physical level to express themselves, and are expressing themselves in an unacceptable manner *physically*. But they are still a spirit; they are still loved by you at a God-level. They are *always* loved by God no matter what they do. So, you have to exhibit that God-Love in being part of the change that must come to them.

Does that make sense to you?

Josephine: Complete sense, yes, thank you — especially the bit about worrying about the Light, the positivity and negativity coming back.

Joseph: Your Light is your armour. Remember, if you will, the vision of the Archangel Michael with the sword of Light, with the sword of truth, with the Light, the armour of Light. And there is a fight going on, but the fight is not a war. The fight is an attempt to change consciousness and the sword is a symbol because the sword cuts through the darkness like a knife and the darkness disappears. Your love for people is your own armour. No matter what they try to do to you that armour is impenetrable, and that armour of Light elevates your soul.

We are tiring Michael. Who would like to ask another question, please?

Doreen Marr: Can I ask Joseph, there is a prolific amount of writings regarding spirituality and other therapies and one thing or another and all coming through at different levels. Earlier this evening you talked of the circle above you and the circle above them and so it goes on at different levels of sort of infiltration, and there's obviously lower levels below you. I find it very confusing and I think it must be difficult for people becoming aware and going into this field. There seems to be no control in the inspiration that comes through to people. Yes, yes, I believe *this* but from my own experience, from when I started to where I am today, I could have gone off at a tangent at the first thing and put a load of stuff out that now I wouldn't have believed.

Joseph: What prevented you?

Doreen: My heart.

Joseph: Your heart! That is the simple question that is the answer.

We are individuals. In this room we are individuals and God glories in our individuality and our ability to see the world uniquely. That individuality does not leave us when we leave the physical and when we leave the physical flesh. And so we congregate slowly, slowly into groups who are like-minded – but like 'heart-minded' not like 'physical-minded'. And, as a result of that, we determine that we will try and get a message through to the Earth plane to our brothers and sisters who are still suffering, because we are still suffering – we are a part of that movement back into the Light.

But we still come as individuals. When we touch the Earth plane we have to, if you like, 'devolve'. The molecules that are closest to the physical body we have to inhabit once again in order to communicate with you and, in doing that, we take on some of the persona that we once had, some of the biases that we once had – and this once again is an effect of the Field. We are, if you like, 'sticking our necks out' into the Field and, as a result of that, the waters sometimes become muddied.

What you should look for in any literature that you put out, in any literature that you read is, is the core the message:

1. Not offending you?

2. Being something that you can believe in and run with into the future.

This is why I always say with *my* book (and it is only 'my' book in the sense that I am a spokesperson for a great many souls – it is not my book at all) the message is underneath the words. Many people say: 'Joseph, I have read your book four times ...five times... and each time I get a different message; each time I see something different in it.' It is because you are getting the message *beneath* the words. We have put into a physical manifestation a spiritual concept. We have blessed the words, we have blessed the book, we have blessed the undertaking and that book can be a different message to a thousand people because it is the message that is tuned to them, *not the words*.

And you can always hold a book over your heart-centre and say: 'Do I agree with this before I read it? How does it feel to me?' Because you will extend, from the heart-centre, those tendrils of energy into the book that will instantly tell you on a spiritual level whether that book is for you. The message, regardless of where it comes from – from literature or from someone else – is at core the same. Unfortunately, it is being transmitted to you through the effects of the Field and through imperfect souls like myself.

Do you see what I am saying?

Doreen: I do, yes, but I also think that there are many ways to tell a story and sometimes the direct way is easier than trying to interpret because everyone is going to interpret what you have just said differently as we sit round here.

Joseph: That is the point.

Doreen: Absolutely.

Joseph: The point is they *should be* interpreting it differently on a conscious level, but on a subconscious level **the message is the same**. The book that you read is a tool of the Field. The voice that you hear ...why am I not standing here with you physically outside of Michael? Because I have to approach the Earth plane through the effects of the Field, which *limits* the extent to which I can get the message across verbally or visually.

And this is why we come because there has to come a tipping point when we can change the effects of the Field so that the message will be simpler to get through and will be universally understood.

But you are the message – no matter what you read, at any time you can go into your heart-centre and say, 'Do I agree with this?' Or, you can go into your heart-centre independent of spiritual literature and say, 'What do I think about this? What does the God-within think about this?'

That is the message you trust – irrespective of Joseph, irrespective of any spiritual book you read – *what is within you.* And trust that what comes through your heart-centre is the universal message and is right for you and is right for others and, if it isn't, you walk away from it until it is.

Do you understand that?

Doreen: Yes, thank you.

Joseph: Thank you. Thank you for your patience.

Pat Jackson: Joseph, can I just ask about the phrase 'gut feeling' – is that gut feeling spiritual or is it largely a physical feeling?

Joseph: It is more likely to be spiritual because it is the spiritual that impacts on the physical so your gut feeling is your instant feeling that something is right or *more often* that something is not right for you. It is like having another 'hand' from your solar plexus that handshakes someone else that you have just met and says, 'I don't like that handshake. I don't like that person.' And don't you feel guilty? Don't you feel guilty! And then months or perhaps years later you say, 'If only I had trusted my gut instinct!'

Now this is not a matter of sending out anger or hatred to someone – it is simply viewing their vibrations, chakra to chakra, and feeling that that vibration that comes to you, that links to your chakra, is not a vibration that you want at this time. Therefore, you need to be steered by that inner voice. That does not mean that you should not pray for the person or love the person – you should do both. But if something says to you: 'Not that direction!' If something says to you on Earth, 'Danger! Quicksand!' what do you do? You avoid the quicksand. But the physical mind says: 'You are being terrible to this person! You cannot perceive of a person you have just met as being as someone you do not want to be with and do not want to talk to.'

Yes, you can!

You shouldn't be guilty about that because you are being given a message. Remember that you have an aura, an energy field that extends from you so that when you come into someone's proximity you touch auras. And the aura contains, sends and receives information and that information goes first to the spirit, first to the heart-mind and then instantly [*snapping his fingers*] to the physical mind and says: 'Don't like that! Shouldn't touch that! Don't want to be in this building! Want to be in this building! Want to be with that person!' And it is showing you that your vibration is *or isn't* harmonious with the vibration of the person or the location that you find yourself in or with.

Take heed. Take heed! We are here; you are here for guidance. You pick up spiritual literature for guidance; you investigate spirituality for guidance. What I am saying is that that guidance is always with you if you know how to listen to it; if you take heed of it; if you obey it. Because you – *the spirit-you* – is telling you – *the physical-you* – something about the situation you find yourself in. If you always align yourself with God, morning and night, then the information that comes to you is correct.

Does that make sense to you?

Pat: Yes, very much. Thank you.

Joseph: Thank you.

We are overrunning Michael's physical body. He often describes it as feeling like he is being run over and he is closer to the body now as the energy wears thin. I thank you for creating this energy that has allowed me to work tonight and, as always, I will attempt to answer a couple more questions, but if I depart during the middle of one, please forgive me.

Who would like to ask something?

Two people simultaneously: Can I ask, Joseph?

[*Audience laughter*]

Shirley Hayhurst: I am dying to hear what you both have to say!

Wendy Loudon: Joseph, this evening you have mentioned, a few times, the Fall and I was wondering exactly what that is.

Joseph: The Fall is a *vast* subject. The Fall is a set of circumstances that happened to the human race a long, long time ago. **A long, long, long time ago!** And the Fall and the information about the Fall explains why the Earth is as it is at the moment and what we can do to *change* that.

It is a vast subject – I am not ducking that subject but we are preparing information on it. We have a section of a book ready now but not the whole book. It is a delicate and yet an explosive subject. It will change the way that people will think about themselves and about the history of this planet but it is not yet ready. My first task is to dictate, is to create with the people who are working with me, the three books in the series [*reference to the Joseph Communication series*]. Those three books are not a 'be-all and end-all' – they lead to the book on the Fall.

So, it is coming! [*Smiling*] The Fall is not coming – the information about the Fall is coming! Please be patient – if I overrun Michael too much there won't be a book on the Fall.

[*Audience laughter*]

Is there someone else, please?

Jayne Lea: Can I just ask – I have been given a 'tool' [*reference to More to Life Magazine*] to try and help people who are realising that they are spiritual, and to achieve it and to reach as many people as possible I struggle to stay in the 'heart' because I have got to be in the 'head' quite a bit to be able to actually do that work. I just wondered could you give me advice about how to keep that balance because quite often it overwhelms me with the amount of work it involves, and it is hard to keep that balance but I know that I have been guided to do this work.

Joseph: This is, again, an effect of the Field. Everything in your lives goes too fast; you have no time for God; you have no time to sit and eat and digest your food; you have no time to think … and the Field wants it that way, *needs* it that way, must have it that way!

Please do not be misinformed about meditation and about going to the heart-mind. **The heart-mind can be reached in a fraction of a second.** You can walk into a room and, very quickly at the speed of physical thought, look at the room, look at the situation, realise that you need an answer and go into the heart-mind and *ask*. You can isolate yourself from the other people in that room for a fraction of a second, you can tune into God – just as surely as you tune into other stations on your television sets in a second simply by pressing a button.

You need that time with the heart, but that time with the heart can be between seeing people, can be when you are in an office, can be when you are driving to and from work. When the actions of the physical body are automatic, you can retreat into the heart-mind and ask and pray and see what the heart-mind is saying to you.

The spiritual path, Ladies and Gentleman, is difficult – it is difficult, difficult, difficult – because all the time the Field is pulling at you. All the time – through the way that you feel (because you are part of a collective consciousness) and the way people react to you when you say you wish to achieve something spiritually – always you are being pulled at, pulled at and pulled at: 'That is not the way! That is nonsense! Come back with us. Be the way you were before!'

And the Field (as I have said earlier) awakens and singles you out. You are not one of the sheep that are going in the same direction – you are the sheep that is making for the fence at the other side of the field and the Field does not like that, and so it concentrates on you – or so it seems.

And it seems, as you walk the spiritual path, that the challenges around you become more and more and more intense and more and more and more demanding. Do not be put off by the Field saying, 'You have no time.' There is *always* time, always a split-second, always a few minutes, always the time between waking and sleeping when you go to bed at night to contemplate the heart-mind and to say: 'No, the Field is not the stronger partner – the heart-mind is the stronger partner. I am working for God. God controls the situation not the Field and I will go with what God tells me to do.' Do you see that?

Jayne: Yes.

Joseph: Do you see that? Do not give up!

Do not give up! So many fall by the wayside; the weight of the Field crushes so many and they go back to what they were ...but they can *never* be what they were. They have spiritual knowledge and they become even more upset, even more depressed because they do not fit into the physical world and they feel they have not time to fit into the spiritual world.

There is only one world and it is a spiritual world. You are right – it is the others who are lost, who are mistaken, who are drawing energies from the wrong source.

You are right!

So you must keep on – each of you in this room – must keep on with the words that you say to people, with the Love that you send out to people, with your own quest to discover more about yourselves *spiritually*. Keep on and you become beacons for the Light and you change this world forever – which is our quest.

Chapter Five

Joseph Trance Demonstration – 9th October, 2009
The Sanctuary of Healing, Lancashire, UK

Spiritual topics discussed:

The reason for accidents.

Illness and disease.

Changing the world through visualisation.

The need for simplicity in spirituality.

The effect of negative thoughts on the collective consciousness.

Is the Earth the only planet to experience negativity?

Indigo children.

The need for respect for the Earth as a spirit.

The imbalance of masculine and feminine.

What will happen to mankind if the Earth comes to an end?

Do new souls come to the Earth?

A brief summery of the Fall.

Reincarnation.

The ego.

Sacred places and networking Light across the globe.

Joseph: Many of you will be interested as to how I get here. I get here very quickly. I know, of course, in advance that one of these demonstrations, one of these sessions, is going to take place and I become very quiet; I isolate myself from my colleagues and I link with Michael over a number of hours and a number of days without him being aware of that. And then there is the in-rush, there is the time when I *connect* to your vibration.

And the first thing that strikes me is the heaviness of this realm, although I was a part of it time and again – **the *heaviness* of this realm.** The second thing that strikes me as I make that transition is the amount of noise emanating from this realm. Not just the everyday noises that you are used to but the noise of thought ...the noise of distress ...the noise of illness ...the noise of prayer ...the noise of anguish ...the vibrations that are given out by each soul.

There is a way to calm that noise; there is a way to heal illness; there is a way to find answers in time of distress ...**and the way is to become quiet, to become silent, to go *within*.** Many of your spiritual philosophies talk about 'going within' but do you understand what that means?

...To set aside, to let go of the circumstances around you *totally* for a short time and to explore the world within yourself. At the centre of your heart there is a comfortable 'seat' and you can sit there at the heart of your soul and become quiet. And, if you become quiet enough, answers to every problem that besets you can be found and *known* as a surety: 'This is the way I must proceed. This is what I must do. This is what I must *not* do.' And then I will not have to make this journey, then I can stay in my sphere because then you will reach answers from within – not from *Joseph*.

Forgive my sense of humour; I like to begin each session with an upbeat vibration. You have come here not to understand more about me but to understand more about yourselves, so I *hope* that you have brought questions for me this evening, and

I would like to invite the first of those, please. Who wishes to talk to me?

Tony Clarkson: Joseph, can I ask a question? It's Tony. In your book [*reference to* **Revelation**] there is a chapter about illness, wellness, and in that chapter it touches upon accidents. Could you explain a little more about accidents and what accidents actually are?

Joseph: Do you wish to know about the cause and effect behind accidents?

Tony: And also what we can learn from those accidents.

Joseph: Everything that happens to you in life is as a result of something that has happened to you previously – **without exception.** You are constantly switching tracks by the decisions that you make and you can instantly see the physical effects of the decisions you make, but there are also *spiritual* repercussions because of the decisions that you make. If you are, for example, distressed, then that distress is a dominant vibration in your aura and in your being and attracts from outside itself *similar* vibrations. If you feel that your life is off the rails, that you are heading blindly into the future, if you are frightened of that future then your fear of the future is a dominant vibration in your aura ...**and you attract more of the same.**

Also you have to consider that your soul is here to learn despite what your physical mind says to you on a daily basis, despite your image of yourself as a physical being. You exist on a spiritual level *first* and your soul knows what it needs in order to learn. And so as you consciously bring out certain vibrations, consciously fear things, consciously draw things to yourself, also at a soul-level you do the same but the two do not necessarily run as parallel paths. You may be frightened on a physical level but your soul will be sure of something, and if you turn away from that something and *need* to meet that something your soul will set up vibrations around you – in conjunction with the

127

karma that has been assigned to you before you incarnated – to draw that thing to you. And your 'accidents' are nothing of the sort – your accidents are cause and effect in operation; your accidents can be turning points; your accidents can be points at which you are placed in the path of different people, different circumstances, and made to take stock of the way that you have lived your life thus far.

There is always some benefit in your accidents and you will say: 'Joseph, that is nonsense! I hurt myself; I was a burden to others; I couldn't operate as I had before.' But consider one example: consider one soul who, through an accident, loses mobility for a time. During that time that soul can only think, can only consider, can only go back over the past and look at life thus far. And if that accident over an amount of time brings to that soul a *wisdom* as to how to act in future, if that soul realises something through that accident, then that accident has been a wondrous event.

You have no accidents! People crash in planes because on that particular day they were supposed to go 'home.' People hurt themselves because of the ways that they have been thinking about the world and themselves. People are brought to a halt because their soul is saying: 'It is time to take stock, to evaluate and to learn something.'

It seems harsh, but remember that the physical body is merely that – a physical body; it is part of the illusion of the Field. You are not *in reality* operating from within that body although, from your point of view, it appears to be that way. It is as though part of your soul – the greater part of your soul – is asleep and a pinpoint of Light is 'you' within a physical body. Once that physical body is withdrawn, once that physical body drops away from you, you return to the higher soul with the wisdom that you have brought to yourself, wrapped around yourself through your experiences on Earth.

It may have been painful for the physical body; it may have been restrictive for the physical body but, through those sacrifices of the physical, the *spiritual*, the soul, the core, has learnt. And you may say, 'Poor physical body – how terrible for the physical body!' But remember that once you withdraw from the physical body the sentience withdraws from the physical body that has kept it in motion, and the differing degree of sentience that the molecules of the physical body contain disperse to come into being again as something else – another body, or an object or another expression of God.

Nothing is lost; nothing is harmed except, ultimately, *yourselves* by returning and not taking the advice that accidents give to you, not learning from them so that you come back into the physical again ...and again ...and again. That is when you harm yourself because in being in the physical you can be harmed through experience. You experience pain, you experience suffering – it is not the true state of your soul **but *you* choose it.**

So, look at your accidents in another way; look at them as turning points; look at them as learning opportunities; look at them as something that your soul *wishes* for some reason. There is some aspect of your approach to existence that needs to be sharpened, needs to blossom, needs to be enhanced and accidents allow that to happen.

No accidents! I wish I could substitute a different word – 'inevitabilities'. If you approach something in a certain way and do not learn from approaching it in a negative way, you will be brought to a point where you will have to look at it and learn from it and move on. Is that a sufficient answer?

Tony: Thank you.

Joseph: Yes, please – another question!

June Proctor: I would like to ask, there seem to be more and more children being born who are being diagnosed with autism.

Are they bringing traumas from a past life or what do you think the reason is?

Joseph: You have a terrible situation! You have a terrible situation in which souls come through to learn, souls come through to learn new experiences and, of course, bring with them major traumas from the past. But the world will not allow them, as I have said, to blossom because the world is set to negative and so the world resonates at a vibration that brings, unfortunately, out of those souls the worst aspects of the situations that have dogged them from the past.

There are many diseases that seem to be escalating at the moment. It is not that souls are bringing them in, in order to experience them – it is that souls are returning and the Earth is resonating at a vibration that harmonises with those aspects within their soul-memory. So, if there is a situation from the past that is negative that has not been resolved then the Earth tends to bring that out. You see that in *every* life, because in every life does it not seem that there are more negative things than positive things that happen to people during the course of that life?

When – not *if* but **when** – the Field has been 're-initialised' (there's a modern word) in the name of Light then the souls who come here, even though they have those soul-memories of negative experiences in the past, will have far better physical lives because the vibration of the Field will bring out of them the higher spiritual vibrations, the ability to overcome and conquer illness, to see past illness, to dispense with illness and say it doesn't exist.

So, it is a combination of two things. It is a combination of past memories, soul-memories that have always been there, and the current vibrationary signature of the Field that concentrates subconsciously on those memories, brings them out of the soul so that the soul suffers again.

It need not be so.

It need not be so, and this is the whole point of my making an appearance here tonight – to say, 'It need not be so!' *It need not be so* means that you do not concentrate on what appears to be wrong – you concentrate on what can be put *right*. And you have to be very blinkered, you have to be very 'straight ahead' – not turning to the right or to the left but straight ahead – saying to yourself, believing, making a hymn of:

There is only Light today.

There is only Light in my life.

There is only Light in the lives of the people that I touch.

There is only Light in the world and I am sending it out.

...And then you begin to change the vibrationary signature of the Field from negative to positive *and people suffer less*. Is that a sufficient answer?

June: Yes, thank you.

Joseph: Thank you. Another question, please!

Shirley: Could I ask, Joseph, what can we do as individuals, besides sending out the Light, to help with the Earth, to help raise the vibrations of the Earth?

Joseph: There are two things you can do. Unfortunately, society wants to make the answer to changing things complicated and complex: 'You must do this ...you must chant every third day ...you must stand in a certain corner of the room ...you must understand certain spiritual equations that are tremendously complex.' The truth – as all your master teachers have said to you over the centuries, over thousands of years – is simple: **You are Light.**

It is as simple as that! **You are God. You are Light** ...and you have forgotten that.

The Field delights in creating complex patterns in your mental field. The Field is delighted when you pick up a book that tells you how, through *complexity*, to get through to God.

You cannot get through to God through complexity.

You cannot get through to life *here* through complexity if you wish to change it. Life here can only change through two things: through visualising and sending out feeling, caring Light into the world and by also seeing, creating a better world in your inner vision.

If you want the world to change you cannot condemn it. If you want the world to change you have to love it. And if you want the world to change, *most importantly*, you have *to see it*; in your meditative times you have to see the world that you want in the way that is unique to you – to see happy smiling faces; to see nations at peace; to see empty hospitals because no one is ill any longer; to see green fields and green trees; to see an end to the industries that are choking your planet; to see blue skies.

You, each of you, is part of God. You, each of you, has the ability to create. You create each moment of your life but, unfortunately, you create *subconsciously* for the most part. And what do you create? You create a perception, a vision of the world based on the news programmes you see, based on the reports you hear, based on what you read in the newspapers. Such wonderful tools for the Field of consciousness – television, radio, newspapers! 'What a good time I can have with the people on Earth. I can keep them held within this negative thrall by making them believe the worst ...expect the worst ...*create* the worst.'

You have to be – as people who wish to see change – *blinkered*, only looking straight ahead and saying, 'This is the way I see things! This is the way that things are!' Turn off the news, rip up the newspaper, pull the plug out of the radio set! Believe in your vision, God's vision, send it out into the world enveloped in Light and you begin to change things.

Remember the imaginations you had as children. Remember how easy it was to become a knight in shining armour, a damsel in distress, and how ordinary, everyday objects became castles and tanks and wigwams ...and it was so *real*. It was real because at that time you hadn't become completely polluted by the negative aspects of the Field. But it is just as potent a thing for you today as adults to imagine in this way. It will take a little while because you are used to coming up against the perceived 'reality' of the Field, but if you persist, if you are single-minded, if you send the Light out **then *you* change this world**.

See the world you want and accept nothing less – that is how you do it. Was that a satisfactory answer?

Shirley: Yes. I am glad that you said that it was simple because I always look for the simple way to do things rather than going into the complicated things that people do... *you know you've got to go into different religions and learn how to do different things.* Well, to simply send out the Light, to me, is beautiful.

Joseph: The Light is the one truth. Sending out the Light is the one truth that changes things. It is not dependent on religion, not dependent on complex creeds ...but it *is* dependent on your *time*. Time is of the essence and, in order to change things here, we have to begin *now*. So, a part of each of your days should be set aside – if you truly care, if you truly want to change things – for sending out the Light, for accepting and creating that vision of the Earth that you want.

It is simple. If anyone says to you, 'God is over here but He is dependent on you learning this, understanding that,' and the words do not make sense to you, the words seem so complex –

forget them! God is not there. God is here [*pointing to the heart-centre*].

God is saying: 'Child, come home! Come within! Visit Me *here*. I do not expect complexity of you. I simply love you and wish you to experience that Love by divesting yourself of the complexities of the Earth-Field around you. I am here. I am always here. I demand nothing from you except that you experience My Love, which will enrich you. And then, if you choose, you can spread that Love to each person around you, to everyone around the globe. It is simple. Coming home is simple. Being a soul is simple.'

I am glad that you have asked this question because it touches on the complexity of the Field and the way that the Field *in so many ways* will try and take you away from the task of sending Light into the world.

Many people in their search for spirituality become trapped in complexity, are sidelined off the main issue. Wonderful that you have crystals that you can use; wonderful that you have objects that make a noise that you can tune into; wonderful that you have mediumistic abilities that you can use clairvoyantly. But very often the Field will say: 'Isn't that interesting – it's so interesting that you don't need to go any further. Become entranced by the crystals, become entranced by the clairvoyance, become entranced by the objects that make a noise! And, whilst you are entranced and whilst you are seeking greater complexities, I am winning, because during that time you have forgotten your mission, which is to send out the Light and see the world and recreate it in the way that you want it.'

No complexities! As someone once said, 'Be ye as a little child if you want to enter the Kingdom of Heaven!' That is what it means – simplicity, no complexities. Thank you.

Another question, please!

John O'Brien: Yes, Joseph, the Field that you are talking about – we feed it, don't we, through our own negative way of thinking and, therefore, it's like really that we attack ourselves with our own energy.

Joseph: Exactly! Originally we fed the Field as souls with a *different* pattern. Originally the Field was to be used as our area of experience, was to be used as somewhere where, in positive vibrations and in Love, we could explore who we were; we could share in God's Creation; we could learn to create; we could love each other; we could have an adventure and the Field responded. We put into the Field daily, every evening, every night – as souls – positivity and Love.

Things were in balance ...until the time when we didn't, until the time when, through our own arrogance at that time, we felt that we knew better than the way things were. We felt that we knew better than the way *we* were, that some of our vistas could be improved, some of our aims could be attained more quickly if we acted in a certain way.

At that time, over a period of many years, we began to change the vibration of the Field from positive to negative. We consciously lost – not at a soul level – but *consciously* lost our connection to God and, as a result of our changing the vibrations, the Field responded to that twisted view of reality that we put into it. When we came back and incarnated again, we expected, we came, we arrived from that time onwards with an expectation built into us that *things would go wrong* – not built into us by God – built into us by ourselves, and so we reinforced the Field negatively.

Yes, every minute of every day and every night, we project into the Field that which we believe to be true. We have always done this; it is just that today we believe so many things to be true that needn't be true. We believe that the world is a bad place; we believe that the world is a place of suffering and pain, and greed, and the attainment of power at any cost.

That is on a global level of belief... Individually we believe that *we* are going to go wrong – our physical bodies, the God-given physical bodies that we have are going to go wrong. Why? It is a two-way conversation. The Field tells us that they are going to go wrong and we believe it, and so we put out into the Field energies that say, 'Yes, my body is going wrong.' And because we create ...our bodies go wrong. How many of us believe that tomorrow is going to be a perfect day for us? Very few! How many of us believe that things will go right – positively rather than negatively? Very few of us because we are conditioned by the Field ...but we, as you say quite rightly, also condition the Field with our thoughts. Which brings us back to the 'mission statement' and the mission statement is this:

I want to change the world, therefore *I* have to change.

I cannot expect the world to change unless I change *first*.

I cannot rely on the negativity that I see around me to sustain me in pursuit of the God-within and the glories without. I have to create them *myself*.

It is such a simple message but such a difficult message for people to take on board at this time. They are used to the Field being negative; they are used to their lives being lived out in a certain way, to themselves decaying and to their energies degrading.

There is only one way. It starts with each of us and we have to pour into the Field more positivity, more Light. So, if you adopt a positive attitude *that* goes into the Field when you are working at something else, when you are in bed sleeping, when you are eating, when you are watching the television. That positivity goes out because you have built it into yourself, you have changed your vibration, you have changed the emanations from your soul, and then you become a worker for the Light and you put a blindfold on as to how the Earth appears to be.

When you are in your bedrooms at night and you close the curtains and you pull up the covers – you are *safe*. You should be peaceful, you should go into a peaceful sleep and when you come out of sleep in the morning, having visited the spirit levels, how wonderful those first few moments are: 'How wonderful. It's bliss! I am awake. It's wonderful.' ...And then your conscious mind brings back to you the things that you fear, the things that upset you. The Field *presses in*.

You have to adopt that feeling of security as you go to bed at night throughout your waking life, knowing that God will never harm you, knowing that God will protect you and knowing that, as a worker for the Light, you will be brought into contact with other people who are working for the Light so that you can spread your message. Not a creed – a message. The message is that the Earth can be different; the message is that: 'I'm proving it for myself. I can pass on that information to you so that you can prove it for yourself. And we join together, and we change the Field of consciousness and we rediscover paradise.'

Is that a sufficient answer?

John: Yes, thank you

Joseph: Thank you. Who else, please?

Sergio Solazzo: Joseph, is the Earth the only planet where souls experience negativity?

Joseph: The Earth exists within a pocket of vibration, and the space around it exists within a pocket of vibration that was formed when souls changed direction and began to invest in a feeling of lack, in a feeling of there not being enough for each person, in a feeling that they had to take what the other person had because they would not have enough did they not do so. That consciousness extends beyond the Earth just as your individual aura extends far beyond your physical body. This 'experiment', if you like, that went wrong is unique. **Unique!** Nowhere else in a populated universe – in populated *universes* – did souls make the mistake that we originally did.

As a result of this vibrational change, *time* is affected within the sphere or bubble of change; normal relationships with the molecules outside of that bubble of consciousness are not established. Other planets contain life because other planets *are life* – even the planets that do not sustain life in the human form are alive. The entire universe is alive, but the experiences of souls on higher physical levels of consciousness (because there are other higher or refined levels of *physical* consciousness) exist in a different way than you do. They exist to create and explore, they exist to harmonise with other forms of life and they exist to understand the relationship between physicality and the spiritual aspects of life.

So, there are lessons to learn if you like, but 'lessons' is the wrong word – there are *experiences* to be had in other frames of reality, but this area that contains many, many, many, many souls is the only one (as far as we are aware in the areas of reality that we have encountered) that suffers in this way. And the suffering is not the result of a vengeful God – it is a result of us turning away in consciousness at a certain time in the past from the reality of us being a part of God.

What is happening to this world now – the violence that you see, the discord that you see, the greed that you see – has happened *before*. You created at the time of 'the Fall' – which is a term that I use for the time when things went wrong – you created a wave that could not escape ...**a repeating wave;** a *repeating* wave that can only be altered by the views of the souls, contained *within* that sphere of altered consciousness, altering their consciousness *back* to how it was before that bubble was created.

The wave emerges, souls are born into this level of consciousness but first they live to a *certain* extent (but not fully) in harmony. The wave expands and, as it expands, the souls within it begin to believe that they do not have enough – they can *never* have enough! The wave expands further and the souls become traumatised and say, 'I need to take this from you because of a fear that I have within.' And the souls take, and take, and take from this area of life and this area of physicality until there is very little left to sustain life. At that point, at the top of the wavelength, the whole concept of 'reality and physicality' collapses, and down you come again.

Where are you at this time? You are not in a physical body. You are not in one of the spiritual realms. You are trapped between living the same lesson, learning the same lesson again and again.

AND I CANNOT STRESS TOO HIGHLY HOW CLOSE TO THE TOP OF THAT WAVE MANKIND IS AT THE MOMENT.

Close to the top of the wave ...but the wave *does not have to* come to its peak if enough of you recognise that something is wrong and place Light and Love and a new vision of this world into your consciousness.

The problem you have is that you cannot do it by knocking on doors and saying: 'I have a new way of life for you.' You cannot get past the consciousness of mankind, the consciousness of the Field. You have to get to the *subconscious* elements of mankind; you have to reach them at soul level, making a bridge of Light across from your solar plexus to their solar plexus and say: 'I love you. Everything is alright. Isn't this a wonderful place that we are creating!' You have to awaken that memory from *beyond* the time of the Fall when things were as near to perfection in physicality as you can find.

...So important that you send out an altered image of reality – which is not 'reality' at all; it is flexible, it is malleable – an altered image of reality and you send it out to other people and on behalf of other people because their physical consciousness is too strong for them to accept a different way of life, but at soul level they know, they *remember* – that's where you can reach them.

Is that a sufficient answer?

Sergio: Yes.

Joseph: We 'bite our nails' metaphorically. We bite our nails; we look at the way that the Earth is progressing and there is a great movement. Children were mentioned – so many children are being born at the moment with the capability to see almost instantly the way that things should be and with the ability to communicate a different way of life to people. They *know*, they are older souls, they have incarnated with the same mission as Michael – and that mission is to change consciousness, to bring Light and a different way into this world.

We grow anxious. Imagine our frustration when we try to bring something of this knowledge through and all that is demanded of the medium is the same old requirement for messages from family members. And because the people in the audiences have free will, we can't alter their request... therefore, we cannot come through. We are there, knocking at their consciousness, saying: 'Let us in! We have something important to say!' So seldom does that happen.

Joseph's soapbox! [*Smiling*] It is a very tall soapbox. I add to it every time I come here – I put another layer of wood on it so that I can stand a little higher and shout a little louder.

Who would like to ask me a question, please?

Art O'Malley: Joseph, I would like to ask a question following on from your ideas about children. I think these children are known as the 'Indigo Children' and I think they give out a special form of vibration, and I am just wondering how we can best receive that vibration to pass it on ourselves? It is this idea of being at one and giving the unified message that is reached at a higher level of consciousness.

Joseph: The children that are being born with this ability are, for the most part, placed in situations where they can blossom quickly – although there is a lot of resistance. There is always the comment: 'You have imagined that! You have not seen that! That is silly! You have to take your place in the real world.' Fortunately they *are* operating from the *real* world.

There needs to be a change in the way people approach the subject of mediumship and spirituality. And there again you have perhaps (forgive me) the greatest enemy of spirituality ...and the greatest enemy of spirituality is *religion*.

RELIGION!

Religion is nothing to do with God!

Religion is nothing to do with sending the Light into the world. Religion is *control*. And the problem we have with children who are incarnating is that many religions will say: 'You cannot do that! You must not do that! That is a sin!'

...To bring Light into the world is a sin?

...To think *freely* is a sin?

The children who have incarnated have brought with them a great deal of strength, have brought with them an 'army' of guiding forces. Our danger point is at the point when they realise that they are spiritually-minded; when they realise that they are clairvoyant, or clairaudient, or clairsentient; when they realise that they can see things, because that *point needs nurturing*, needs blossoming. And those children in the short-term need teachers who can say: 'This is what is happening to you. This is *why* it is happening to you. You are special. You have a mission.' And there are so few teachers at the moment.

You need to set up like-minded people with the knowledge of how to change the world; groups that will accept children to bring out that knowledge that is already within them; groups where children can say to you: 'I have seen someone. I talked to someone. I feel things. I know things' ...**and not be ridiculed.**

And in your individual groups, in your villages, in your towns, we should work to the time where you will actively pray for those children, actively encourage those children, and hold regular meetings to see how those children are progressing and discuss how best to open up their spiritual abilities.

What a great task they have, but you must understand that it is not a task that necessarily will fail because many of those children are from specific soul groups; and at night, when they are asleep, they are linked again as *who they really are* to the full knowledge from within those soul groups; and then those soul groups are linked to other soul groups of children around the world. So, they have their own private 'battery' regardless of what people say to them, but things would happen so much more quickly, so much more effectively if they were nurtured, if they were encouraged.

If you know such a child *pray* that their guides will get through to them clearly. Pray that, at the point of their acceptance of their spiritual gifts, there will be a blossoming, there will be people around them who can advance their knowledge. Pray for protection for those children because there will be the unscrupulous ones who will try to feed off their power, try to manipulate them, try to make them into a circus act – always the Field will try and impinge on anything that is working for the Light.

Pray for their protection, see their protection, ask – if you feel that you are of a sufficient spiritual background, if you have sufficient knowledge – ask that you be led to those children you can help and they to you, that they be placed near to you or their parents be placed near to you so that you can give them the knowledge that you have and help them to understand what their children are going through, and what their children, more importantly, are *capable of.*

Very difficult – you are witnessing a time of great change because we are climbing that 'arc' to the top. And the reason that so many children are being born with so much spiritual knowledge and the ability to access so much spiritual knowledge at such an early age is because *time grows short*, and a loving God and loving souls do not want mankind to repeat the pattern again – to in effect go 'to sleep' for a great deal of time, to be awakened again in physicality and to climb that curve again to make the same mistake again.

No. Not this time!

Please, not this time!

So, you begin to see the amount of work that you can do and you can do all this work – helping the children, changing the world, sending the Light into it – without anyone else ever knowing, without ever leaving your house. 'I cannot move. I am crippled' – as a soul you *can!* As a soul you can go anywhere, you can do anything. As a soul you can bring Light to anyone. A silent, quiet, effective 'army' that creeps up on the Field from behind and grabs it by the scruff of its neck and gives it the good shaking that it deserves ...and shakes all the negativity out of it and resets it before it is too late.

I can feel the soapbox under my feet but there are souls with me tonight – as always I do not speak for myself. I do not speak because I like the sound of my own voice (which at the moment is Michael's voice) – I speak for many, for thousands, for millions. And why do they come? ...Because they are part of you. Why do they come? ...Because they have escaped, for the most part, the physicality, the Field, but they cannot return to the Godhead without you, without *each* of you. They love you – they want you back. God loves you – wants you back. We have to work for that.

Tonight I am pleased that questions are coming out that allow me to say – **only *you* can do what needs to be done.** Only *you* can change the world. The Field, throughout your life, will say: 'No, you are reliant on us! You are reliant on this person and that organisation.'

No, these things are dust! You are reliant on the God-within, and the God-within changes hardened hearts, moves mountains, changes the Field …and your children will teach you that in the next generation.

Does that sufficiently answer the question?

Art: Yes, thanks.

Joseph: Thank you. Yes, please another question!

John O'Brien: Joseph, about the Earth… if we are going to develop as a human race we are going to have to start thinking of the Earth as a spiritual being as well as one that has got the same chemical processes – you know… it's got a physical body and a spiritual body as well.

Joseph: We are very arrogant in that we believe the human form is superior and we believe the human form is the only one that matters. We have divorced ourselves – again because of the Fall – from the fact that *everything is alive.*

Everything that you see, feel, sense, hear, smell, is alive.

Always *was*, always *will be*, because you create the things around you from the living atoms of the Field. The Earth is plundered; the Earth is disrespected; the Earth is turned away from and yet without the Earth you would have no physical existence. The Earth supplies the oxygen that you breathe; the

Earth has supplied your physical vehicle, the Earth supplies every experience you have on a physical level and yet you treat it *abysmally*.

You treat the great devas – the nature spirits – abysmally. You carve into mountains; you carve into the Earth; you burn the trees; you pollute the clouds ...**not realising that all these things are *not* under your charge.** They are under the charge of the devas, the great nature spirits who live silently, quietly, invisibly side-by-side with you to balance things. You cause them pain and distress; you banish them from the areas that they have been allocated to; you wound the Earth; you cause it pain. Never do you touch it with your hands and say, 'Thank you!' Never do you touch it with your mind and say, 'I wish to heal you.' Never do you touch it with your heart and say, 'What can I do for you?' Never do you look at it and say, 'You are *so wonderful!*'

The Earth that was created by human souls millennia ago, created by human souls working in the name of God, human souls in their angelic form – the Earth that was created in this way should not have had to suffer as a result of the Fall but you covered it in a 'bandage' of negativity; you confined it; you restricted it. The Earth is supposed to evolve as you are evolving – as you are *supposed* to evolve. The Earth should reach a point where it is 'Christed', where it transforms, where it elevates, where it exists on a different level of physical and spiritual matter ...**but it cannot.** It is trapped because you are trapped, and you have trapped it within the Field that you create day by day.

How terrible! What has the Earth done to you? *Despite* the way that you treat it, it continues to give of itself, to sacrifice itself, to provide for you ...until that point at the top of the 'arc' when it can provide for you no longer.

...And then it is not destroyed. It does not cease to exist but it becomes fallow again, it needs to rest. You have infested it for long enough, abused it for long enough! It needs to rest and it may rest for a million years, two million years, whilst you await physical form again to start your plunder of the planet again.

Certainly there should be respect; there should be *awe* for this planet – for the spirit that this planet is. There should be thankfulness for every day that this planet sustains you in physical form. There should be conversation between you and the planet:

'I am sorry that I have to dig here. Please will you restore the energies to what they were once I have my vegetables and my fruit?'

'Is there somewhere else I can build so that I am not disturbing the haunt of a great deva, a great nature spirit?'

'Would you mind possibly if I do this or do that? I will restore it after I have taken what I need. I will replenish it, reproduce it.'

'Would you mind if I heal you?'

'Would you mind if I listen to you?'

'Would you mind if I love you – precious, *precious* planet Earth?'

You can see how the time runs out on every level. You can see how the respect for this planet is dwindling ...and dwindling ...and dwindling until the planet tries to give ...and give ...and give, and on a certain day cannot give any longer. And at that point a sweep downwards into sleep and re-creation within the boundaries of the Fall starts again ...**unless *you* stop it.**

Love ...Light ...respect ...re-creation ...thankfulness – these are the tools that you need as 'gardeners of the world' to create a new Eden.

Does that run along your thoughts?

John: Yes, thank you.

Joseph: Another question, please!

Bridgette: This afternoon I was looking through one of your books, and there's a chapter on feminine and masculine that you talk about and also man and woman, and the differences and how they come together in harmony – can you talk a bit about that?

Joseph: What aspect of that would you like me to discuss?

Bridgette: About male and female on this Earth plane and masculine and feminine – because I got a bit confused on it.

Joseph: There is something that I would like to say and there is something that perhaps is not realised in a lot of spiritual books, and perhaps is not realised from the first book [*reference to Revelation*]:

Each of you is masculine and feminine.

Each of you has a masculine half and a feminine half. The dominance of one or other of those halves results in an imbalance, which leads to a certain set of problems for you to solve during your life.

Originally before the time of the Fall you were *balanced*. Masculine and feminine charges were used by you to create on this level of physicality. Originally you were neither masculine nor feminine – you contained within yourself a perfect balance of the two.

Now the two are poles apart. There is a duality to each human being – there is an imbalance of masculine and feminine. But there is also the physical appearance because, of course, as a physical being you appear to be either masculine or feminine. So, you have a certain set of traits that were assigned to you karmically (in other words – so that you can evolve and discover more about the masculine and feminine imbalance and put that balance right) when you took on the guise of either a man or a woman. In reality you are not a man, you are not a woman – you are a spirit, you are energy, you are God.

So, if you are a man in this present incarnation physically – you are a man for a purpose. If you are a woman – you are a woman here for a purpose. And there are certain challenges in life that will connect with your masculine physicality or your feminine physicality. That is the *surface*.

Within you there is the ability to bring out masculine or feminine aspects of creation – or a balance of the two so you are learning to deal with the creative aspects of male and female *inside of you*.

What is happening at the moment in your world is that the roles are becoming blurred and there is dissatisfaction. There is dissatisfaction with certain of the male populace with the roles that they have as men. There is dissatisfaction with the feminine members of the populace because they are feminine. They fight against the very attributes that they have been given so that they can learn as souls and evolve.

This is nothing to do with traditional roles on a physical level or perceived male domination or female approach to life. No, this is to do with you having a very certain, precise set of circumstances to meet as a male or as a female and then to use, from within that framework, your understanding of male and female creatively to solve those problems, those riddles, those karmic challenges that come to you.

To make things simple – **you are what you are at this moment for a purpose.** Why would you want to be otherwise? *Why?* And so, in embracing the charge – either male or female – that you have been given as a physical soul, you are doing yourself and other people around you a service – you are living out the life you are supposed to live.

Do not bolt from your charge!

Now your charge, as I have said, can be physical – you may *appear* male or female – but can also have a soul-charge of male or female and that too has been frowned upon in recent times. We have what appears to be a male that has a predominantly female outlook or what appears to be female with a predominately male outlook – so many layers to be true to and to balance.

The one to go to, to balance the other, is the soul.

How do you feel about the projection that you are putting out? Are you comfortable with your masculinity? Are you comfortable with your femininity? If not – why not? If you are uncomfortable, is it because you have something to learn within *the body* you have been given? Learn to seek *within* for the balance; learn to seek *within* for an approach to your life through the physical appearance that you have been given, which is there for a purpose.

I hope I haven't confused you further!

[*Pause*]

Can you talk to me again please?

Bridgette: The one who asked the question?

Joseph: Yes.

Bridgette: No, that actually makes sense. It makes more sense.

Joseph: This is nothing to do – and I have to seek to divorce one level from another – this is nothing to do with society's perception of male and female ...and yet it is everything to do with society's perception of male and female because that is what throws people off. They buy into trends – they feel that it is not right to be feminine, it is not right to be masculine in certain circumstances and they throw things off.

I am not talking about stereotypes – I am talking about *spiritual* types. You have a charge of predominantly male or predominantly female and you have female and male within you as two – not contradictory forces – two *complementary* forces that allow you to create and balance things. And you are here in a specific body because it is judged by yourself, as a soul before you incarnate, and by the people who govern your karma, that that body is the right one and that *mind* is the right one – because the male and the female mind look at things from a different aspect.

Welcome the way that you are, welcome what you are and ask your soul in meditation: 'What am I supposed to be learning? What are the patterns in my life?'

And I welcome a time when I am addressing a congregation of angels – not males, not females – but angels who know *once again* that they can create by using positive and negative ...the male and the female... to put in front of them and around them whatever they desire. And I hope that by that time, that desire is to be more aware of *the God-within* and the beauties that can be created *without* by drawing on the God-within.

Is that OK?

Bridgette: Umm, yes, I think so.

Joseph: Are you sure?

Bridgette [*laughing*]: Umm, I think so. I think so. But there's some question ... because I work with children as well and I've obviously got my own children... I see a difference sometimes in males and females. And also the roles they think they should take on maybe, or biological make-up maybe they have to take on, and I just wondered if there's a difference in the lessons to be learnt in the bodies they are put in?

Joseph: There is...

Bridgette: As the male body is different...

Joseph: There is, by complicating...

Bridgette: Because they all have different experiences – they are forced somehow I think...

Joseph: Society complicates that by saying: 'This is the male role! This is the female role!' This is not what I am saying to you. I am saying that by going within you will understand what the male role is if you are male, by going within you will understand what the female role is by linking to the God-within, and that those two roles are not necessarily what society says is the role of the male and female. **It is what the *soul* says.**

I am saying that you are in a certain body for a reason. It is not coincidence that you are male or you are female. You are in those bodies so that you can learn and deal with and overcome a certain set of circumstances that will bring you closer to the time when you are completely balanced as two forces – as male and female – to the time when you incorporate them within yourself and you become both and neither; when they once again become *tools* that you can use rather than an exterior expression of a conflict. Do you see that?

Bridgette: Yes, I think so.

Joseph [*smiling*]: I shall go back this evening and they will say to me, 'Joseph, did they understand you?' And I will say, after a pause, 'I *think* so!'

[*Audience laughter*]

And they will say, 'That is not good enough! Did they *understand* you?'

151

...'I *think* so.'

...'Go back!'

...'No! No, *never* to go back!'

And were you to take the journey that I must take inevitably at the end of this session and see the circumstances that I live in, which *are not yet perfect* but are considerably more perfect than they are here, you would not wish me to go back [*to the Earth plane*] – neither would *you* wish to come back.

And that is a good comment – 'Go back!' I would like to encourage you by saying that there is something worth working for, that the Light that I ask you to put into the world and into each other is a worthwhile pursuit. Not just for this level of consciousness (that you must bring back from the precipice) but for the next levels of consciousness that one day you will live in, in closer harmony to each other and to God, and you will witness a way of life that is as far away from the way of life you are living now as you are from the next galaxy. Completely different and completely freeing!

...But not *completely* freeing – let me rephrase that. Not 'completely freeing' because you will feel the pull of those souls who are still on Earth. You will be in a beautiful place, you will be able to create a beautiful place for yourself but you will feel the pull of the Earth, and you will think: 'Those poor souls are still there. A part of me is still there' – because a part of you *is* still there, is still on Earth. And this is why we come back because we have to free *every* soul; we have to make every soul see.

EVERY SINGLE SOUL – there are no exceptions!

We never say: 'You have been a bad boy – I turn my back on you' because we understand *how* that soul has got to that point, *why* that soul has made the decisions that have brought it to that point. Could you go up into a beautiful loft-room and leave one of your feet behind? Could you go and lie on the roof on a summer's night and leave one of your eyes behind on a lower level? The souls that inhabit the Earth are part of you and **at the deepest level they *are* you** so you have to, in order to be *whole*, collect every single soul. That is our purpose.

Even *if* the curve goes past the peak and starts to slide down again and souls are put into a kind of 'limbo' until the Earth can sustain them again, we do not, we will not abandon them. We cannot – no matter how long it takes.

You would not expect advanced souls (and I mean 'advanced' in terms of spiritual evolution), you would not expect us to grow weary, would you? But we *do* because we stand in front of you and we say, 'This is going to happen unless you change!' And because your minds are so full of the noise, the clamour of this world, you don't see us. Or if you do see us you don't listen to us. You say: *'There's* a pretty light... I think I've seen someone ...it must be one of my relatives.'

Not if we can help it!

...If we can help it, it is one of *us* saying, 'For goodness sake, change is needed *now*.'

Is that sufficient?

Bridgette: Yes, that's fine, thank you.

Joseph: Who would like to ask me a question, please?

Shirley Hayhurst: Could I ask, Joseph?

Joseph: Of course.

Shirley: When you talk about the Earth going into a rest period for – say – two million years, and then it starts up again, would humankind come back to the Earth and would it be a different body that souls would use?

Joseph: Humankind – as in the expression of the soul that is the male and female – would *have to* come back to the Earth.

That is the point – you have *trapped* yourselves in a sequence and you repeat your past patterns that bring you from an emergence into physical consciousness to a time when you have abused that physical consciousness so much that it cannot sustain you any longer and it collapses. The system collapses – it cannot sustain you. You then go back into a period of sleep and of waiting (and I am not talking about *you* specifically but for the souls that have not reached beyond the Earth in understanding) until the Earth reaches a point where it can sustain souls again ...and then the whole exercise happens again.

This is as a result of the Fall. It is as a result of a vibration that became a 'loop biting its own tail', so that instead of the evolutionary course that you are supposed to take, instead of being able to visit physicality, experience certain – shall I call them – 'fairground rides' and *know* that they were fairground rides and then exit physicality, and then visit some *other* area of physicality – instead of this you became trapped.

The 'record' plays itself again ...and again ...and again, and it can only be broken – you can only play a *new* record – by changing the perception of the souls around the Earth. Outside help has *always* been there. For as long as you have existed it has always been there, but there comes a point where you can either listen to it or the Earth cannot sustain you any longer. That has happened twice before – we don't want it to happen a third time.

You talk about the manner of body that you will have – here you have to understand that you are likely to come back into a physical body that is *very similar* to the one you have now. Why? ...Because you were the original creators of the Earth. As angelic beings you created the Earth as your playground and so, being locked into that pattern, you can only create from your soul-memory. So [*smiling*] you will not come back as a fox ...in clothes; you will not come back as what you would consider an 'alien' life-form. You have to revisit the territory that you have ploughed before in order to play out the same set of circumstances and be given a chance. You are giving yourselves a chance to change things again.

We have to say at this point that certain of you in this room will be saying: 'Well, is that my fate? Is that where I am going?' Not if you embrace the Light, not if you understand the spiritual path and, most importantly, **not if you don't want it to happen.** On leaving this world this time round, take with you, please, a very definite desire *not to come back*, not to be pulled back into incarnation, not to let the desires that you have now (whatever they may be) pull at you, to the extent where you say: 'I have a choice of going this way or that way – it's got to be *this* way.' Take that with you in *full consciousness*.

That is another of our missions – to instil into people in full consciousness that they have a choice, whereas many souls return to the spirit realms and give in to their subconscious, give in to the view of the world they've always had that it's the only place they know. Therefore, it is the place they want to go back to.

Educate yourselves during the time that you are here in the ways of God, in the ways of Light. Prove to yourselves by sending Light into situations that what Joseph is saying is *actually* truth. Don't take it from me or anyone else – prove it for yourselves. Build into your conscious mind the fact that there is somewhere to go, that that 'somewhere' is better than here, and that *here* can be manipulated for the good by your thoughts, by your beliefs.

Then, when you depart this level of consciousness you will take with you that knowledge, and you will sit with your advisors and they will say: 'What do you want to do? Do you want to stay here and evolve through certain cleansing levels to go back to

God, or do you want to go back to the Earth? Do you want the pain or do you want the perfection? Which do you want?'

And you will not be pulled by that subconscious desire that so many souls have, and you will say, 'I want to stay here.' And then you can start to progress through the spiritual levels, but you will also have, as part of your make-up, that pull for the other souls on the Earth. But instead of being pulled back towards *them*, you can work for them in the spiritual realms to pull them towards *you*. That is the difference!

Is that a sufficient answer?

Shirley: Yes, it is. Also, are there many souls waiting to come to the Earth that have not been here already but they want to experience the Earth?

Joseph [*smiling*]: Here in Britain you are used to queues...

[*Audience laughter*]

You adore many 'gods' and queues are one of the gods that you adore. Were you to see the queues that form to come back to the Earth plane, you would be in absolute awe of the 'great god of queues' because many souls almost instantly, having departed this level of consciousness, *choose to come back*.

At present – to answer your question – the only souls from the higher realms that are queuing up to experience the Earth are *not there to experience the Earth*; they are there to help – like the children we have spoken about tonight. So, you have a mixture of souls. You have the souls who want to get on the fairground ride again (the 'ghost train' at the moment – not a pleasant fairground ride) and you have those souls who *selflessly* choose to come back here in order to be a torch, a beacon, for the others to follow.

God is *in-finite* ...**infinite.** Therefore, the numbers of expressions of God that God is capable of are *without number.* As I said earlier, you have furniture that is alive; you have other animals that are alive; you have opportunities on other planets to experience once you have escaped this twist of consciousness on the Earth.

There is *never* a finite number of souls but there is a finite number of souls that will visit the Earth, because most of those are souls getting on for 'one more ride'. The additions are those who are coming back to say: 'Please listen to us! Please see the Light! Wield the Light! Turn your back on the world as it is – not on the world *but on the world as it is* because you can restructure it.'

I tell you that if this message went across and was understood and accepted by every soul around this globe, the Earth would change *now.* The Earth that you stepped out into following this demonstration would be completely different than the Earth that you left before you came into this building. **Such is the power of the Light!** It is simply a matter of igniting all those souls to change the Earth *now.*

And then souls would want to come back here but not to be trapped here – to experience what the unique vibrational signature of the Earth had to offer them, and then go back to God and perhaps choose to experience in some other physical realm or in some other spiritual realm. The journey is endless. Unfortunately the journey *here* is looped – that's the difference.

Is that a sufficient answer?

Shirley: Yes, thank you very much, Joseph

Joseph: Thank you.

Mike Sly: Could I ask you to talk a bit more about what you described as 'the Fall' earlier this evening and what your understanding of that is, and how we might have a better understanding of what that involves and how we may be able to reduce the likelihood of that happening again?

Joseph: Yes, it is a *vast* subject but, as I have said standing here before [*reference to the previous demonstration*] we are in preparation of a book on the subject. And the reason that it is being put into a book is because we want Michael to be advised by a number of guides (not just by me) and to get the complexities of the Fall *correct* to offer to people **a complete explanation of why things are as they are now.** That is in progress, has been in progress now for two years and will be in progress for perhaps another two before it is made available. To condense it is difficult, but I will try.

The origins of the mistake were rooted in goodness, *in good intent.* Certain souls – a certain hierarchy of souls – felt that they could establish God's plan for physicality in this area of physicality more effectively than He could, more quickly than He could. And that was suggested to the communal consciousness as something that could be achieved. More and more souls allied with that change of the way of creating, and did not realise that they were shoehorning themselves into a 'reality trap' ...into an area of physicality that would become more 'real' for them than their link with God.

And so, as a result of this volition *through free will* to act in a different way, the vibrational quality of the Earth and vibrational quality of physical matter – including the human body – was changed, became denser, became... 'corrupt' is the wrong word ...became *stuck*, so that the natural journey through this level of physicality for the soul became a difficult one. Instead of dipping into this consciousness, experiencing what this consciousness had to offer and then retracting one's consciousness back into the spiritual realms, it became a matter of incarnating into this consciousness **and *instantly* losing one's knowledge of who one was.**

The vibration of the Earth – the vibration that resulted because of the Fall – trapped souls between two aspects of creation ...between positivity and negativity ...between male and female so that they could not escape. They could not create positively and they could not escape the capsule of vibration that they had created. At that time the creative Field that responds to those souls changed its vibration from positive to negative, and it became the norm and became accepted that things were going to go wrong ...that there would be pain ...there would be suffering ...that the other person was an enemy ...that the other person's power needed to be taken because you didn't have enough for yourself – and a pattern was created. The souls could not escape beyond that vibration that they had created – *the Fall.*

The only way to counter the effects of the Fall is by bringing in God-consciousness again. But because you have free will, because God has given you free will, whilst you turn your back on that other possibility of reality, the world continues *as it is.*

Not only that but the world operates – humankind operates – by drawing power not from the Godhead but from the Field of conscious, and (like your oil fields and your gas fields) that Field that is set to negative and feeds them with feeble energy compared to God-energy **is running out.**

So, the trap is that the souls incarnate into physical matter, they then forget who they are and they draw on the physical Field which is set to negative. It makes them ill; it makes them depressed; it makes them angry; it makes them aggressive – and they pull, and pull, and draw, and draw from that Field until the Field cannot sustain itself and the Earth cannot sustain them. Then, because they have not learned to step outside the effects of the Fall, through free will on a subconscious and on a soul-level, they are forced to remain within that vibration until a degree of physicality that can sustain them in physical consciousness is created again.

...And then the cycle begins again.

The effects of the Fall would be transmuted today, as I have said, if every person believed in the Light-within and transmitted that Light into the Field – it would rectify itself.

It is simple!

We are back to the beginning of this event – keeping things simple. But, because of the Field, because of lifetimes and lifetimes reincarnating back into the negativity of the Field, souls don't want simple. They want complex, they want upset, they want, 'See, I told you things were going wrong!' They are *subconsciously* perpetuating the effects of the Fall that they first instigated.

It is our mission to change that vibration but we can only change it by assuring people they are a part of God, that they can draw on Light and that they create reality. We are not allowed to sweep through this world with a torch of Light to change things. We are only allowed to talk to people in the faith and hope that they will listen to us, will take on board what we say, will practise what we preach, will prove it for themselves and will get at least *themselves* out. ...Because for every soul that gets out of the 'game of snakes and ladders' the other souls are pulled a little closer to that time when they *too* can understand the Light, can understand their God-heritage and can understand that this world needn't be as it appears to be. When you elevate yourself, you elevate everyone else because **you** *are* **everyone else.**

A very complex subject! We sit with Michael, when we can find *time* with Michael, to put down that subject to the nth degree, to explain how it was in the beginning, what went wrong and how we can put it right.

I hope I have been able to give you some glimpse of what happened in the 'abridged' version. Does it make sense?

Mike: Yes, it does. I guess I'm struggling to link that into a physical dimension and what timescales we are looking at.

Joseph: Ah, there has been much talk by the members of this group that bring through this information [*the Band of Light*] about Atlantis, because if you have read the book [**Revelation**] you will understand that I was once a citizen of Atlantis. And I can say something nebulous like: 'Atlantis was a state of mind'. It *was* but Atlantis was not a point on the Earth as you have the configuration of the Earth now. **The Earth was completely different.** Remember I have said that civilisation has risen and fallen twice – and that is going back in records as far as we are allowed to go back…

[*Pause due to a break in the communication*]

…I am sorry we are running out of power. Please talk to me again – I want to try to establish the link for as long as I can.

Mike: Right, thank you. Yes, just to re-iterate – it's trying to understand the concept of a shift in the way in which people see themselves, see their relationship with the spirit world and the fact that we are tied into the physical dimension and the time dimension.

Joseph: Yes, of course, the time involved. Time is not important because time does not exist. You gauge the times to the time of *this* civilisation, and your scientists look back and say: 'Such a thing happened, and there were dinosaurs and this creature and that creature.' …They have *no* idea. **They have no idea!** The Earth has re-formed itself many times and looks completely different now than it did in my day.

Mike: That does make more sense, thank you.

Joseph: The timescale that *concerns* us at the moment is **the hand is at five to midnight** …that you are running out of time in which to put things right again before you make the same mistakes.

As a result of the Field, you always see your civilisation going back to ancient history. No, quite *modern* history, in fact, compared to the aeons that have passed since man first walked this Eden – since angelic beings first walked within the Earth, around the Earth. And at that time going back so very, very far the angelic beings were in complete communion with the Earth, with the devas, with nature, with each other, with God. And there was not the fear of physical death that there is now because the fear of physical death is another product of the Field trying to hold on to you.

And it is right that you should be here for a certain amount of time, but there shouldn't be fear in transition, because when the time comes you will find that the transition is so easy, is so blessed, is so wonderful. And you step out of this murky, dim world that appears so bright to you on a sunny day but really is not ...into Light, into a landscape that is so vivid, so wonderful, so personal to each of you. You will marvel at it and that transition is easy. It is only difficult when you move across to the higher side of life and feel the pull of such silly things:

'I didn't resolve that relationship – maybe I can next time.'

'I really like the taste of things on Earth – I think I'll be drawn back to taste them again.'

'I liked the house that I had – I think I will have a house like that again.'

Unfortunately, you might be drawn back into the same circumstances but not into the same house, because your karma will decide how best you can evolve, and sometimes you have to evolve by doing *without* those things in the subsequent life. But it is like a lottery, it is like the one-armed bandit:

'I'll try again – maybe I will get the house back this time.'

[*Joseph pulls an imaginary lever*]

House ...house ...*karma*!

'No house this time, I'll pull again!'

Karma ...karma ...*house*!

You cannot win on that physical level; you can only win when you want to change that physical level and change yourself from within.

Am I making sense to you?

Mike: Yes, thank you very much.

Joseph: I don't mean that in any disrespectful way. I mean am I – as a spirit that is about to be pulled back to my sphere of reality – impressing words on this level to such an extent that they are resonating?

Another question, please... I always overrun Michael.

John O'Brien: Joseph, was the Fall considered the start of the ego, the separation, the *I am*?

Joseph: The ego first exhibited itself in mankind's stance that it was right and God was wrong. At that point there was a shift, but the ego established itself more and more strongly in subsequent incarnations with the enhanced belief via the Field that *there was not enough*, 'I must survive!' rather than, 'I *do* survive. I cannot do otherwise but survive – I AM.'

I AM – capital letters – **I AM.**

And so the ego was a survival mechanism that, due to the effects of the Fall, overran the physical consciousness; and all war, all conflict, all cruelty, all torment of souls is carried on through insecurity, through a soul-insecurity: 'I do not have enough, therefore, I will take yours. I am frightened of your point of view, therefore, I will squash it. I do not like you, you are different to me. I seek to survive.' And all the time these thoughts are going on, the Field seeks to perpetuate them – more war, more torture: 'This is wonderful! This is what I need to sustain myself in my present form.'

You see, the Field is our 'slave' but it is our *sentient* slave and we instruct it, unfortunately, to be negative. Once enough of us turn it into a positive Field of energy, it will accept that, too, and it will deliver what we expect from it again. It is our tool – it will deliver to us the Utopia, the Eden, that we want from it, the peace that we want from it, the harmony that we want from it, the lack of war and the abundance of everything else *for* everyone else. So the ego, yes, originated at the time of the Fall.

Before the Fall there was a universal consciousness. The individual was aware of itself as being an individual but the consciousness that flowed through the individual linked it to every other individual or 'seeming' individual in complete harmony. And you can imagine the security of knowing that you are part of everything else – including the spiritual realms, not just the physical level – that you are part of everything, that you can never die, that you can never be parted from anyone, you can never cease to exist, you can never be out of harmony. What a wonderful place it was but we flipped it – you flipped it, I flipped it – and we have to reinstate the positive aspect of the Field.

[*Pause*]

...It is now becoming a 'telephone line' – from controlling Michael it becomes a telephone line at the point where his consciousness must come back in because he is not yet supposed to go to the spiritual side – so as I withdraw is there one last question, please?

Art O'Malley: One last thing – I've read that different people are trying to anchor higher levels of consciousness in physical locations about the world that can act as a network, as a matrix, as a grid to enhance the communication across continents and so on; what advice would you have if we could have like-minded consciousness connect in that sort of way?

Joseph: You can make places *sacred* places – there have always been sacred places. What disturbs me or worries me a little is that if people are striving to do this, they must have first anchored within themselves *totally* the new way of thinking. So, the Earth can be replenished, the Earth can be changed **but in order to do that you first have to change yourself** – *then* you band together to love the Earth.

This is a terrible analogy, but imagine that you have an infestation of some kind in a house – you cannot change the house until the infestation has gone. It is no use putting in new carpets because the infestation will come back and overrun those carpets. It is no use putting in wallpaper that looks nice because the infestation will eat the wallpaper. You have to get rid of the infestation. **The 'infestation' is not man – it is the way that man *thinks*.**

So, first you approach the house by taking off your muddy shoes, by leaving the overcoat that is covered in branches and leaves in the hallway. Then you approach the house and renovate the house because you are having respect for the house and for each other.

So, yes, you can alter the Earth – you *have to* alter the Earth – but you have to change first yourselves, and if you change yourselves the desire to change the Earth and the ability to change the Earth comes as that change in personal consciousness.

You cannot change over to God-consciousness *without* respecting the Earth.

So, your greater task is to stop people from plundering the Earth and destroying the Earth by changing their consciousness. You cannot do that by standing in front of them with a banner – you can't! It is wonderful, it is brave, it is marvellous, but they cannot see what you are seeing, they cannot see your point of view.

You have to talk to them through your prayers; you have to send out Light to them; you have to explain to them in those parcels of prayer – Light – that you send to them what you want and why you want it. You have to, not argue, but state your case in Love on a subconscious level (conscious for you because you are actively doing it but on a subconscious level for mankind) and you have to link with other like-minded people so that there comes a point where the subconsciousness of the people who will not change at this point *has to react* – has to react to that Light and begin to change.

And at that point then the Earth becomes a more beautiful place, a more protected place, becomes recognised as the sacred place it once was because, if you recognise it as being sacred ...**it is sacred**. You are creating that sacredness and vibrating at the same level as the Earth. You are feeding that sacredness, you are feeding the Earth's ability to feed you, to love you as you love it but it begins first of all with people.

If people have fully changed in consciousness then they should set out sacred places and say: 'The Field does not come in here! This is our community. This is our town. This is our house. This is our church *and within these walls God reigns* – the God that we really are ...perfection reigns ...creativity reigns ...peace reigns ...Love reigns!' And then you can spread out that network to change the entire globe.

Is that a sufficient answer?

Art: Thanks, yes.

Chapter Six

Joseph Trance Demonstration – 16th December, 2009
The Sanctuary of Healing, Lancashire, UK

Spiritual topics discussed:

The nature of time.

How to discern whether channelled material is correct.

Sending out Light as a group.

God-Light.

Sacred geometry.

Joseph's soul group.

Pre-destiny and choice.

When does the spirit of a baby enter the body?

Contact from loved-ones in spirit.

Exorcism and spirit rescue.

Nurturing children with psychic ability.

The reason for disability.

Elevated souls who come back to teach.

Saving the world before it is too late.

How best to serve humanity.

The meaning of 'Ascension'.

Joseph: There is no appointment book, no diary – I simply know the time to come. No one knocks at my door and says: '*Joseph you have to go to Earth!*' I *know* – it is written into my vibration and one second, as you would measure it, I am *there* and the next second, as you would measure it, I am *here*.

But I do not come empty-handed this evening because I bring with me a waterfall. I have placed – and others who work with me have placed – this waterfall in this room to bring spiritual power into the room, to bring spiritual power into your hearts and above all to *cleanse*. What a peculiar thing to say 'to cleanse' – particularly at this time of year.

This time of year is difficult for spiritual communication. It is difficult because there is such a focus on material things. There is such a panic within so many people wanting to do so many things so quickly for so many others to *please* them, to give them a little of themselves in the form of a present that is instantly forgotten. The vibrations at this time become very intermeshed, become difficult to penetrate and, even with the best view possible towards Christmas, you become *contaminated*. You cannot help but do so because you are part of the Field of human consciousness.

And so I bring the waterfall to cascade down silver and golden Light, to cleanse those vibrations from you and to put things into perspective. This is what we are here this evening to do – **to put things into perspective**; to [*help you*] realise that festivals should be festivals of Light; to realise that what you should be giving to each other is Light – is Love; to hold those presents, to imbue them with Light before you give them out; to say: 'I am sorry this is just something material but within it is something eternal, something that will serve you all your days on Earth ...it is my love ...it is Light.'

So, in Love and Light, I welcome you as I ask you to please welcome me and I ask for a question, please.

Ben Hamilton: From a karmic aspect are all our lifetimes running at the same time?

Joseph: Everything runs at the same time because there is *no* time.

Ben: Does that mean that in our present instance that will affect our past and future at the same time?

Joseph: You are accumulating at any second, as you view it, richness to your vibration or you are accumulating at every second, as you view it, a heaviness to your vibration.

You have to exist on this level of consciousness within what seems to be a linear adventure otherwise you could not take advantage of the opportunities, the challenges that come to your soul along that adventure. But in reality – in *spiritual* reality – you are living that adventure, the other adventures you have had and the adventures, from your viewpoint, that you still will have **...at the same time.** But time is such a deceiver, time is such a darkening concept on this level of consciousness – it disguises the truth.

Your life on a spiritual level is still, to a certain extent, linear but without the influence of what you call 'time', so you will anticipate certain events and you will peruse certain events that you have already experienced.

...Perhaps a better word is 'experience' – every life that you live, every adventure that you undertake is an experience; it gains experience for your soul. The soul knows this but the point of consciousness within any lifetime can only take in so much of that *eternal now*. The over-soul – the *real* you – understands the potential of the adventures that you are going through but can only draw on your experience. You are sent out into matter to gain experience. As a result of that experience your consciousness as an individual (which is also an illusion) and your consciousness as an over-soul is heightened, your vibration speeds up and you are taken into new adventures on other levels of consciousness.

Everything exists now because there is only now but within *now* there are perspectives, within *now* there is an ability to say: 'I have done this. I will do this' and to draw on the experience that you have to elevate yourself. And anything that is in your 'future' is simply, as you view it, a lack of experience – you have not had that experience, you have not absorbed that experience thus far in your consciousness. Does that make things easier?

Ben: Yes, thank you.

Joseph: It is a terribly difficult subject to get across. As I explained as I came in, I know when I have to reach you, when I have to touch the Earth plane again – it is within my experience.

Ahead of you (and 'ahead' is a term that relates to the Earth plane and not to the spiritual planes) there are different experiences that will enable you to elevate your soul, to elevate your consciousness, to absorb and understand more of the nature of Creation and Light.

That is how we define past, present and future: 'Experiences I have had, experiences I am having, experiences I have yet to have.' But they are presented to us spiritually as though they are one 'painting' in front of us and we can look at different aspects of that painting. We look at the past and we see experiences that are familiar to us. We look at the present and we see experiences that we are beginning to understand. And we look at other parts of the painting and see experiences that we do not *yet* understand – it is like an abstract art form. The painting we see that is the present and the past is a photo-realistic art form, so we move from photo-realism that we understand to abstractism that we don't *yet* understand. But it is all the same painting, all the same 'canvas of opportunity' that we are looking at, at the same time.

The concept of time is terribly difficult to remove from your consciousness, but you must experience timelessness when you meditate. When you meditate there is a shift and you *feel* different – you feel that time has moved away from you, and you are in a state of peace and growth and understanding because you have lifted yourself out of that concept of time. When you meditate you are looking at that 'canvas'. Meditation allows you to see more of the canvas than you normally do from a daily perspective, and then you can bring that knowledge back with you to understand more about the experiences you are having and the experiences you have yet to have – as you measure time.

[*Smiling*] I think I have succeeded in making it far more complex! Do you understand what I am attempting to get across?

Audience: Yes.

Joseph: Another question, please!

Debra: Joseph, I'm Debra.

Joseph: Hello Debra.

Debra: There are many channellers in the world. How can we discern who and what information is actually right?

Joseph: This is a difficult question for me and one which I have attempted to answer in the past [*reference to a previous demonstration*]. The short answer is **any information that is given should have a resonance with you.** It should – rather than be *thought* about in the correct way – be *felt* in the correct way.

There are many points of view in the spirit world. There are many people who would like to contact and *do* contact the Earth level of consciousness. You have to remember, though, that they create their own worlds (as you will as you walk up the spiritual steps of progression) and so their perspective is influenced by the world that they have created.

On the lower levels (and I do not mean 'lower' in a derogatory way) the souls who are learning to create have only their unique perspective to draw on. If they choose to create their vision of 'Heaven' that is what they have to draw on and transmit to the Earth plane.

As they lose more of their individual perspective (but not their individuality) they begin to link up with other souls and their perspective changes. They are still creating their own world but it is a world that they begin to share with others. They gravitate towards others who have the same ideals, the same perspective, the same goals. So, there is a *shared knowledge* and they begin to function as part of what they already are – which is a group soul.

That group soul, because it is made up of hundreds, thousands, millions of individuals, has a richer perspective, a richer insight into what lies beyond and what has gone before. Therefore, you find channelled information that comes from group souls comes from *elevated* spirits (and I do not mean 'elevated' in a grandiose way – it is simply a fact). They have experienced more, they have gone on further and they have a different perspective, which is not as individually biased as it would be on a lower level of consciousness.

And so you have many communicators vying for your attention, do you not? ...including those who are of a rather baser nature who will attempt to communicate any way they can – through a Ouija board, through chaos being brought in the form of phenomena. Would you listen to them?

What is it that stops you from listening to that low form of communication?

It is your heart.

It is your intuition. It is that part of you that says, 'This is wrong!' Similarly, when you are receiving information that resonates your heart says, 'This is right!' ...Not your mind – your *heart* – and so you have to listen to your heart.

You also have to understand that, as your heart accumulates more experience, your perspective changes and the information that was given to you on Tuesday may not be the right information for you on Thursday, because your viewpoint will have elevated itself and you will have filtered out of that information those aspects of that information that do not resonate with you.

I cannot and will not put down another person's point of view. Were I to do so, it would become 'The Joseph Show'- it would become Joseph's point of view only. All I can say to you, in talking about the communication that I bring through, is that I am not alone in bringing it through. I am part of a group soul that consists of millions of souls and those millions of souls have elevated themselves to such a height that they can see certain things that the souls below them cannot yet see – they will one day but cannot *yet* see. Therefore, I am presenting knowledge that comes to me in collaboration with millions of other souls who share that point of view.

Also, the knowledge that comes to me and to the other souls in the group is filtered from a higher group soul ...and that group soul filters information from a higher group soul. So, we feed you information in instalments because that is how the information (apart from our own perspective) is brought to us – in instalments when we are ready, when the heart is opened a little more.

You should always test the communication that comes through to you. You should always look at it carefully and see whether you feel comfortable with it. That is not to say that, if you are discomforted by it, it is wrong – it is simply *perhaps* that you have not reached that point yet at which it will seem comfortable to you. If you feel that a barrier goes up instantly when you are reading something or watching someone **then take notice of your** *own* soul telling you what you are ready for and what you are not ready for.

And above all, use – if you are using your physical mind – *logic*: 'Does the information I am being given make sense?' Does the way in which it is presented seem right? Is there the Divine in the equation? Has God been invoked? Is God in the midst of this communication? Is this communication to do with personality or spirit evolution? Is it to do with Light or is it a cult situation, a club situation, where you are invited in but then when you get in you are not allowed, within the dictates of that information, to consider anything else?

You are on a journey. Spiritual knowledge is a journey but you always have your own guard in your chest and you must go to that guard and say: 'Does this feel right?' If it does – embrace it until it feels wrong. If it doesn't – push it away until it feels right or it may never feel right.

Do not look outside of yourself for protection in communicating with spirits, with God, with the spirit realms. Look inside – you are connected to God and God will tell you what is right, what is wrong and protect you always if you go along that route. Is that sufficient information?

Debra: That's wonderful, thank you very much.

Joseph: Yes, please, another question!

[*Pause*]

Debra: Joseph, it is Debra again. I've got another question. At a previous session here you mentioned about us networking points of Light across the globe to make a stronger Light – what's the most effective way for us to do that? Also, is it better for us to work in a group like this? Is it better for us to work with a few people to raise consciousness higher or to work with many people and limit it to a lower level?

Joseph: First of all, when you send out Light, the most extraordinary, exquisite thing you can do is send it out *without bias*. It has to be Light that touches every soul; it has to be Light that touches every situation; it has to, again, be Light from the heart.

You are polluted. Each of you is polluted... and I do not mean that in an insulting way. You are polluted by the Earth plane because the Earth plane has given your physical mind that you are used to relying on a particular spin during your life. It has a political spin; it has a religious spin; it has a spin with regard to culture; it has a spin with regard to what *you regard* as being right or being wrong. And as you send out the Light, if you are sending out the Light from your mind (which you cannot really do) the beam of Light you send out will have within it those biases, and subconsciously you may de-select certain groups of people. Unfortunately, you will de-select the ones that need the Light *most* – the ones who are the most violent, the ones who are the most entrenched in this physical life, the ones who seek power at the expense of others.

So, sending out Light has to be an unbiased thing and again you have to connect with your God (with whatever your view of Divine Universal Intelligence is) and you have to say: 'I send out Light unconditionally. I select those areas that are difficult for me – perhaps I cannot come to terms with certain crimes people have done – I seek out those people in Light, in protection, and send out my Light unconditionally to them.'

How difficult!

You can select certain nations that may, as you feel, have an attitude that is injurious to this Earth and send out your Light to them. Become used to sending out Light into difficult areas for you and you will grow, and the amount of Light you will be able to send out will also grow. Of course, include those people you love, include those people who are behaving, as you see it, 'correctly' according to your world view. But also include those who don't, those who aren't – because those are the situations that can be compared to a 'cancer'.

Those vibrations hurt the Earth, those vibrations hurt you because people in praying exclude them; they become dark spots – do you see? It is easy to pray for someone who is like you. It is difficult to pray for someone who you perceive as having committed a crime that is terrible to you. But those are the people, those are the situations, that need the most help ...that need the most Light ...the most prayer. Remember those situations link up – just as the Light-filled situations/vibrations link up around the Earth – the negative vibrations link up. How powerful they are because they are ignored by most religions, they are ignored in most prayers.

You have talked about where it is safe to give out the Light and how to give out the Light. Do you give the Light out in a group? Do you give the Light out as an individual? **You do both.**

But similarly in groups *initially* as you begin to evolve spiritually, there are problems because people are used to looking for power, are used to looking for a reason to shine, to be the one whose voice is heard and they bring those biases, they bring those 'needs' (as they see them) into a group situation. So, in a group situation you have to be extremely disciplined and you have to say to the people in that group: 'You leave your biases and your expectations with regard to you and your ego outside that door. Then we can harmonise, then we can send Light out because we are harmonious, we are not discordant any longer.'

And it is important within your groups (as it is with you as an individual) to remember that you do not create the Light – **you channel it**. You talked about channelling – you channel the Light and you channel the Light by connecting with the God-within. And in your group situations you say: 'You are not powerful. I am not powerful. It is matter of connecting with God. God is powerful. God is bringing through the Light. He is in charge – He/She/It is in charge of our group.' Then, after your group meeting has been completed, you can pick up your worries at the door if you so wish to do ...but not within the group.

Love each other, love the world, love the difficult areas particularly, especially, love the challenge and you will change things. Is that a sufficient answer?

Debra: Yes, that's a great answer. Thank you very much.

Joseph: Please, another question!

Dennis: Dennis here.

Joseph: Hello Dennis.

Dennis: This God-energy – Einstein told me that he discovered it as a grey cloud. Other people have described it as a White Light. Which is correct?

Joseph: Any viewpoint is individual, but from my viewpoint and the viewpoint of the souls that connect to me, and from our plane of reference, God is the most brilliant Light you could imagine ...and then *beyond* that.

God is the Light we carry within us that illuminates our chakras. God is the Light within us that we carry around into all our projects, all our challenges. God is at the heart of the Light ...*Light* ...**Light** that we send into the Earth plane. God is at the centre of the Light that enables me to communicate with you this evening because we create a beam...

Dennis: Is that balance?

Joseph: ...Is that balance?

Dennis: Yes, what end of the spectrum is it?

Joseph: God contains within the Light that you see *every* colour of the spectrum. There are new colours that you will discover when you leave the Earth plane. God is an amalgam of all the colours, it does not create grey as far as our perspective is concerned. It creates White Light and within that White Light are the coloured rays that we use to heal and to change things. Is that a sufficient answer?

Dennis: Thank you, yes.

Joseph: Let me extrapolate... let me go further into 'Light'.

Light can be measured by the amount of harmonious feeling within you as you approach it. Lack of Light, or cloudiness, or murkiness, or fogginess creates within you – within your soul, within your instincts – a feeling of discontent, a feeling of *not being sure*.

When souls emerge, there is more than one emergence upon leaving this physical plane. You first of all emerge into your own world that is visited by other spirits, yes, but it is essentially *your* world and it is a world that is painted and coloured by the effects of your life whilst you were on Earth.

You then climb higher in knowledge as you absorb more Light, and there comes a day when you experience a second 'awakening' – an awakening into the brilliance of God-Light and your life, your experiences are illuminated. It is not just the Light that is physically 'switched on' – it is a Light that burns within you, it is a Light that illuminates all your challenges you have had thus far and makes sense of them. It is a Light that you see in other people and changes your view of other people.

And that is only the beginning – as you climb the steps of spiritual evolution you experience more Light, greater Light, *only* Light ...until there comes a point when you understand that **you are Light,** that all that was missing from your existence until that point was your knowledge of that fact.

You are Light – wonderful, brilliant, pure Light and within that Light you create, within that Light you bring in the balance of creation that you were talking about and you direct it to others; you construct your own world around yourself; the group soul that you are part of constructs a world around you. And you are able to channel and direct that Light into the hearts of men and women on Earth to eliminate the darkness, to eliminate the greyness, to eliminate the blackness, which is created in the minds of men and women and taken with them when they depart this plane into the next stages of their existence *...until* they can see past those darknesses and through those darknesses into the Light that they really are. Is that sufficient?

Dennis: Reasonable. Is sacred geometry appropriate for us to use at this time?

Joseph: No.

Dennis: Could you explain?

Joseph: *It is not!* The ancients knew how to use sacred geometry. The ancients had knowledge that has been blocked from you at this time, and you have pulled yourself into materialism to a greater extent than any civilisation has before you.

A little knowledge, they say on Earth, is a *dangerous* thing – and the power of sacred geometry has to be in the right hands and has to be used by the right souls for the right purpose... otherwise you get, creeping into the equation, the misuse of spiritual power and the lust for earthly power. It is barred from your knowledge except here and there and in small, tiny drips at this time. Depending on how the next generations progress, depending on what you do with yourselves over the next sixty to seventy years that knowledge would be added to your knowledge *...if* **you are still here.** Does that answer your question?

Dennis: Thank you.

Joseph: Thank you – God bless.

Another question, please!

Dorothy: Greetings, Joseph, my name is Dorothy.

Joseph: Hello, Dorothy.

Dorothy: May I ask or enquire – could you explain to us where you originate from or the souls or group of souls that you work with where they originate from?

Joseph [*smiling*]: I originate from God, first of all, as do you.

If you are talking about my *earthly* existence – I have been a soldier; I have been a priest; I did exist (as I say in my books) at the time of Atlantis. But I must make this clear: Atlantis is a different vibration of the Earth plane than the one you are used to. And people say: 'Point to Atlantis! Tell me where it is, tell me where it was!' It was '*other where*' – it was of a different vibration.

We were of a far more spiritual (not 'spiritual' with regards to arrogance but 'spiritual' with regards to *knowledge*) perspective than mankind is at the present time. We had mechanisms, we had equipment that was powered *spiritually*. We were, if you like, standing with one foot on the Earth and one foot in the spirit worlds, and we knew that the two connected. And we knew that the two would bring balance to us and we knew how to use spiritual power to change our environment. We did all this with an eye towards our God-heritage and we channelled God-power after asking carefully and peacefully that we might be able to use it. We respected God-power. Our mechanisms, our 'equipments' were not intrusive; they did not affect the Earth negatively. They were used in harmony to create our society, to further our society and to allow us to experience the Earth plane for what it really is – an area with opportunities to give us knowledge, an area with opportunities for us to explore ourselves within but not harming anyone, not destroying anything.

This is the life that I *choose* to remember. There are others but I push them out of the way as though I am selecting clothes from a wardrobe: 'Not this one, not this one, not this one, not this one ...*Atlantis*!' ...because I am comfortable with it and it is closest in vibration to what I am trying to communicate to you. That time is closest in vibration, so that earthly vibration that I must (because of certain laws) inhabit again when I come to speak to you is already half way there to what I am trying to communicate. Therefore it is easier for me to cut through the heavier vibrations of the Earth plane, in order to communicate, with that particular persona intact. I have been a woman (you have been a man) but I do not select those lives – I select the Atlantean life.

You asked me about soul groups. Soul groups... you can imagine that we have millions of family members, millions of brothers and sisters, and each one of them has a story to tell; each one of them has gone through several lifetimes at least; each one of them has decided to turn his or her back *physically* on the Earth but not *spiritually*. In other words they have decided that they do not want to return. (Unfortunately *Joseph* has to return!) They do not want to return but they do want to channel the information that is available to them to the Earth to those who will listen, and the idea of changing the Earth through the promotion, the movement of Light – this is their task.

The group soul is composed of individuals and is composed of one entity – just as you in this group are composed of individuals but are, in reality, one entity. They have, as do I, their separate worlds ('worlds' is perhaps the wrong word – perhaps a 'house' is a better word... but not a house as you would have on Earth), they have around them a set of circumstances that they have created and are comfortable with *for now*. There is also a group perspective, just as you can go outside now and enjoy a panoramic view of hills, for example, or can go to another country and each experience the same view. So, the members of the group soul are able to either experience their individual view or the group view at will ...or a *combination* of the two.

There are people within the group soul from all walks of life, from all cultures, but they will tell you (as I have told you) that those cultures and those walks of life are, for the most part, 'hung in wardrobes', are 'pressed in books' like flowers. And they may go back to them and say: 'I refer to this because there is a certain challenge that I am not quite sure about but I can find it here in the records of my life.' But they do not for a moment say, 'I am this!' They say, 'I was this as part of my education spiritually and now I am something else.'

But when they return to Earth to talk to you as guides, they have to (because they are lowering their vibration, slowing down their vibration) return via – but only via, only as a surface vibration – a persona that they once had whilst they lived on Earth. And so you have the Native American Indian because that is the persona that they choose to come back through in order to talk to you. And that, in the case of many Native American Indians, is the most spiritual of their experiences and so the most appropriate persona for them to pull back on from the 'wardrobe' in order to talk to you.

Group souls are also evolving. Group souls connect to other group souls. There is always a longing to be more than you are; to experience more Light and more Love; to move up closer to that Light, closer to that Love so it is a migration always. It is always a step up that we seek but you are part of us. You are, unfortunately, encased in the heavy matter of a mistaken society and, in order to elevate ourselves, we have also to elevate you. It is necessary and we do it because we love you. So, we have one eye on the next step and one eye on the Earth. And *oh* if we could bring to you now – instead of dripping the knowledge to you – all the knowledge and have you open your heart to it, then we would have *both* eyes on the next step because you would not wish to be here. You would elevate yourselves from this level of consciousness and the darkness, the violence, the disease, the pollution, the harm to the Earth would disappear instantly. **Instantly!**

Soap-box for Joseph! Another soap-box for Joseph, please, I have worn this one out!

Does that answer your question?

Dorothy: Yes, thank you.

Joseph: I must say (as a coda to what I have said) that I am not that Atlantean. I was but I am not now. It is simply one of those 'suits of clothes'... very nice suit of clothes and some very nice memories, but not what I am now. But you need a focal point... if I say, 'I am Light,' you would say, 'Where are you, Joseph? *Where are you?*'

I am Light. You are Light. But I can choose to be that Light or, if I come back to the Earth plane, I have to compress; I have to give an impression of a human being and the Atlantean persona is the one that I choose to reunite to.

A further question, please!

Deborah: Joseph, my name is Deborah. I don't really know how to word this – is anything pre-destined in our lifetime? Do we have a soul knowing where it wants to get to before it leaves or is everything just created moment by moment?

Joseph: First of all you have to *choose* to come back. That is a revolutionary thing to say – many cultures, religions say that you *have to come back*. **You don't.**

You choose to come back for one of two reasons:

Either because you want to teach and bring through Light to the other souls on the Earth plane who are still in the darkness of the mind...

...Or because you want to come back because there is something about this life that pulls you back into it.

It might be a yoghurt! It might be a love affair that you feel has not been concluded successfully. It might be what you consider to be a missed opportunity: 'I was almost at that level of promotion and I had a heart attack. I can go back. I can do it again.' And we say, 'Please don't!' We say, 'Hello,' and we knock and we try to get in, and we say: 'Please don't – it is so much better here. You have extricated yourself from the Earth plane, you have extricated yourself from the 'experiment' that went wrong and is still wrong. Now don't, please, go back.'

You see, it depends on the dominant vibrations of a soul after that soul has passed over. If the Earth plane is such a *major* player in the vibrations of the soul then that is practically all that soul sees and wants when it crosses over to the primary levels of spirit evolution.

'I want to go back.'

'*But it is beautiful here.*'

'I want to go back!'

And so, if all else fails – if all counselling and guidance fails – then that person is sent into stasis; is taken apart from the spiritual realms and apart from the Earth realm and has to wait until the Lords of Karma (those spirits who are entrusted with the great 'computer' of life) decide where best to place that soul so that the experiences that come to that soul through a myriad of interconnecting vibrations – the opportunities that come to that soul – will give that soul the best chance of this time round saying, 'This isn't for me really' so that when they get back they can say, 'I have learnt enough. I want to move on.'

So, there are certain key points built into the energy matrix that surrounds and guides the soul through its life on Earth – not every instance, not every circumstance, but *key* ones, and that soul will meet those key experiences (unless something goes seriously, *seriously* wrong with the intended life plan for it). How often, for example, have you had an experience that went terribly wrong and you distanced yourself from it and said, 'Thank goodness that is over with' only for that *exact same experience* in another guise to open up for you further down the path of your life? Because you have to meet certain challenges; those challenges are programmed into your life's journey and you can hide behind the tree and you can dig a hole and you can encase yourself in lead **...but you will still meet those key challenges.**

There are certain circumstances – very rare – but there are certain circumstances where souls are pulled off course by the pull of the Earth plane. Those circumstances present themselves to the soul, but the soul is so immersed in the heaviness of the Earth plane that the soul within does not recognise those challenges and bulldozes through them or avoids them, and then goes to them the next time and does something that is counter to their spiritual evolution time ...after time ...after time ...after time. This is why you have guides; this is why you have the voice in your ear that says: 'Perhaps *this* way is the way to go – not *that* way.' Unfortunately many of those voices are blotted out by the effects of the Earth plane, many of those voices are blotted out by the logical mind and you do not recognise the challenges as what they are.

So... pre-destiny? An 'inevitable journey' is perhaps a better term. An *inevitable* journey but the things that come to you in life come to you for a purpose and that purpose is to elevate you. If the only purpose of your life is at the end of it to say: 'Well, I have had a good life. I now want to go somewhere different.' – **Hallelujah!** The Lords of Karma have succeeded in extricating one soul from this matrix of darkness. Does that answer your question?

Deborah: Yes, thank you.

Joseph: Thank you. Yes, please, another question.

Cameron Collinge: It's Cameron, Joseph. At what point does the spirit actually enter the body – obviously either when the baby is conceived or born?

Joseph: It is a difficult concept but the *body* that the spirit enters is spirit. The body of the mother is spirit; the body of the baby is spirit. It enters at a time that is most beneficial within the term of the pregnancy for it to experience its first earthly experience. By that I mean that the circumstances of the mother that the baby is linked to are also part of a karmic pattern. So, the soul intelligence – the spark that will inhabit the 'diluted' spark, if you like, that is the baby's body – comes in at a time that is most opportune for the baby and most opportune for the mother and the father and everyone whose lives they touch.

It is so complex. If you were to look at the world from a karmic point of view, if you could put a grid down that showed lines of karmic energy your mind would be unable to take in the possibilities and the connections that are taking place second by second; and the effect of connecting two points of karmic lineage together: the enhanced energy that flows if evolution is taking place; the stifled energy, the energy that bunches up that fails to flow, if the *wrong* choice is made, or a choice that lengthens the experience is made.

So, the spirit inhabits the physical body at different times according to what that spirit and the lives that it will touch and is touching ...the spirit of the mother and the lives that she touches ...and the spirit of the father and the lives that he touches – *need* karmically.

There is a greater question here – there is the question of spirits returning before, to *your* view, any knowledge has been accrued. **You cannot judge that.** Every spirit that comes into contact with the Earth plane leaves footprints, even if that spirit is only here for a few days. That spirit is a teacher and a pupil. And those spirits that go back to the spirit realms having only inhabited a physical body for a few hours, or a few days, or a few months, have had an impact on someone, have had an impact on the mother, an impact on the father, and there has been an impact on *them* by the sheer experience of being here.

All these things are calculated so that the spirit who is visiting will influence as many other spirits as possible within the time of its life, and so that *that* spirit itself may be influenced as positively as possible by the experiences that come to it.

Nothing is ever lost. No child is ever lost. No life is ever lost. No life is ever worthless. No life is ever in vain. 'They died young,' you say here, 'how terrible!' ...Not terrible at all when you see that child taking up its former persona on a spiritual level in a wonderful world of Light, in a wonderful world of ability, in a wonderful world of creativity, taking back with it to that world the experience of having touched the Earth plane perhaps for only a short time.

You can never judge. Of course you feel the grief if you lose a child. If you lose *anyone* you feel the grief but you feel the grief because you can only see from this earthly perspective. You miss the physical presence but the spirit presence has gone on into a glorious existence and is waiting for you if the love-link has been between you. You cannot lose anyone. It is right that you grieve but you should grieve for yourselves because you are still here, you are still learning. One day you will be there and the grieving will be over. Is that a sufficient answer, Cameron?

Cameron: Yes, thank you very much.

Jackie McCann: Can I ask a question, please? It is a two-part question – my name is Jackie, by the way. First of all I would like to know if people in spirit can *at will* look at the lives of their loved-ones on Earth. And also is it within their power to choose whether or not they can contact those people?

Joseph: It is indeed a two-part question.

You look at the lives of another person only *if* you are given permission to do so. And sometimes you will be given permission to do so because you are the *only* person that can get through to that person who is still on Earth, via a clairvoyant link. They will listen to you so a guide will say: 'Come with me' and will take you into a great hall and will show you a 'book' with some *aspect* of your relative's life in there. Some aspect – the rest will be blank to you; the rest will be shielded from you. And they will say: 'Look, I have tried to talk to your relative on Earth but they will not listen to me – perhaps they will listen to you. Will you please tell them this – will you tell them that some aspect of their life will shape in this way if they follow this particular path according to their individual will?'

And then, in those circumstances, you are allowed to look into the records – but the records are not public. The records depend on your level of evolution spiritually and your reason for wanting to visit them. You also have to understand that many people on Earth do not accept the concept of having (for want of a better word) a 'book' – a vibration that contains within it all the knowledge of what they have done. It is a sobering prospect to many people to think, 'Somebody knows what I have done.' Well, yes, they do but only the *right* people, only the appropriate people with regard to your spiritual growth.

You were talking about is it allowed – is that correct – for people to communicate if they want to with someone on the Earth plane?

Jackie: Yes.

Joseph: In a correct set-up (and a 'correct set-up' mediumistically is one in which guards and safeguards are set in place between the person who wishes to communicate and the person who is doing the communication – the medium, the channeller) a message goes out to those people who it is thought are most likely to be of value to the person on Earth and whose communication is most likely to help them in their quest for spiritual evolution.

Now that sounds quite strange when you consider the nature of some of the messages that are brought to you – when we talk of 'broken fences' ...and 'there is a door that needs painting' ...and 'there is shopping that you have just put away' ...and 'there is a picture you have just straightened.' It is dependent on what can be brought across to the person on Earth and their level of acceptance.

And so, if a person on Earth only wishes comfort from a message, doesn't wish to know about the spiritual realms, only wishes to know that someone has survived, then something personal and simplistic will be given to them via the person on the other side working through the guides towards the medium (to protect the medium – that is why they are there). And there is a criticism that is levelled on Earth towards mediumship always: why is it so simple, why is it so bland? But within that simple message that brings comfort to the individual is nested a series of vibrations that that individual needs but is not aware of having received... healing, for example, Light if they are depressed, inspiration if they are seeking. And all those things are channelled, by the guides, by the spiritual family that links to the individual on Earth, whilst the relative of the individual on Earth is transmitting his or her message through the filter of the guides to the medium.

There is only so much time allowed for spiritual communication to take place – 'allowed' with regard to the collapse of the bubble of vibration that allows that communication to take place, that penetrates the darkness of the

Earth plane and surrounds the church, or the individual, or the meeting with enough Light so that the communication can happen. So, a message goes out *psychically* to those relatives that it is thought will have the most power in changing the life of the individual on Earth for the better. All the relatives *who wish to* may share in the experience of seeing, of feeling that communication take place but only the key ones will be allowed to communicate, and they have to communicate through the correct channels.

You have, of course, other circumstances on Earth where spirits attempt to communicate. Very often spirits will attempt to communicate with a person on Earth irrespective of going through the right channels, and will move something or drop something or blow across a person's forehead to say, 'I am here.' In those circumstances, once they are located, we very politely tell them that they should not be doing that and take them back to their relevant sphere.

Communication has to be controlled or the energies that can be brought through by spirits not going through the right channels can be destructive. They account for poltergeist activity; they account for activity where certain entities or other spirits who are not well-versed in the ways of the Light attach themselves to the vibration of the communication and then 'bedevil' – in the literal sense of the word – those people that have been communicated with on Earth.

So, it is a very complex set-up. It has to be to operate in the right way but you can never say in a spiritual communication, 'That was absurd! That was simple.' ...because you can only see and hear the base communication, not the vibrations at the core of it that are being sent along that beam, along that vibration of communication to help the person who is receiving the communication. Is that an acceptable answer?

Jackie: Thank you very much, yes.

Debra: Joseph, can I just ask you as a follow-on question from that – when you say you can cast out spirits that have come not via the right channels, can anybody move those spirits on or do you have to get specialist help from mediums? What is the best way of clearing those spirits?

Joseph: You have to understand the *nature* of the spirit. It is not enough to know that there is a spirit there – you have to understand what they want.

Are they communicating simply because they want to create chaos and be a part of the Earth plane and the dominant vibration of the Field?

Are they communicating because they simply have not been located yet and wish to pass something on to a relative on Earth?

Are they communicating because they are lost because their views, whilst they were on Earth, were tightly *against* there being a life after this existence? And so when they moved on they found they had surrounded themselves with situations they were familiar with that were so entrenched in their spiritual minds that they could not move on from them, so found themselves still walking the stairs, still sitting in the armchair, still waiting for someone to appear at the door.

In all cases you need someone who can see into that reality that they have created, someone who can discern: 'Is what I am dealing with a thought-form, a base spirit at the moment (because there will come a time when they will not be a base spirit), a lost soul (literally), or someone who is trying to get across a message, and the only way they know how, through desperation, is by going 'over the fence' rather than trying to set up a correct method of communication?'

You need someone who can see.

You also need someone who has a very tiny ego. In much communication with the spirit world you find individuals who do this – who communicate for their own aggrandisement. You have in situations people who are perfectly capable spiritually – clairvoyantly, clairaudiently, clairsentiently – going into those situations and saying: 'I know what to do. I don't need my guide. I don't need my God (*most importantly*). I know what to do.'

No. You don't!

Each situation is different, so it is not just a matter of seeking a medium... someone who can see beyond the Earth plane. You have to seek *the right kind of medium*, because the right kind of medium says: 'I don't know what's happening here but someone will tell me. I don't know how to move this spirit who is stuck but someone will tell me. I go where angels fear to tread because I take my God with me, and I rely on my God and on my guides.'

Those are the people you should be looking for and this is the discipline you should be looking for in your spirit communication. If you, who are developing the spiritual gifts, realise day to day that wisdom is in admitting you have no wisdom; knowledge is in admitting you have no knowledge and that you cannot do a thing without the go-ahead, without the inspiration, without the say-so of the God-within and without.

Your mediums and those of you here who are progressing spiritually **work for God!** And you are told when to work and you are told when not to work, and when you are told not to work *you do not work*. You work when God moves you and you do what the God-within and the guides around you tell you to do ...and then those people are moved on.

It is very dangerous, for example, to experiment with spiritual communication. It is very dangerous (as is the trend at the moment) to take equipment into a house and try to prove that there is a spirit there because you are inviting – if there is mischief in that house – mischief upon the heads of those people who are carrying out the experiment. You are bewildering, confusing any lost soul that might need to be moved on to the Light by aiming transmitters and equipment at them, by not communicating with them.

Above all God should be taken into any house, any situation where you have to communicate with the spirit realms, and also (Isn't it wonderful!) in any situation where you have to communicate with *this* level. You should be bringing Divine Love into every situation in your life. Every time you go into a room light that room up with Light because no one else will. It is your task, it is what you are asked to do, and it makes all the difference. Is that sufficient?

Debra: Thank you.

Joseph: Another question, please.

Sandie: Good evening, Joseph, my name is Sandie. It is interesting what you have just been talking about. I actually work with children and young people with what are described as 'mental health problems'. I have noticed more recently there are more and more children and younger children who are describing seeing quite a lot in terms of people, figures and beings, but what they are describing are actually quite frightening experiences for them. Although I can work with the Light and obviously help them in terms of protection, I was just wondering... two parts to this question ...one is – is that to do with the vibrations of the Fall that these younger children are being much more influenced by the negative nature of those entities – whatever they are? That is the first question. Also, is there more that I can do and my colleagues can do to help those young people?

Joseph: The young pile in at the moment ...it is like one last football match that all the supporters want to go to. The young are the most sensitive because they come here from the spirit realms and have not had time to be polluted by the Earth plane. They are *highly* susceptible to spirit communication; they have not been told that it can be otherwise; they have not been told, 'This is silly. This is wrong. You are imagining things.'

Unfortunately, as you have said, because of the Field those sensitive children are reacting more and more to the dominant vibrations of the Field, which are set to negative, which are set to violence, which are set to materialism, which are set to personal power. So you are combating – not the children *per se* but the effects on the children of the people that they link to, and their own ability to receive information from the Field.

To best help children who are influenced by visions who are spiritually aware, you should in a morning *pray* for them, in an evening *pray* for them and surround them in your vision, with God's permission, in a capsule of Light. And pray that all the knowledge and experience that comes to them on that particular day or through that particular night comes from God, from the soul-within, from the Light-within.

You also have a difficult task in that you need to pray for the parents, because the parents are steeped in a society that says, 'This is all there is. Get more! Experience more! Live today!' So, you need to pray for them and similarly pray in God's name that they *literally* **begin to see the Light.**

You asked about the nature of the visions that the children are seeing. There is a very base level of communication; there is a beginning to clairvoyant communication and that communication links to the Earth plane and the successive lower planes above it. Until those children have been trained to see higher than that – to connect with angels, to connect with their guides and above all to connect with God – that is what they will *initially* see.

There are many, many children at this time, who are ready to blossom into full spiritual knowledge, who are ready to be trained. Spiritual knowledge and spiritual sight without training and without discipline is useless. So the third thing that you need to pray for is – not that their facility closes down so that they no longer see things – but that they see the *right* things. And the way for them to see the right things is to be connected to a teacher who will show them what to do, how to control their gift, how to be disciplined and how to communicate with higher levels of reality.

So, your third task (having prayed for the children and encapsulated them in Light, having prayed for the parents and encapsulated them in Light) is to pray that the pupil finds the teacher and the teacher the pupil. To encapsulate the child in Light and the teacher in Light and say, 'Please God, let them find each other.' ...Because without a teacher each of those children blossoming now into spiritual knowledge can so easily be taken off the path. Their facility can be shut down and will not be given to them again within this particular lifetime.

So, it is good that you are experiencing children who are seeing things; it is bad that they are experiencing the effects of the negativity of mankind and of the Field at this time. But you can do *everything* – you can treat them on a physical level and you can change them, uphold them, nourish them and sustain them on a *spiritual* level. Is that a sufficient answer?

Sandie: Thank you.

Joseph: Thank you. Is there another question please?

Honor Wearden: Yes, Joseph, I would like to ask... you talked about people coming back to this life, but people coming back with disabilities – mental and physical – do they choose to come back for their life experience or for the families because their disabilities, whether mental or physical, do impinge on the family and how the family then works?

Joseph: First of all they choose to come back within the context of what we have discussed earlier. They choose to come back either because there is a pull to the Earth plane that they cannot resist or do not want to resist, or they come back to teach. Now within that context there is always – after their 'karmic package' if you like has been put together around them – there is always an opportunity for *them* to learn and for the people around them to learn from them.

You *now* are a teacher in this room. Each of you is a teacher in this room; each of you is a pupil in this room because you donate experience to each other. You have something to learn from each person and they have something to learn from you. So, in the case of disability it is a blend of the two. It is that the spirit who is undergoing the disability is learning something but also (quite rightly as you say) that the people whose lives are touched by that spirit are also learning something.

It is like that with each life and nothing is wasted. That disability is not wasted no matter how much grief it provokes on a physical level, no matter how much heartbreak it seems to generate on a physical level. On a spiritual level there is a reason for it and that reason is not judgement ...that reason is experience, and evolutionary... evolution of the spirit, evolution of the people whose lives are being touched by that spirit. **Nothing is ever wasted.** Does that make sense?

Honor: Yes it does, thank you.

[*Pause*]

Joseph: I feel I am overrunning Michael again but I choose to do it.

Another question, please!

John: My name is John and I would like to ask a couple of things. You talked about dissuading people from coming back and you said that there are two reasons they might want to come back and the first one was to help and to teach. Does this dissuasion process also apply to those teachers who want to come back and feel that they have an ongoing purpose?

Joseph: You have to consider from what point of view the person who is coming back is operating. Are they operating from a lower step of evolution or a higher step? Usually it is from a higher step and usually it is in conjunction with the wishes of a thousand, a million souls in a group soul who say, 'Wouldn't it be good *if...*' and there is a volition within that soul to come back to try and change perception.

Sometimes the soul that wishes to come back is not the soul within the group soul who eventually does come back, because the volition of *one* in the group soul is to a certain degree the volition of *all* in the group soul. When it is decided through discussion, through measurement, through much deliberation, that someone should come back it is always the person who is *best equipped*, who has the best chance of teaching a particular lesson or giving out a particular value of Light-vibration who is selected to reincarnate with, of course, their permission.

There is an interesting question here: is the need to come back and teach also a pull from the Earth plane? Is the need to come back and teach as much a pull, as much a difficulty, as the need to come back and have that yoghurt [*reference to a previous question*] again?

No, because it comes from a different place. It comes from a desire – *not* to return because the group soul members who come back to the Earth plane do not want to return – it comes from the desire to *change* things and to change things from within; to be a receptor for information and for Light from within so that the Field can be changed from within – which is the most effective way to change it. **So, they are coming back *not* because they want to.**

And you should see the tearful reunions when someone returns to a group soul having successfully negotiated that terrible 'crocodile pit' called the Earth once again, and have come back into the fold of their spiritual family. You should also see and feel the trepidation with which (metaphorically speaking) a member is 'waved goodbye to' to incarnate on the Earth plane because it is a dangerous place. And they stand to gain much on behalf of mankind but they can also be injured. They can also be, to a certain extent, polluted and *always* are. And this is explained to them before they incarnate: 'It looks fine here. It looks easy to do *here* but once you incarnate to a certain extent you will experience, you will absorb, you will mop up, some of the pollution of the Field. It is inevitable because you are linked to the Field through your physicality. These are the dangers that you are taking on.'

So, people do choose to come back, but from a different perspective ...not because they want the Earth plane... because they want an end to the suffering on the Earth plane. It is dangerous but the rewards and the ability to change the Field increase so much more when you have someone in the Field – a 'Field Agent' if you like – able to give out Light by linking, *subconsciously* often, to the group soul that they are a part of so that that group soul can channel Light through them to change things on a physical level. Is that a sufficient answer?

John: Well, if I could ask you because you referred to this Field being a 'matrix of darkness' and you also talk about bringing in God-Light – so is the aim to change this Field of darkness or just to enable the maximum people to escape from it?

Joseph: If you place enough lanterns in a Field of darkness – the darkness no longer exists. So, if people are in dark corners and the Light is brought to them there are no longer dark corners and they don't wish to hide in them any longer.

The purpose of reincarnation from a group soul (to bring Light into the world) is to *speed up* the process. And as I have said in the books that I have communicated to Michael, **there is only a certain amount of time left before the energy within the Field** (which is the energy that most people exist within and feed off because they cannot link to any higher energy) **expends itself and civilisation ends.** And this is the importance of what I am saying and very often it escapes at meetings:

'...Did Joseph talk about the end of civilisation?'

'...I don't know.'

YES, HE DID.

There are signs already within your world – very serious signs – that things are taking a turn very definitely for the worse. With the children coming in – many of whom are members of group-soul projects to bring Light into the Earth – there is a 'rush', if you like, there is a stampede, there is an imperative to bring Light in to change things within this society before it is too late for this particular society ...and the whole thing has to start again.

We are tired; we are weary of it. *You* are weary of it – you just do not realise that fact or realise **how *close* to the end of your particular cycle you are unless you change things,** unless you re-energise and, therefore, change the Field.

And *if* and *when* the Field is changed successfully to a sufficient extent then the souls will escape because they will no longer wish to stay here. They will realise, rediscover, remember, who they are, why they are here and will wish to move on to the spiritual realms. Is that a sufficient answer?

John: I hope so. Thank you.

Joseph: Is there one final question, please?

Dorothy: Yes, please Joseph... my work has changed considerably over the last few years and I wondered, if whilst I am still here on the Earth, is there a main focus as to where I go in the future to assist and be of service to humanity?

Joseph: Bless you for your question! In all matters where you seek to serve humanity you have to turn around your thinking. You have to look, not at the physical manifestations of what you have been doing, but at where the Light is leading you. It is very difficult. One of the traps of the Field is that you are encased – almost 'embalmed' in some cases – in a certain set of vibrations, and you feel that you have to operate within that set of physical vibrations in order to make a difference. And the vibrations *solidify* around you and hem you in.

The most effective thing to do is to become quiet. That is *always* your first daily directive – for all of *you*, for all of *us* – to become quiet first every day. The second thing is to then distance yourself through your meditation from the conflicts and complexities of your physical life – even those that you think you are investing God's time into. You push them away; you become quiet; you enter into the void **...where there is just you ...and Light ...and God.**

And then you say: 'My God ...my Father ...my Mother ...my Creator ...my Everything ...Me – I wish to serve You. I do not know how to serve You, but today if there is a direction You wish me to go in, if there are people You wish to bring to me – point me in that direction, bring those people to me and give me the words, the volition, the strength and the Light to do what I have to do in each circumstance. I am willing to work for You today, tomorrow, all my tomorrows and then beyond my earthly life when I go back to You via the ladder of progression. I am willing to work for You.'

And you have to be quite certain and I know that you are. When Jesus said **there is no greater gift than to lay down your life for a person** he did not refer to *dying*. You are not able to influence the Field as well when you are outside of it as when you are in it. 'Laying down your life' means laying down *the days of your life* for others, for this world, for the planet. And you have to be very certain and say: 'Father, today I lay down my life for You. Take my hand and show me, lead me into the experience that I need in order to help.'

And you will find that your spiritual pattern changes throughout the course of your life, that there are certain things you will be asked to do at certain times and they will fall away. Then certain things will emerge at other times and they will fall away. But they fall away because you are ready for something new, something greater, some greater task that God has entrusted you with.

'Be ye as a little child in order to enter the Kingdom of Heaven' ...the Kingdom of Heaven is where you reside *always* but the complexities of adulthood, the complexities of the society you have created say, 'No! No, it is far more complex than that – far more complicated!'

That is not the case – the case is that you have to strip away that complexity, push it at arm's length once a day, twice a day and say:

'Father, I am here. Father, what do You want me to do?'

And if it is nothing, you do nothing – if it is something, you do something.

'Father, organise my life so that I can be the best use to You.'

It is sacrifice ...It is discipline ...It is Love.

But *ultimately* it is the only rewarding thing you can do if you are spiritually minded – which you are. Does that help?

Dorothy: Yes, thank you.

[*Pause*]

Joseph: I am pleading with Michael for one more question. One more question, please!

Two members of the audience [*simultaneously*]: Joseph...

Joseph [*smiling*]: *One* more question, please.

Elaine Kellet-Harrison: Joseph, my name is Elaine.

Joseph: Elaine, hello.

Elaine: Hello, Joseph. I am not sure how to put this across to you ...in the next few years... we have heard a lot about the evolution of the planet, this earthly place where we are – is it going to be made into two different Earths with the light on one side and the dark on the other? Can you enlighten me also about 'ascension' and what this actually means to the different earthly planes?

Joseph: Yes, I would like to talk about ascension because, unfortunately, the Field has grabbed onto this title. And it is a title bandied about in much the same way that '2012' is bandied about.

2012! ...Ascension! ...Ascension!

You ascend by absorbing more Light. You ascend by understanding the things that we are discussing today. You will still follow your normal path of having been born, traversing this plane until you 'die' to this plane but you will have ascended to a certain extent dependent on the Light that you give out, the Light that you absorb and what you understand.

Ascension is freedom and freedom is not a point in time. Freedom is an experience *within* that has been earned through challenge, through understanding, through seeking.

The Earth is already two Earths. The Earth is the thick crust of the Field, and the Earth is the planet that it once was before the

Field weighed it down. Nested within the darkness, the pollution that you see, there is the spirit of the Earth. And, as ascension applies to the human spirit, ascension applies to the Earth. The Earth is struggling to maintain its *physical* children against the effects of the Field and their own thoughts; is struggling to emerge into spiritual Light once again as you are attempting to emerge into spiritual Light once again.

The situation that I have spoken about is in flux at the moment. The outcome is not set in stone. Were it set in stone, I would not need to communicate with you. The outcome that we *desire* is that society rethinks itself ...'Christs' itself ...elevates itself ...ascends itself through the instruction that is coming through so many points and so many people at this time. That is what we hope and pray for and work constantly towards **but it is not set in stone.**

The worst possible scenario is that mankind will take itself to the brink again – not necessarily through weapons but through an extinction of the facilities of the planet needed to sustain human life.

Should that happen then the cycle will be set into motion again. The souls who have not enlightened themselves to a sufficient degree to want to *leave* the Field will find themselves in stasis until such time as the planet can maintain them anew and they are born anew. *Born anew* but with the same set of karmic circumstances to work out so that they can transform the planet, transform themselves and escape from the effects of the Fall.

I know which option I prefer.

I will leave you this evening asking you to consider which option *you* prefer.

And, if what I am saying feels right to you, then work each day of your life to ascend yourself but also to ascend others. Don't be the one who starts an argument. Don't be the one who bears a grudge. Don't be the one who allows bias to influence which souls you pray for and which souls you don't pray for.

Remember the Earth. How many of you remember the Earth on a daily basis? The Earth needs your Light, needs your prayers in order to sustain itself.

And remember that what you are seeing – the pollution that you see now, the crime that you see now, the lack of discipline that you see now – are effects of the cause, the prime cause, the spiritual cause, *the Fall* – the mistaken use of vibration that trapped you between evolution and reincarnation.

And because you have free will we cannot intervene other than to say: 'Here is our point of view. Accept it or throw it away.' ...But we can warn you that **an end** has to come – which end is it? Is it the end that transforms things into Light so that society and the planet heals itself? Or is it the end that takes away the right to live here until such time as the planet has repaired itself with work from angelic forces and can sustain you again?

These are the things that I come to talk about; these are the things that I want you to consider; these are the things that are important in spirit communication and I pray on my knees that you will at least, *please*, consider them.

Chapter Seven

Joseph Trance Demonstration – 24th March, 2010
The Sanctuary of Healing, Lancashire, UK

Spiritual topics discussed:

Sexual energy.

The spiritual mechanics of a trance demonstration.

The role of animals in ascension.

The effects of the Fall on the environment.

How much time is left for the planet?

An alternative approach to conventional medicine.

Living within the Light.

The trap of repeated incarnation.

DNA Theory.

Balancing practical and spiritual action to help the world.

Combating the trap of the head-mind.

The nature of God.

Meditation techniques.

Joseph: Do I turn left or turn right to get here? Where do I come from? Where do I go to?

I don't *go* anywhere. I simply make the connection. I simply move that part of the universe that is me into and around that part of the universe that is Michael – and Michael, for a while, has to share my thoughts and I his.

None of you ever go anywhere!

Isn't that amazing? *None of you ever go anywhere.* **The experiences come to you.** You exist at any one time within spheres of energy that bring to you the progress that you need in order to go back to God; in order to become less physically-minded and more *spiritually*-minded; in order to forget this place; to forget the Earth plane... not to forget it through loss of memory but to forget it through loss of *desire*.

I come back because I love this planet but I remember the planet as it was, not as it is now ...strangled ...polluted ...*dying*. I remember its people as the noble beings they once were and *still* are deep beneath the surface. I come back because this is not a happy world. I come back because you are not happy people, and because *you* are not happy people *we* are not happy people. We belong to you and you to us – we are a part of each other.

Change has to come! I come here to instigate change, to suggest change, to bring change. And that is all I can do – suggest it, bring it, deliver it to your door **and then it is up to you.**

But this is a two-way exchange tonight; it is a two-way conversation and I would like you to ask me whatever you want to ask me, and to the best of my knowledge and ability I will answer those questions. Who would like to talk to me, please?

Ben Hamilton: What is the effect of spilling the 'Cup of Hermes'?

Joseph: I am sorry, I don't...

Ben: What it means is sex and the male ejaculation – how does it affect the outer body?

Joseph: How does the male ejaculation affect the outer body?

Ben: Yes.

Joseph: Are you talking from the point of view of a male or female?

Ben: Male and energy.

Joseph: You have been both male and female in your infinite existence. The means that bring you here are simply *means to bring you here* in heavy matter. The sex act is steeped in heavy matter at this time. It was not always so. There was a time when you came here through volition and not through physicality; therefore, my degree of interest at the moment is with *spirituality*.

I see a lot of terms bandied about and I see a lot of people gathering together into clubs, into groups, into small areas where they feel that they have anchored onto something spiritual. That is not to say that they haven't, but it is important in what we do to look at the *whole* picture and not a small portion of the picture.

You are brought here through a physical act on one level only; you are brought here through a *God-act* in actuality – you are drawn into the physical world as a spirit being, as Light into an area of denser Light. On other worlds the connection to physicality is not as strong; on other worlds it is known that you can bring yourself through without having to touch the physical to such an extent.

I am not familiar with your term and, therefore, not familiar with how to answer that on a physical level. Is there some way that you can expand that question for me?

Ben: The sexual vibration, the sex in itself, does it create energy for ourselves?

Joseph: Energy creates sex – sex does not create energy.

Ben: Right, so the actual spilling the 'Cup of Hermes' does that higher or lower our vibrational level?

Joseph: As with everything on this physical level, it is what you put into it in terms of *intent* that determines what that object and what that act is. If your intent through physical sex is to grow closer to a person in love then the effects of that act (be the effects of the act nothing at all, or the effects of that act another physical being) will be imbued by your core desire, *by what you wanted at the point of the act*. But this is so with *all* things physical – it is what you put into anything physical that determines what that object is and what you get out of it.

Sex is a use of energy; it is not energy in itself. Everything that you see – the carpet in this room, the lights in this room, the clothes that you are wearing, the chairs that you are sitting on – are all acts of energy; they are all expressions of energy. A chair is energy but energy is not a chair. Energy is only a chair whilst it is perceived to be a chair because *you* bring through the image of the chair – you make the chair what it is. And there was a time originally when a chair would have been created and would have been a loving object, and each object created would have been a loving object, because there was a time when we imbued *everything* with the Love of God.

Now we say: 'I am simply making a chair' **...But you are not!** As you create the chair – or the car, or the television or whatever the physical object is – you imbue it with your *intent* at that time, so you channel energy from God through yourself in order to make the chair. But how do you feel at the moment that you are making the chair? Are you angry? Are you sad? Are you worried? If you are worried you put a little of that worry into the chair,

Left: Why so serious?
Ever the thoughtful little boy, I
always felt 'different', and even at
this tender age regularly (and
uncharacteristically for one so
young) contemplated such
weighty issues as death and the
meaning of life.

Below: Joan, my teacher and
mentor, a few short years before
her death. She remains an
inspiration, and is one of the
wisest, most spiritually and
physically disciplined souls I
have ever met.

Right: *Little Miss Cheeky Chops* (and she hasn't changed!). The Lady Jane, aged 8, and, below, the cover and an excerpt from her 'Spirit Contacting Society'. Naturally its members were expressly forbidden to contact spirits. See appendix.

Opposite top: Jane and myself are snapped on the couch prior to a private Joseph circle.

S.C.S
Book

SCS

Ofcorse you know SCS stands for Spirits contacting Society. But we are not going to contact the Dead. It is realy Just a Society were you tell ghost storys and Sing ghostly Songsles for no good corse or to raise money for Something. Its for are own benefit and enjoyment. most of them will wunt to contacted the Spirts and play weger. But you dont realize how dangerous this could. It could Kill

Pto

Above: Always subconsciously co-ordinated... this photograph was taken shortly before 'An evening with Michael Reccia' – a regular event held at the Sanctuary of Healing where spiritual topics are approached and examined in – hopefully – unusual and entertaining ways.

Top: An impressionable infant school David watches entranced (or is that in disbelief) as his portrait is rendered utterly unconvincingly (see result left) by a visiting councellor. Above: Setting up recording equipment as I prepare to go into trance at home.

Above: David works on one of Jane's *Band of Light* newsletters at the computer.

Right: A young Tony poses for his grammar school photograph.

Below: Tony and myself test the Skype connection to legendary UK DJ Johnnie Walker, who subsequently interviewed me for his *Alternative Johnnie Walker* website.

Bottom: Not a scene from an action movie car chase... just Tony expertly driving us to Ireland and the Joseph event in Wexford which he had suggested and subsequently organised.

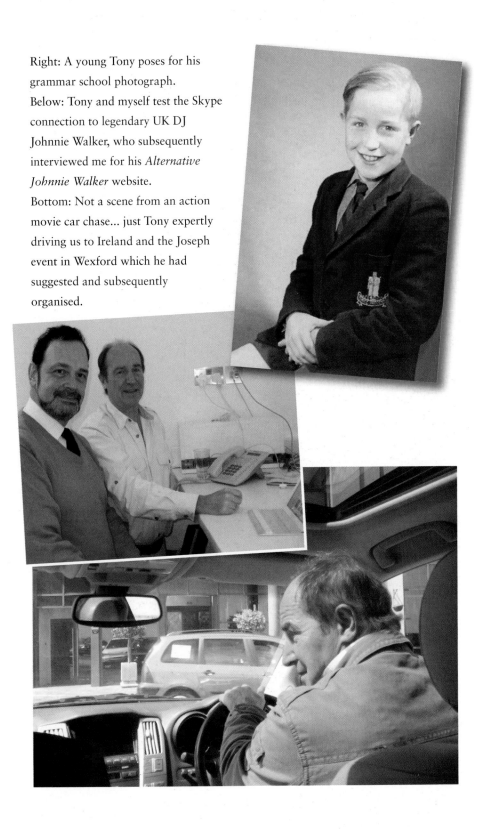

Opposite top: "Turn off your mobile phones and refrain from eating sweets or talking to each other, please." The 'halo' is, of course, a light behind her... but I think it's appropriate (don't tell her). Opposite centre: I'm completely out of the picture at this point – that's Joseph addressing the spiritual seekers in the room.

Opposite bottom left: The aftermath – bleary-eyed and vacant, a post-trance Michael decimates a slice of cake.
Opposite bottom right: More post-trance ravages are evident in this photograph, taken on the ferry back from Ireland the day after a demonstration.

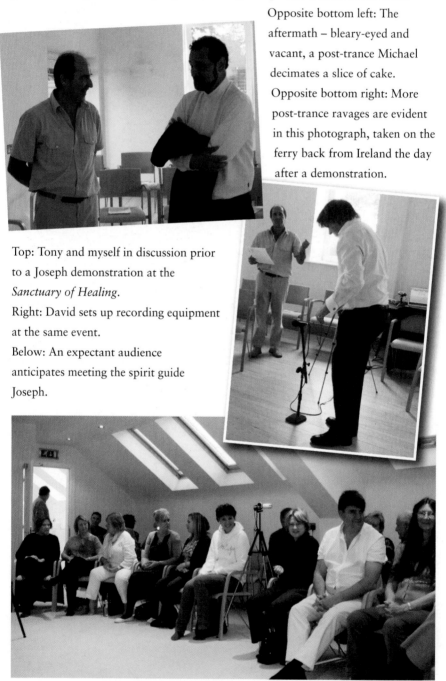

Top: Tony and myself in discussion prior to a Joseph demonstration at the *Sanctuary of Healing*.
Right: David sets up recording equipment at the same event.
Below: An expectant audience anticipates meeting the spirit guide Joseph.

It's not all hard work, however... Jane and myself enjoy good food and fine company at Chez David... ...and three of us make a spectacular entrance at David's fiftieth.

you create a 'worried' chair. If you are angry, you create an 'angry' chair. If you are loving, you create a 'loving' chair.

And this is the point and the core of my argument: you have to begin to put into the physical world more of what you want out of it. If you want it to be angry, want it to be worried, want it to be depressed, then continue to place those things in the objects that you make and the objects that you imagine. If you want it to return to its God-like state, to the paradise that it once was, you have to imbue *everything* – everything that you make physically, everything that you think about physically – you have to imbue it with God-Love and with *your* love. Then there will be no angry chairs; there will be no neutral chairs. There will only be chairs that have been imbued with God-Love. And you will feel the Love from those chairs; you will feel the Love from those objects – from your car, from your house, from your window, from your television, from the glass that you drink out of, from the spoon that you eat with.

Energy is transmitted via God through you. You then decide the energy that you are putting into the things that you make and the concepts that you turn your attention to – be those concepts sex ...or war ...or Love ...or peace ...or harmony.

Is that a better answer?

Ben: Yes, thank you.

Joseph: Who next, please?

Grayling Barraclough: Hi, Joseph!

Joseph: Hello.

Grayling: You warned people in the second book [*Illumination*] that there may be phenomena at these meetings and that was because of the thinning of the barriers between your world and ours so you said there could be manifestations of some sort. I was just wondering what kind of manifestations you were talking about and whether it is something that is out of your control or something you can affect?

Joseph: It is the equivalent of a sonic boom; it is the equivalent of going faster than the speed of sound; it is the equivalent of two differing vibrations having to be married up and there being, at times, cracks around the edges. That is why there are guides here tonight who are protecting you and protecting Michael, because at the edges of the difference of vibration there are people who gather to see what is going on. There are crowds at the edges of vibration.

Some of those people know that they shouldn't be there; some of them are attracted to the Light. And then there is the juxtaposition of differing vibrations – the lower vibration and the higher vibration that we use to meet the lower vibration, and between those two vibrations you sometimes get phenomena, because between those two vibrations the will of those who should not be here, perhaps, and have not come through the correct channels in order to be a part of this gathering, *creeps* though. And, because they are creative souls, they bring with them that act of creation, so if they wish to impress on the people here that they exist, that they are there, then they will bring forth *energy* – energy that will create noises or lights or a disturbance of some kind.

Also, the same thing is true when the two vibrations are separated; there is a rupture between the vibrational levels that can again cause interference – as you would get a crackling on a radio or a disturbed picture on a television-set ...except that *in this case* the disturbance is caused by life, is caused by people, is caused by minds that perhaps should not be in the gap between the two worlds.

There is a vast set-up of protection when such a demonstration is being given, and there are guides whose purpose it is to stabilise those vibrations to allow communication to take place.

But there is a buffer zone, there is a level of vibration between the vibration that is outside of this room and the vibration that is inside of this room and, as it were, at 'the backs' of those guides there are people who attempt to get through whilst they have the opportunity.

There are also people that do not realise that they have passed but are attracted to the Light that such a gathering creates – and you are creating Light now by joining together. They have to be kept out unfortunately; each of them will be dealt with; each of them will be loved and taken to the place they are supposed to be in *eventually*, when their mind comes to that point where they *wish* to be helped. But that is not the purpose of tonight's gathering and so they are kept out – they are at 'the back' of the guides.

Does that answer your question?

Grayling: Yes, thank you.

Joseph: A further question, please!

Deborah: Joseph, my name is Deborah. I was just wondering what part do you feel that animals play in raising awareness or in affecting consciousness, or even in ascension?

Joseph: I feel that animals are wonderful, perfect, innocent souls. And you might ask the question: 'If they are wonderful, perfect, innocent souls, how can they kill each other? How can they kill each other for food? How can they be so wild? How can they be so unlike us?'

Actually they are *exactly* like us in one respect: **we donate the vibrations into the Field of consciousness that is around the Earth that make the animals violent.**

We donate the vibrations into the Field of consciousness that is around the Earth that make the animals *need* to express that violence in the collection of food, through the absorption of energy from other bodies. **We do it ourselves.**

There was a time when we didn't. It is all to do with the power-play that is going on within the limited Field of energy that is around the Earth. We *want* – we feel we *need* – someone else's energy. We feel that we have to take someone else's energy ...at work ...on the phone ...face to face ...whilst we go to bed ...as we wake up. It is always a power-play at some level because that is the way that the Field is set up.

The animal kingdom is apart from this but, because they are encapsulated for a time within the Field of consciousness, they are drawn into that violence. Not that they want to be violent, not that they want to kill each other – they *have to*, and the savagery that you see is because of us and not because of them.

What would they eat, otherwise?

What would they eat, otherwise? ...Wonderful question! What would *you* eat, otherwise, if you did not eat meat, if you did not take power from each other?

...You would take power from *beyond* the Field; you would take energy from beyond the Field. And originally animal forms were less condensed than they are now, were more angelic than they are now and sustained themselves by absorbing Light ...**as did you before the Fall**, before the 'experiment' that went badly wrong that trapped souls for so long within the sphere of consciousness known as 'the Field'.

Animals have a separate destiny; it is a linked destiny but a separate destiny. They have different goals. Their goal is to bring back knowledge and energy to the devas that they are a part of. And devas are nature spirits – wonderful, great nature spirits – that are integrated with, that are a part of, many forms of animal life around the planet. And the animals take back to the devas as they become ...not absorbed ('absorbed' is the wrong word)...

as they *become one* with the deva, and yet still retain the individuality that they had as that certain animal form and many other animal forms that they have had in their soul past, they take back to the deva *knowledge* that allows the deva to progress.

As the animal forms are trapped, as their life-force is trapped once they incarnate, by the energies of the Field so the devas that are linked to this planet – **and the planet *itself* is a deva** – those devas are trapped by the trends of the Field. Those devas seek to escape, but they have in their charge the animal forms that they are a part of and the planet itself on a natural level.

And so, when the Field is changed, not only do the souls escape – not only do *we* escape, do *you* escape – but the animals escape too and, ultimately, the devas. But they will be back, and you will be back, because the ultimate aim is to release souls from the experiment, from the Fall, from the things that have gone wrong, so that they can return to God and decide where next they want to be, where next they want to experience. And if that is in reparation, if that is as part of a new spiritual project that permeates this planet, *so be it – you will return*, but not immediately **and certainly not now**.

And I hope in that answer you see how the dear animal forms are severely mistreated – not only by those that do violence to animals but also by those who say: 'I do not eat meat. I love animals. I am fine with them.' Because, whilst you are part of the Fall, whilst you are part of the Field, until you have changed your vibrations towards *everyone*, you are channelling and maintaining the violence that is shown to each other and to the animal forms, which is another *key reason* that I come here, that I return to say: 'Think differently!'

Do not be part of the crowd. Do not invest in the crowd's worry ...the crowd's uncertainty ...the crowd's violence, and **simply be, each day of your life, a Light**. Then that Light will be guided by your inner-self, by your soul, to where it is needed – to the animal that needs help but also to the human that needs help, to the planet that needs help, to the deva that needs help. Your energies will be used by that part of you that has greater knowledge and greater wisdom than you do as a physical being.

Is that sufficient?

Deborah: Yes, thank you.

Joseph: Another question, please!

Mike Sly: Can I just follow up your comments about the Fall, which you referred to last time you spoke here, and I am particularly interested in any link between the Fall (which I think you suggested may be something that happened all at once in our existence) and the environmental condition of the planet, and whether or not the two are linked.

Joseph: You are asking whether your present state is affecting the planet?

Mike: Yes.

Joseph: Yes, *absolutely* your present state is affecting the planet. The planet – if you were to see it spiritually – is shrouded in a mantel of grey. The planet seeks to push trees up, seeks to widen streams into rivers, seeks to glorify and celebrate the God-within it by being what it is ...an evolving and changing world that says: 'Look, Father! Look what I am! And I am what I am because of You; and I am glorious because of You; and I rejoice because of You.' But it is shrouded; it is crushed; **it is restricted by *your* thoughts – by the thoughts of the people living on this planet.**

You have to examine, in order to change things, what the dominant thoughts of society are. Is it not true that the dominant thoughts of society are that you will never change ...there will always be war ...there will always be sickness ...there will always be poverty ...there will always be lack ...there will always be

Godlessness? And, because you are God *in essence*, you bring through those thoughts as a belief – **as a *creative* belief** – and you push them out into the matrix of the Field to join all the other thoughts that are thinking the same thing and, therefore, creating the very atmosphere that is strangling the planet.

It is right that you should attempt to heal the planet. It is right that you should clean up the atmosphere. It is right that you should plant trees. It is right that you should clean up the skies. It is right that you should re-use materials ...but these things are the Band-Aid on the wound. You have to tackle the physicality but you also have to tackle the *spiritual* aspect of this world.

You have to tackle the root cause of what is wrong with this world. If you channel Light into this world, if you channel Light to each other and to the planet and to *everything* that you come into contact with on a daily basis, then the pollution disappears because suddenly, unexpectedly, a soul that previously has said, 'We will pollute. It is our right to pollute! We need the things that we are making that cause pollution,' will say, 'I am not doing this any more!' And suddenly a soul over here will say, 'I am not tipping things into the water any more.' And suddenly a soul over here will say, 'I am not polluting the heavens any more.' And suddenly a soul over here will say, 'That material is dangerous. Why didn't I see it before?'

...They didn't see it before because the Light wasn't there for them to see it before. Governments will change; heads of state will change; the polluters, the destroyers, the manglers of this planet will change, but you have to put Light in first then you begin to change things.

Is that a sufficient answer?

Mike: Yes. I am just conscious of a comment you made last time you spoke in relation to the description of the Fall, and I think you used the analogy of 'the clock' being set at five to twelve.

Joseph: Yes.

Mike: Is 'five minutes' a long time?

Joseph [*laughing*]: That is a wonderful question – is five minutes a long time? Our ... I don't want to say 'knowledge' because knowledge then puts into your mind a *fact*... our musings and our vision into the spiritual elements of this world *suggest* that there is – if the world continues on its present course, if no more Light is put into this world, if things are as they are now – suggests that there are three generations left ...around seventy to eighty-five years. But that, of course, is only our view and not to be taken as *a fact* that would speed up the Field and make that fact even more concrete.

There is an urgency *now* ...an urgency *tonight* ...**NOW** to do something; to change something; to take your thoughts individually and to look at them and to say: 'How much do I love this world and how much do I love my fellow man and woman? Do I want there to be three generations left or do I want things to change?'

If you want things to change they will not change via the ballot box; they will not change via the rifle and the sword; they will not change through *physical* revolution ...**they will only change through *spiritual* revolution.**

And that means becoming a 'soldier' for God. Being a soldier for God is *oh so difficult* in its early stages, because you have to put yourself in a tunnel of Light and say: 'Whatever is to the left of me I do not believe in any more. Whatever is to the right of me I do not believe in any more. I am a channel for the Light and I channel Light down this tunnel. The tunnel is behind me (a tunnel of Light that goes back to God); the tunnel is in front of me (a tunnel of Light that shines Light into the world) **and that is my only purpose.**'

This does not make any difference on the surface to your professions, to your families. It will certainly make a difference to your hopes and dreams, but you will find that slowly, and then more rapidly, you will invest every single action and thought with Light. You will retreat from those thoughts that are argumentative with people that seek a difference in people rather than a sameness. You will retreat from those thoughts that make you different and look for those thoughts that make you the *same* in Light, in brotherhood, in sisterhood, in Creation.

Three generations ...*but I haven't said that*!

[*Audience laughter*]

Is that a sufficient answer?

Mike: Yes, thank you.

Joseph: Another question, please!

Rosia: Joseph, hi!

Joseph: Hello.

Rosia: I am on a mission. Four years ago I had cancer and I didn't go down the conventional route. At first I was devastated and just wanted to go back to God, then I started getting better and better. I found a camera from America that actually shows up breast abnormalities ten years before mammography does, and it actually helped me with my healing process. I could see, as my tumour shrunk, the body is just a magnificent machine.

Also I basically feel that I have become enlightened from the experience – it has been the best experience I have ever had in my life. I am on a mission now because people keep coming to me that have cancer and I try and get the word out there. And for the last two years I have been to see oncologists and been all over the place knocking on people's doors who I thought would help me with my mission to empower women to help them make changes in their lives – not major changes but changes in their diet, changes in their whole attitude to life, and I feel inspired to be here and to do this now.

Before, when I first found out I had this big tumour, at that time I thought, 'Oh my God, I know I am here for something special,' but I haven't actually got there. So, now I am here for reassurance that I am on the right track and also protection because I am being spoken to all the time; I am getting messages all the time. I know now that I have to start with each woman and get out there and educate each woman. I have been told to do this speech and I have written a speech, which is being filmed and is going to be sent out through various other 'Earth angels' that are helping me get this message out to send it round the world. I know I am on the right path but I do want your reassurance that I am on the right path, though. My family are frightened for me; my family are frightened that something is going to happen to me; my family are frightened of pharmaceutical companies but I have to do this quest. I have to get information out there that has been suppressed. Well, basically that is what I am here for. I wanted to see if I am on the right track but I know in my heart I am and I know what I am here to do.

Joseph: There is your answer: **'I know in my heart I am.'** That is the answer that will take you forward. In this area of knowledge there are many dangers. You are going against – or will come up against – people who are still locked into the Field, who will protect to the *nth degree* their way of life because their way of life brings them money, brings them the power that I talked about earlier. But, for every hundred that are entrenched in their ways of life, in their professions, in their beliefs, you will find one who will listen to you. And I tell you that the one who listens to you and the one who takes up the way of the Light is far more powerful than a hundred or a thousand who don't.

Every situation in your life exists to teach you something, to bring you to a different point of *now*, a different perspective of *now*. This can come through illness, this can come through loss. And you might think: 'Why does God teach you through suffering?'

He doesn't!

Remember that the Light can only get in *dimly* at this point. And remember that many, many souls choose to reincarnate into this world, into this Field, for another 'ride', another go, another lifetime, because there is something they find so appealing about the Field that they cannot yet leave it.

You, therefore, have to listen to the *real* source of knowledge **which is your heart.** God can only influence you through His purest chamber, His purest expression in physical man and woman ...which is the *heart*.

God uses the material in people's lives to try and shake them out of the way of materiality, out of the way of physicality, and so the suffering that happens to you only happens to the extent that you buy into the physicality of what is happening to you. Once you transcend that physicality (as you have just talked about) then you step away from the suffering, and, *more importantly*, the suffering steps away from you because you recognise it for what it is – a 'stepping stone' that has brought you to a point where you look at things differently.

It is dangerous.

What we are saying here tonight is dangerous. What you are doing is dangerous. But each day, in bringing through the Light, you start the day by asking God for protection; you end the day by thanking God for protection and asking for His protection during the night. And you ask God to bring *to you* the people and the circumstances that you need in order to get the message out. **And then you take your mind off the subject and you wait.**

And the stepping stones will be put in front of you; the building blocks will be put in front of you; the key people that you need in order to further the message of Light that you are bringing through will be brought to you.

It is a change, a turn-round of thinking. You are used to, on this level, thinking, 'I have to go from point A ...to point B ...to point C in order to achieve D.' No, once you have accepted the way of Light, the route is there **and the route comes to you.** You simply have to recognise that it is there – against everything that the Field is saying to you; against what your family is saying to you; against what the medical profession is saying to you; against what big business is saying to you – and say, 'No, this is my way!' And on certain days God will bring you *nothing* to do and on certain key days He will bring you *everything* to do, and He will bring you the people and circumstances that will further your cause.

So continue! Know that you are blessed; know that you are supported; know that everything that you do is known – not only by the Godhead but by those who are guiding you. And if *your heart*, every morning and every night, tells you to go in a certain direction – follow that heart because it will never, ever lead you astray. And at the end of the day *if* you lose your house what does it matter?

Rosia [*laughing*]: I've already lost that!

Joseph: If you lose your physical life – as you perceive it – what does it matter? If you lose these things and gain the pathway and clarity of your soul then you have gained everything. Everything else is transient. Do not be afraid to ask, either, to say: 'God, I need X or Y or Z today. Thank you!' and then leave it. In saying *thank you* and leaving it, it will be brought to you in God's timescale and in your soul's timescale.

Does that answer your question?

Rosia: Yes, I think I wanted to clarify that the message that I am getting is that the speech is about how I visualise the future; it's not about what is happening now because I feel that I can't change that. And people around me are frightened of me being ridiculed and all that sort of stuff, but I just know that that is the way to go and that it is the future and how I see the future. If I can keep on track with that then, hopefully, as you say I'll attract the right sort of people in.

Joseph: Please bring the future into now. There is no difference between the 'you' that is today and the 'you' that is in ten years' time – except your point of perception. Do not view it as the *future* – view it as the *now*; and view it as each day bringing a degree of that now into being through your thoughts, through your prayers, through your actions.

In seeing it as the future, there is a danger that you create it always as the 'future' within the confines of the Field. **It has to be the now.** Whatever you want, according to your heart and what God is saying to you, you see as being with you now, *because it is.* You are an infinite being; you are already in that period of time; it is simply that your perception hasn't caught up with that period of time. See it as now: 'The world is changing *now* Father, thank you! The world is different *now* Father, thank you!' ...and you bring it into your life by degree each day of your life.

Does that make sense?

Rosia: Yes, it does. Thank you very much.

Joseph: Another question, please!

Chris Quartermaine: I'd like you to clarify a little bit more about what we can actually do practically to spread Light into this world.

Joseph: First of all you have to *unlearn*. You have to realise that a great many of the concepts that you have been brought up into are wrong.

You have to understand where you come from, and you have to understand where you are going to. You have to understand that you are a part of God, that you are a Light, that you are an angel. You have to understand that this world is sticky; this world is seductive; this world wants you to be a part of it for as long as it can possibly hold on to you.

Why?

Because if you leave it – if you move on from this planet, if you decide that your pathway from this point leads through the spiritual spheres and back to God – it has lost a degree of its power. So, it is in the interests of the Field to instil in you a sense of ageing, a sense of sickness, a sense of *what can I do*, a sense of poverty, a sense that it is all futile.

You have to unlearn. You have to go into the quiet by yourself, envelop yourself in an envelope of Light and say, 'God, talk to me!' And the God-within will move you in different ways... either through speech, or through images, or through a wonderful silence and sense of wellbeing that you have not known thus far in your life. Once you feel that and accept that then you can move forwards in saying: 'This is more powerful than the world that I have known up to this point.'

It is very convenient... when a soul incarnates on Earth the memory goes. The memory begins as a child here, but the memory of what lay *before* goes because the soul is enveloped in the negative Field of consciousness. If you had that memory now you would not ask the question – you would send Light to everyone, *be* Light for everyone, imbue Light into everything that you experience to change things now, **but your memory has been cruelly taken away from you by the Field.**

It was not always like that. When you were an angelic being encased not in matter but in Light, you came here to experience, to play, to understand your creative tendencies, the power of your heart-mind, the power of God flowing through you. You came here to look at different vistas, different horizons, and you had a connection to God that you knew *consciously*. That feeling of peace was with you consciously and always, because you knew where you had come from; you knew that at a certain time you could move out of this area of play and return to another sphere of consciousness. Unfortunately, none of you has that luxury now; you return here and your connection to God is still there but your memory of God, your memory of things beyond this physicality, is taken away from you.

So, your key to changing things is **to begin to remember** because, as you begin to remember who you are and remember the God that is at the heart of you, you begin to forget the effects of the Field. And the stronger you grow in God-memory, in an assurance each day that you are a part of God, that nothing can harm you and that you are Light, the stronger you grow – the effects of the Field grow less on you.

You will shrug off illnesses that would previously have brought you low; you will not invest time and power into political movements that you now see to be mistaken; you will not invest time and power and *anger* as you watch the 'box' in the corner. You will withdraw from all those things, and *instead* you will remember who you are and you will remember who everyone else is too. And in remembering who the 'old friends' are around you, you will greet them with Love, and you change the world and change *their* world from within. It is a wonderful thing!

It is a wonderful thing but so hard for so many people to do because they are steeped in the illusion; because they are trapped in the 'play' – they can't get off the stage, they can't see the audience, they just keep repeating the same lines again ...and again ...and again. It has to stop!

Does that make sense?

Chris: Yes, thank you.

Joseph: Another question, please!

Debra: Joseph, could I ask (I'm Debra)... you mentioned about the world wanting to hang on to people. Do we still have new souls being brought into the world or have we got like a circulation of existing souls that keep reincarnating?

Joseph: That is an excellent question! God is constantly putting out tendrils of Himself – 'children'; is constantly sending out fragments or facets of Himself into all areas of physical and spiritual universes so that those fragments can bring back to Him the sum of their experiences, so that those fragments can discover more about each other and more about Him. **And, as they bring back those experiences, they add to the experience of God.**

That is a terribly difficult concept to understand isn't it? Because your religions tell you that God is perfect and, yes, He is **but God advances.** If you are part of God and you progress – which you do during your life – if you are made in God's image, if you progress, doesn't it follow that God progresses? And God progresses through new experiences, through new delights experienced through the 'sparks' that He sends out into His Creation and *your* creation because you are creators too.

The problem with the Earth at the moment is that, because of the effects of the Field, souls who return to higher levels of consciousness also wish to return to this planet. They are presented with a full story when they arrive on the 'steps of spiritual evolution' as it were, and they are given a choice because in all things God says to His children: 'I will not control you – it is your choice. It is your choice *how* you want to be. It is your choice *where* you want to be.' And many, many, *many* souls are here now because they chose to come back.

This again turns on its head traditional views of reincarnation where *you will come back.* ...**You will come back *only if you want to come back.*** And you will stop coming back when you see the Field for what it is and wish to progress away from it, or wish to help those souls within it from outside of it through spiritual means.

So, the system is clogged. The system is clogged with souls who are the equivalent of 'queuing up' in order to come back time ...and time ...and time again.

Elevated souls, new souls, do not have to come here at all in their first spark of *implied* separation (because souls are never truly separate from God – there is no separation; there is no separation in this room). In their first moments of implied separation they are given a choice at soul-level as to where they go. Those are the new souls. **Many, if not all, new souls choose not to come here.**

You have souls who feel, upon returning to the spiritual realms, that they must come back – not as I am coming back tonight – but must come back into *physicality* because that is their best chance to make a difference. I believe the term is 'fast-tracked' and those souls are fast-tracked to come here. It is only in the cold light of an earthly day when they wake up and think: 'What have I done!'

[*Audience laughter*]

The mechanism of souls coming back, going back to the spirit side of life and coming back to the earthly side of life has to be stopped. There has to be a crow-bar put into that mechanism, but it is *painfully* slow work because you have to convince souls that there is *more* than this illusion. You have to convince souls that there is more to *them* so that when they come over into the spiritual realms they do not simply operate from a skewed vision of the earthly life being all that they are about.

Many of the souls that are here are old souls; you hear the term 'old souls' and it is an accurate expression. Many of the souls that revisit the Earth time and again are old souls, but they are not old souls in *wisdom*... they are old souls *because they keep coming back*. Those old souls need to reconnect with their soul-memory of who they have been since the moment that they were pushed out gently from the loving 'nest' of God. When we can do this – when *you* can do this then that merry-go-round will stop, and the souls that come here **if there is time left** will come here to repair this world and will have far greater power than the ones that are coming now because they will be able to influence people who are just waking, just lifting up their eyes to 'Heaven' and thinking: 'What if?'

So, new souls for the most part are not waiting to be born into this level of physicality, onto the Earth plane. However, new souls *are* constantly being put forth into all areas of God's Creation. And I have seen some of the areas of God's Creation – not all of them but some of the wonders, some of the beauty, the Love, the bliss, the new experiences of being beyond this Earth plane. And yet so many souls wish to return to it time and time again. It is [*smiling*] like opening the box, putting them in, shutting the box, leaving them in the dark – like mushrooms – for seventy or eighty years and hoping that they have grown when you open the box again.

[*Audience laughter*]

...And yet many souls just want to return to the 'soft earth' to become another 'mushroom'.

Does that answer your question?

Debra: Yes, it does, and I was wondering from that, when a soul has incarnated does every soul have the same number of strands of DNA because there is talk of having 'transposed-strand DNA activation' and raising your consciousness that way?

Joseph: I hear so many things. I hear so many formulas. I hear so much that links to the *physical*.

The fact is that each of you is a spirit ...the number of strands of DNA you have is not important.

The number of strands of DNA can be likened to the number of threads in the coat that you are wearing. Would you consider yourself to be the coat or something more than the coat? When you take the coat off, what is the coat? The coat is only a covering; the coat is only an aspect of physicality. Here you can see how easy it is for the Field of consciousness that is set to negative to influence people... 'Ah, I will involve them in a little spin. I will convince them that there is a certain number of strands of DNA they should have. I will tell them that there is only one form of healing and that they should invest all their energies in that. I will tell them that *here* is a 'master' – *there* is a 'master' and if I involve their physical minds I have them. **I have them for life!'**

Your physicality is not important; your physicality is simply there as a shell to enable you to react to the level of vibration around you; it is a 'space-suit'; it is a 'suit of clothes'. The reality lies beyond that. The reality is *simple* and the reality is:

You came from God. You go to God. You *are* God.

You were an angel. You are an angel. You will be an angel again.

The timescale is up to you but do not engage, do not allow – see through the subterfuge – do not allow the physical mind to be entrapped by complexity. The spiritual truth is simple. The way to God is simple. The connection to God is simple. You do not have to go through a priest; you do not have to go through a set of circumstances; you do not have to go through a ceremony – **you simply connect *within*.**

Test everything that you have been told. Test what I am saying to you. Test the new theories that are exploding here, there and everywhere – the terminology, the phraseology – and test them from the heart. Don't test them from the mind or you are testing from the very trap that has been set for you. You cannot think out into the spiritual realms from here [*pointing to head-centre*]; you have to take any information that you are interested in into here [*pointing to heart-centre*] and you have to ask yourself in the quiet and in the peace: 'Does that feel right?'

If the answer is 'yes' and you have given it long enough; if you are truly saying, 'Does that feel right?' and not allowing a thought to jump instantly back into your physical mind and say, 'Yes, it does.' If it *feels* right from here, over a length of time in the peace and with you relaxing your biases towards the subject that you are bringing into the heart-mind, then you can proceed. If you take away those biases and go into the heart-mind and say, 'Does this feel right for me?' and the answer is 'No!' ...avoid it at all costs.

Avoid it at all costs!

Avoid complexity! The Field controls you through complexity – witness the number of forms you have to fill out; witness the number of people you have to talk to in order to get anything done on a physical level; witness the complexity of your politics that excuse bloodshed, excuse poverty, excuse cruelty as being *something that we are getting to eventually; something we are working on; something there is a plan for*. If there is a plan for it and it comes from the physical mind – avoid it. *You* make the difference! *You* make the difference now through keying into your God and sending out into the world – transforming yourself, transforming this world.

Does that answer your question?

Debra: Perfectly, thank you.

Joseph: A question, please!

Hilary: Joseph, this is Hilary. For many years I have felt that the spiritual path is important to me. I also have paid attention to the truth movement which is going on, and there are a lot people who don't believe our politicians any more and don't believe all the lies that have been told in our name. I am going in a few days to join a conference of *hopefully* like-minded people. So, I hear what you are saying about, yes, we have to do our own spiritual practice to connect with the Light, but also, on a planetary level, somehow we have got to come together to make the changes.

Joseph: Absolutely you have but you have to have a core-energy. In order for any concept to take hold and to have longevity – any concept that is steeped in Light and has at its core a wish to change things for the better – you have to imbue that concept with strength in *energy*. If you do not, that concept will fall. That does not mean that you should not get involved in the movements you are talking about. Absolutely you should! But what I am saying to you is that you should be aware that there is a duality to everything and that the world will change when there is enough spiritual energy, positive energy, from outside the Field that will make it change.

Therefore, as I have said, into everything that you do – whether it is a conference, whether you are working for truth, whether you are working to protect the rain forests – take with you, as your constant companion, *your true self*. Then, if you are sitting around a board table, because you are taking with you your true self as a companion, you imbue everyone around that table and the concepts that come out of that conference with Light. And they have strength against the Field; they have energy that can combat the Field because the Light is stronger than the fogginess of the Field.

Of course you must make changes, but you must also recognise that you will be drawn into organisations; you will be drawn into areas that reflect your spiritual evolution. When you are ready for such a thing you will be given the means to change things. And you should again go to the heart-mind and, by using the heart-mind, assure yourself each day that what you are doing is correct for you and correct for the planet. And if your heart-mind (which is *you*) says, 'Yes,' and if there is a feeling that this is what you must do **then that is what you must do.**

I am not saying abandon your society; I am saying imbue your society with Light and, in doing so, you will change it. But it is essential that you do so because otherwise, if you do not do this, you are only treating the surface; you are applying a Band-Aid; you are applying a plaster. You have to apply the plaster, yes, but you also have to dress and heal the wound and it is this duality that I bring to you – a *remembrance* of your duality. Yes, you operate as a physical being and you will each go back to a house tonight and you will each sleep in a bed that is familiar to you, but that is not who you really are. That is part of your journey – that is not you. Once you imbue every aspect of your journey with Light then you uplift all the things that you are involved in – from talking to someone, from having a drink, to changing the world through clearer thinking than we have had for generations.

Do you see that?

Hilary: Yes.

Joseph: Are you sure that you see that?

Hilary: ...It's easy to get involved in the mind, to think things out so it's good to keep remembering, I guess, yes.

Joseph: The mind ...what a travelling companion is the mind! What a travelling companion:

'I am comfortable – no, you're not!'

[*Audience laughter*]

'I am happy – no, you're not!'

'I am rich – you're poor!'

The mind is connected to the minds of everyone else around this world. The minds of everyone else around this world are connected to the Field of energy that feeds those physical minds. And the Field of energy that is conscious (as all things are conscious) and is sentient seeks to keep you controlled, loves the arguments that it can get into through your physical mind with yourself. You don't need anyone else to argue with, do you? [*Audience laughter*] You can do a perfectly good job of it yourself.

You do not have to be a slave of the mind; you do not have to be worried by the mind. It is time to take the harness and say, 'I am leading you – you are not leading me.' It is time to take a 'whip' of Light to the mind and say: 'In line! *In line*!' And you will have to do this on a daily basis because the Field will always want you to revert to the thoughts of the physical mind, which are confusion, which are a merry-go-round, which spin around ...around ...around. And whilst you are thinking and spinning around ...around ...around in here [*pointing to the head*] you are doing *nothing* here [*pointing to the heart-centre*].

Come to the place where there is stillness and allow that place of stillness to guide you both in here and out there. And you will begin to recognise when the mind is attacking you, and then you will be powerful enough to say: 'Enough! I still hear you but you are in a box somewhere and you are not worrying me!' And eventually you will re-program the physical mind too because the energy comes through you out through the heart-centre, but also can be drawn up into the physical mind to cleanse the physical mind. And you will find that certain aspects of your past come to you and you will be able to let them go – then you know you are on the right track. You will query whether your thoughts are your own or the collective's thoughts – then you are on the right track. And you will have times each day when you can go to the heart in silence and experience peace – then you are on the right track.

Does that answer things more fully?

Hilary: Yes, thank you.

Joseph: Another question, please!

Rose: My name is Rose and I've got a question about God. I know that God is the sum of Creation and is within each of us and, as such, is probably quite frustrated, but is there an independent and a more powerful God that can act independently of each individual? You were saying there is a greater God, I noticed in one of your books.

Joseph: What there is at the moment, around this planet and within each of us until we *recognise* it, is what we would describe as 'the lesser God' or 'the sleeping God' or 'the God not recognised' because the effects of the Field dampen our ability to open up to God. But you have to remember that, once you have left this planet and chosen to leave this planet, you then have to slowly cleanse yourself from the effects of having lived on it for so long. You have to cleanse yourself of the effects of living within the effects of the Fall so your experience of God grows as you heighten your vibrational rate.

To encapsulate the essence of God in words is *impossible* – I can only say that we grow in knowledge of God. We, in our sphere and the spheres above our sphere, grow in knowledge of God the equivalent of 'daily' because we discover something else about ourselves that reveals something of God. And as far as we are aware (and I am a hundred percent *certain* of this but I can only give you *my* viewpoint) there is just the One Field of Energy ...I am wrong... **the One Field of *Creation* behind the Energy.** The Energy is the tool. There is the One Field of Creation – there is the One Creative Urge. Again, words do not explain this. There is the Creative Urge that comes forth as you ...as me ...as the worlds of creation ...as this world ...as the spirit worlds.

You are able, however, to experience God – your view of God – because you will push into the matrix of God your own viewpoint of what He ...or She ...or It is by becoming quiet, by divorcing yourself (as I have said) from the physical mind and tuning into the heart-mind. There in the silence, there without anyone saying anything to you on a physical level, you will, if you persist, experience *through a glass darkly* an aspect of the God that you are and the God that He is.

God, we find, is more and more within ourselves. As we travel upwards (and 'upwards' is an earthly concept that does not apply), as we hone our vibrations, as we move closer together and yet embrace our individuality to a greater degree we discover, through the tasks that we put ourselves to, through the experiences that we go through, that God reveals Himself not *out there* in the wonders that we see but *in here*, always through the heart, because, as we go closer back to God, He expresses Himself more easily through us.

I cannot encapsulate, I cannot put a projector in the middle of this room that will show you the glory of God, but I can, through looking at you as spirits, experience that glory, through feeling and seeing a oneness with each of you that you cannot see because you are encapsulated in flesh. I express my God in the joy that I have in existence and in the joy that I have in experiencing the aspects of God that are my friends, that are my colleagues, that are the members of my family – the other members of the group soul that I am a part of.

God is glorious and, to the extent that you can channel God here tonight, you will change this world. From our point of view the mechanism of changing this world is a simple, a slight and a small one. From your point of view it is a mountain because you are trapped within – again I am repeating myself but I have to –

trapped within the dampening effect of the Field ...the Field that takes away your God-knowledge.

...But you can get it back through here [*pointing to the heart-centre*]. If you want to know God – the *One* God – **here is the One God!** If you want to know the One God in the spirit spheres – the One God-within – *go within*! Ignore the Field and transfer the seat of control from your physical mind to your heart-mind, and you will find Him ...but *only* in facets.

The discovery, as we progress through the spheres of spiritual consciousness and creation, is that those facets are added to as we leave this place behind, as we leave the experiment that went wrong behind, as we progress out of the effects of the Fall. And then at the 'end' (if such a word is appropriate) of the 'staircase' there is another staircase – each set of steps more glorious than the one that preceded it. And, as far as we know, those steps are infinite and yet 'steps' are a three-dimensional concept. The understanding of God expands on many different levels, through many different dimensions. Again you are trapped in this area that only allows you to see in a certain way. We are here – *you* are here to take the blinkers off.

Does that help in some way?

Rose: Yes, thank you.

Jane: Joseph, could we make this the last question because Michael said you haven't to overrun him?

[*Audience laughter*]

Grayling Barraclough: Joseph, could we talk about something practical, maybe, for the last one? In the books you talk about doing the meditations – so this is drawing in Light through your head and is going out to the world through your solar plexus. Now I am assuming, as it is the head it is something to do with the crown chakra, but when I have done meditations in the past

I have sent them out through the heart, and you have talked a lot about the heart tonight. There's lots of different ways of doing meditations that are sending Light out to the world, but I was wondering if you could maybe fill us in with a bit more detail about your specific meditations and the thinking behind them.

Joseph: My specific way – and this applies on Earth and not through my sphere – my specific way is to give you an image that will allow you to 'reach up'. So, I am saying: draw in the energy through your head, *reach up*, burst through the effects of the Field and draw down Light into your heart. Then, when you have accumulated Light (and you can do this breath by breath) in your heart-centre ...**savour it for a moment** ...experience it ...experience the Love that you have brought into yourself ...the vitality that you have brought into yourself ...**and then give it out**. Send it out from the heart because, in sending it out from the heart, you are sending it out from the purest vessel you have as a spirit that is made up of a physical body and a spiritual body.

It is necessary in the early stages of meditation for your physical mind to have something to do *other than attack you*, and so the meditations in my books are designed to give the physical mind something to do so that sneakily you can connect with your God whilst the mind is unaware of that.

[*Audience laughter*]

Any set of visual aids that allow you to connect with God and bring through Light from the heart are ideal, are fine. My meditations are simply *suggestions* for those of you who might find this difficult in the early stages. There will come a time...

...I must return to something: you will find that many people think meditation should go on for quite some time in order for you to *benefit* from it. Again the mind is saying: 'We must meditate for half an hour or an hour or there is no good in this.' As you progress, as you use the visuals and are able to connect more quickly with the heart-centre, you will find that you can dispense with the visuals. You will find that you have trained the physical mind to switch off and you can get directly to the heart of the matter.

Then you breathe in, you take in and you give out energy **for as long as you *feel* that energy to be there**. Once that energy begins to wane, once your connection to God is being overtaken again, embraced again, blanketed again by the effects of the Field ...*let go*, or you will give out your own life-energy and deplete yourself. And, depending on what is happening to you physically, that amount of time that you meditate for (maybe a half hour on one day, maybe two minutes on another day)... you have to recognise when the energy is fading. **And when the energy is fading *you go no further*.**

And you will think, because you are used to living in a finite physical world, 'I can't possibly have done anything of worth today in ten seconds.' Remember that you are an infinite being and that when you connect to the God-within you are bringing through Infinity. And that Light that you are sending out, that Light that you are *being* (for eventually you will just sit to *be* Light – not even striving through the physical mind to send it out – you will send it out naturally) that Light is going to a hundred, a thousand different points, decided upon by your soul and by the God-within.

And remember that that connection through meditation allows you to open up for the period of your meditation until the energy goes, until you feel it go, but also allows you to be used by your greater self and by your God at other times during the day because you have invested in the discipline necessary to connect to the God-within.

It is often said, 'Nothing happens in my meditation!' ...and I have to say: *what do you want to happen*? What do you want to see?

If you want to see something you are pandering to the dictates of the physical mind. If you want to hear something you are pandering to the dictates of the physical mind. In your meditative state you are there simply *to be*, to draw in Light and to give it out. If one of us wishes to talk to you, we have to ask permission: 'Please, Sir – please someone higher than me – can I talk to this person on Earth?' And if the answer is 'Yes' then we will come through the correct channels and we *will* talk to you during your meditation, but not because you are seeking something – because you are *needing* something, because we want to add something to your experience.

Remember to meditate each day to give some time for God, and please don't say, 'I don't have time!' How can you not have time for yourself? How can you not have time to bring into your life the joy that you constantly say you are missing? How can you not find time to bring into your life the healing, the health that you say you are constantly missing, the harmony that you say you are constantly missing? If you strive to find it only on a physical level you will come up short. If you strive to find it on a physical level but are bringing into your physical experiences the Light of God, then you will find the peace ...and the Love ...and the bliss ...and the direction ...and the comfort ...and the support that you are looking for.

So, the meditations exist for those who wish to follow a narrative. But if you take up the meditations in the book today and still need them in three years' time then you are not doing them correctly. In three years' time you will say, '*Joseph*, I don't need that any more.' And that is wonderful! [*smiling*] I can then put my feet up; I can then play cards; I can then drink coffee – or the equivalent of these things in my realm.

Now, it is quite right that I have been overrunning Michael in previous demonstrations and I have been brought to task for it! You see, from my point of view, I have all the energy I need *plus* Michael's energy, but Michael is a finite being on a physical level and, therefore, I have to respect that I have to vacate this vessel so that he can use this connection again in the future.

Chapter Eight

Joseph Trance Demonstration – 13th May, 2010
The Talbot Hotel, Wexford, Ireland

Spiritual topics discussed:

What happens if we deviate from our spiritual path?

The trap of repeated reincarnation.

Combating fear.

The role of animals in our evolution.

God.

Bringing the God-within into our daily work lives.

Recognising how God speaks to us.

The need for respect for the Earth.

Changing the planet through Light.

Assessing our spiritual progress whilst on Earth.

The true meaning of the 'sins of the fathers'.

Joseph: I always begin by asking Michael to stand ...actually that's wrong – I begin by *telling* Michael to stand, and I tell him to stand because the energy flows better between us when he does so.

So, I begin by standing his body up, and I begin by talking for a little while about the sea. In order for Michael and his companions [*reference to the other members of Band of Light*] to have arrived here tonight they had to cross the sea. I love the sea. I love the sea because it is part of my background, but I also love the sea because it reminds me of the way that God works. It reminds me that from that friendly, wonderful, loving shore God pushes out energy; pushes out His 'children' into the four corners of His Creation. But He does not leave them there alone; they are always reached by His information on the next wave and, ultimately, they are brought back from their experiences by a tide that brings them back to Him.

...Or so it *should* be.

Things, at the moment, are a little slower than they should be in bringing His children home, but perhaps we can talk about that at some length here tonight. Also I am reminded by the sea of the energies that we bring *to you* this evening; the energies that come out from the God-centre via us into this room to bless each one of you; to contain you within the bubble of vibration that we are using in order to communicate; and to wash away, as we begin, those worries, aches, pains, stresses, dilemmas that you may have so that whilst we commune here this evening you are safe; you are at peace; you are filled with healing-energy; you are uplifted, and I look forward to our conversation this evening.

As you will know I like this to be a conversation. I don't want to dictate to you. I don't want to say: 'This is *Joseph's* way and, therefore, it must be *your* way. I want to hear from you. I want us to discuss things. I want us to learn things together as the family that we truly are – you and I – and so, in God's blessing, I ask for a question, please.

Michael Morrison: Can I ask a question?

Joseph: Yes.

Michael: It's regarding the soul. What happens to the soul if they ignore their path, and how does that impact on the family soul?

Joseph: The path is quite a complex subject to talk about because the path exists on *many* levels. There is, for each of you, the 'apparent' path – the path of family, and friends, and work, and relationships, and aspirations on a physical level. But *beneath* that path there lies a stronger path and that is the path that you, as a soul, have chosen to tread whilst you are on Earth. Unfortunately, this path is hidden from you for most of the time because of the effects of the Field that surrounds you on a physical level – a Field of energy that is confusing; a Field of energy that makes you forget who you really are ...**a soul on a journey**.

In order to access the path, in order to understand your path, you must at times, *as often as possible*, go into the silence. Go within yourself and be still – no television, no phones, no radio, no distractions, no conversations – just you and your God and the quiet. And if you do that don't expect the path to be revealed instantly to you as a broadcast, but expect yourself *by degree* to understand more about why you are here; to draw energies into your physical life that will allow you to connect to the people you are supposed to connect with in order to react with them and play your part in undertaking the mission that you chose to undertake before you came here.

Do souls always fulfil their mission?

No, unfortunately not, but there is always another 'goal' (that is not what we want for souls; we want souls to come back home) ...there is always another goal, always another chance, always another lifetime to get things right. And, if a soul decides that it does not want to come back to the Earth plane in order to fulfil its mission **then it does not have to.** It can fulfil that mission on the spiritual levels of evolution, within those spiritual levels, by undertaking tasks that are *different* than the tasks it would have undertaken on Earth but culminate in the same result.

You could say that most souls on Earth at the moment are a little lost; you could say that some souls are *considerably* lost, but there is a mission for each soul. And if I was to simplify that mission into a few words, I could say that **the mission of each soul is to return 'home'** – to return home as a soul to God, to return home as a soul by reaching within and creating that home once again in this physical world.

Is that a sufficient answer?

Michael: It's brilliant, thank you.

Joseph: Another question, please!

[*Audience silence*]

Michael Morrison: And are we corresponding with that program?

Joseph [*smiling*]: That is a wonderful question, and you might not like the answer.

The answer is no – not as a whole, and this is the point of my communication: to make you understand that you are a whole; that there is no such thing as one soul alone out on the Earth plane, out in the wilderness. **You are a soul connected to every other soul.** Every other person that you ever meet is part of you, because *you* are part of God and *they* are part of God so you have to look at the whole experience.

Are souls learning as a whole at the moment?

The answer, unfortunately, is NO.

That is not to say that certain souls are not escaping the Earth plane and going back to their God, taking the steps up the levels of spiritual evolution. That is happening but not *enough* souls are doing that, and the reason they are not doing that is because of the 'glamour' of this place.

It is difficult to see glamour in the Earth at times isn't it? It can be a very dark place; it can be a depressing place; it can be a cold place; it can certainly be a violent place; it can be an angry place. But many souls invest so much of their consciousness into the Earth plane, into *this* life, and believe that this life is all that there is when they pass over, when they pass on. When they find themselves on another level of consciousness they ignore the beauty of that level of consciousness and wish to return to the Earth plane. They may want something as insignificant as a television! They may want something, which to them is far more grave – they may want to conclude a relationship or to fix something that they feel they didn't fix before they moved on and left the physical body. They may be obsessed with the physical sensations of this world – with drugs for example, or with 'love' in its impure form – **and they, *by choice*, decide to come back one more time.**

Unfortunately, as they do so and as they immerse themselves in those experiences that they felt they needed so much, they lose their memory of who they really are all over again and they contribute – via their anchoring thoughts of this plane being 'real' and there being nothing else – they contribute to the solidity and the controlling qualities of the Field of energy that you live in. In other words, they reinforce for everyone else – only by a tiny degree – but they reinforce for everyone else **the view that this is all there is.**

Would that we could convince souls that when they move on, when their physical body wears out, when they find themselves on the other side, **they *should* move on.** But that is a difficult task, and that is why I choose to come back and that is why I choose to use Michael to reinforce that argument, to say: 'When you arrive on that side – whether it be this evening or in forty … or fifty …or sixty …or seventy years – take a good look around! See that where you are is *far better* than where you have been and act accordingly! Understand that the desires that you have are physical ones, are material ones, have no purpose in your evolution as a spirit, and try and let go. Try and walk away from the Earth plane.'

…And you will then let in some of the master souls who wish to come here to spread Light, to change things, to work towards a time when *everyone* remembers who they are and this planet changes …war no more …violence no more … abuse of the physical and mental bodies no more …abuse of the emotional bodies no more …abuse of each other no more! That changes with the spreading of Light on this level, and that is why it is so important that souls realise that this is a passing phase – it is not everything; it is a journey that you are moving through and a journey that you influence via your thoughts and desires.

Does that answer the question?

Michael: Thank you.

Joseph: Please another question!

Female member of the audience: So, is that because of an attachment to fear that stops a soul progressing?

Joseph: Yes, fear is such an enemy, and the 'Field' that I talk about a lot [*smiling*] is not the field out there – the meadow – it is the Field of vibration that controls mankind.

Let me take you back to the beginning …the beginning of mankind on Earth or what mankind was at that time, which was angelic – make no mistake – mankind was angelic. Each of you *was* and also *is* angelic. And at that time the Earth was a sphere of beautiful experience; a sphere in which you could discover what you were and what you were not; a sphere in which you could 'play', as it were, in full consciousness of your connection to God and your connection to each other. **At that time there was no fear.**

After mankind had existed on this level for a certain amount of time, it felt that it could understand God's plan for the unfoldment of this area of Creation better than God could. **Better than God could!** Not that mankind felt it was going *against* God …mankind felt it was helping God by finding a better way – something that God would appreciate. And mankind speeded up the vibration of this planet with the result that it became out of phase with the rest of Creation.

As a result of that, the creative energies that souls used in that time to bring forth whatever they wished in front and around them became a trapped Field of energy. Mankind began to experience anger, and fear, and violence – all born out of a need for *enough* Love, *enough* power, *enough* spiritual energy. And there wasn't and there isn't because the experiment – 'the Fall' as I call it – trapped mankind within a bubble of energy that they constantly contributed to. And instead of contributing creation, and beauty, and Light as they had at the beginning of their time here, they began to contribute fear, and anger, and upset, and aggression …and the bubble of energy filled with such things.

Now you also have to understand that your thoughts are alive; you give each thought that you push out from your mind, through each passing second, a purpose, a resonance, an attraction. Your thoughts of fear are alive because everything is alive. Your thoughts of anger are alive because everything is alive. So, you pour into the Field, minute by minute (and have done for countless, countless years) …fear … anger …upset …doubt …feelings of lack …feelings of poverty …feelings of illness … feelings of decay.

So, within the bubble that was created by mankind all those years ago, you now exist within what you have created. Souls are afraid because they know no better, and we – myself and other souls around the globe at this time – are trying to show a better way.

What is the better way, *Joseph*? If we can live without fear, how do we do so?

You do so by transferring your seat of power from the 'parliament' here in your head [*pointing to the head-centre*] to the 'parliament' here in your chest [*pointing to the heart-centre*]; from the physical mind that is a slave to the wishes of the Field to the spiritual heart that connects you to God.

You do this in meditation; you do this in the quiet and, when you do this, **you awaken your God-mind.** You see beyond the Field; you experience beyond the Field. You let peace in; you let quiet in; you let a certainty and a lack of fear in so that, from that point onwards as you connect with your heart-mind each day, the Field will have less of an effect on you. You will be less afraid; you will feel stronger; you will be able to combat the aches and pains and diseases that the Field tells you that you have to have at certain ages. You begin to free yourself from fear, from anger, from negative vibrations.

Not only that but, as you begin to use your heart-mind, you begin to open up the heart-minds of the people around you because you become a beacon for God-Light. And you use that God-Light subconsciously and consciously through your heart-mind – **as you did before the Fall** – to spread God-energy, positivity, creative energy around and throughout the globe. And that is how fear is combated and that is how this world changes.

Have I explained myself sufficiently?

Questioner: Yes, thanks very much.

Joseph: Thank you. Another question, please!

Joe Kavanagh: What is the role of the animals in our evolution?

Joseph: Poor, innocent, lovely, wonderful animal forms!

...Poor, innocent, wonderful, lovely animal forms!

The animal forms are created by angelic beings of a different nature to mankind. They are created by devas – by great, wonderful nature spirits. And just as you are a part of a group soul – in other words you are part of a family of souls that work together with certain purposes in mind to elevate themselves and others – devas become animal forms; they extend themselves into consciousness expressed through animal forms.

The animal forms are as relevant as you are. Each form of nature is as relevant and as important to God as you are. But, again, an effect of the Fall is for mankind to believe that they are the pinnacle of evolution in physical matter.

Not so!

As a result of the Fall you ignore at best – you dominate and cause cruelty to at worst – the animal kingdom. They have a right to be here too because they bring back to the devas that they are part of *evolution*, so that the devas evolve, move on, move upwards, create new forms. It is a cycle: the consciousness goes back; it brings with it experience; the consciousness is brought forth into new forms and new experiences. That is how things should be.

So, from the point of view of the animal kingdom, they are existing on this planet as they should. But I should qualify and tune that a little because there are animals, are there not, that are violent? There are animals that feed on other animals, and you look at the animal kingdom and say: 'Why is there such violence? Why do they have to kill each other?' It is not in order to survive.

They are acting and have acted for years and millennia on the instructions of the Field that seeks always more discord and more violence; on the instructions of the Field that say: 'You have not enough power. You have not enough energy. You need to take it from that form, from this form ...or you will not survive.' And so we – mankind – through our thoughts, through the Field, have harnessed, shackled animals with the need to survive by preying on other animals. We have polluted their thought-processes whilst they are on Earth.

Originally there was a harmonious blend between all physical animal forms, including yourselves, because originally you did not need to kill to eat. **You did not need to eat!** You simply needed to recognise and take in and give out energy. In the harmonious time before the Fall you took in energy from the Godhead, you sent it out from your heart-centre and you *created*. There was energy for all because the misconception that you were separate from God hadn't yet taken place. And the animal forms that were part of Creation and were as loved as you are, were free to come and go and exist without violence, without preying on each other.

So, the animals are extremely important but I have to say to you that everything that is of nature in your world is extremely important. God does not say: 'This blade of grass is more important than a human being. This human being is more important than this tiger. This tiger is a bit more important than this penguin.' God sees you as the Whole of Creation that you are. God sees you as parts of Himself – integral parts of Himself. There is only one organism in this room tonight. There is only one organism in this town tonight. There is only one organism in this country here tonight. There is only one organism in this continent here tonight. There is only one organism around the globe tonight – including the globe itself...

...GOD!

...God who is missing from so many prayers; God who is missing from so many intentions. We hear people praying to us – to guides. 'Oh, just help me in *this* direction! Just help me in *that* direction! My guides will take care of things. Oh, I am praying to this saint, this angel or this guide.'

First, *foremost* – GOD – please! Because, in praying to God, you channel the highest vibration and intent; your life straightens out and you can do no harm.

It begs the question, doesn't it, regarding what I have said with regard to animals whether, if animals shouldn't really be consuming each other, *you* should consume animals; *you* should cause them pain in the name of the next meal; *you* should invoke in them fear that the Field wants you to invoke in them so that you can have a package on a shelf that you can enjoy? It has to be a decision for each of you but *really* **at this stage of the Earth's evolution you should not be considering eating animal flesh:**

Because you should not be doing harm to anything if you can avoid it.

Because, as people who in this room are seeking to advance spiritually, you are more likely, more certain, to contact our realms, our spheres, if you stimulate the higher atoms of your physical and spiritual bodies via the things that you eat.

And, therefore, the things that you eat should have sunlight in them. The things that you eat should have a lesser degree of sentience in them. The things that you eat should be vegetables and fruits; and you should have respect even for those and thank them for being part of God, and pray over your food. And eventually – not now, not today, not tonight – but in many, many years' time, it is hoped that you will return to a situation where you do not even harm the vegetation, where you are so evolved that you are able to take in God-energy and exist healthily and perfectly on that.

We have strayed away and back to the question of animals – does that answer your question, please?

Joe: Yes, thank you.

Joseph: Thank you. Another question, please!

Heather Hadrill: Can you talk about the role of the goddess, please?

Joseph: I come across, in visiting this plane, many terms: there is the term of the goddess; I have been quoted certain rituals and certain cults and certain movements and, whilst I acknowledge those rituals and cults and movements, my message seeks to strip them away.

God is masculine ...God is feminine ...God is *both*. ...God is *neither*.

And I want to say to each of you – although you are encased in a specific form of flesh at this moment in order to learn certain lessons – each of you is masculine; each of you is feminine; each of you is both; each of you is neither.

The masculine and the feminine vibrations are tools in order to bring you back to perfect harmony, and you learn certain things by being masculine in appearance but not in reality; you learn certain things by being feminine in appearance and not in reality. You are a blend of both. God is ALL. We come through and I say, 'My God,' and I say, 'Father,' because I was used to saying that at certain times in my past. But there are also lives that I have visited the records of from the distant past when I acknowledged God to be the sunrise, when I acknowledged God to be the Earth, when I acknowledged God to be that feeling within me that I knew was there, knew was something, but I could not express.

And there have been times on this planet when God has been approached and treated in a very different way than He ...than She ...than It ...than the 'Vibration' that is God (that is too small a word to describe God) is now. For example, before the Fall God was an enveloping warmth, an enveloping belonging, an enveloping wisdom, an enveloping creativity and you – we – *each* of us was at that time, **because we *were* there,** able to acknowledge God as little children would acknowledge a parent, with that degree of security that comes from putting your hand into a parent's hand and saying, 'Lead me!'

That is not to say that the souls that existed before the Fall were naïve; they were naïve of modern society, of the things that you have now, but they were aware of where they came from, aware that there was nothing they should fear, aware that they could trust *completely* in the God that they were created by and were a part of.

So, I look at terms – 'God'...'Goddess' – I look at phrases that relate to a certain part of the knowledge, and I ask that we be careful not to label ourselves. I ask that you be careful always to allow your mind to open up to more possibilities. And the problem with labelling God in a certain way, or a religion in a certain way, or a spiritual movement in a certain way, is that inevitably, once it becomes a movement in your minds, it becomes a movement within the Field. And it becomes a movement that has *no movement* because you may have a glimpse of the truth but say for security's sake – often for fear's sake – that this is what I understand; anything else is not of what I understand, and so anything else must be pushed out beyond the barriers of my movement, of my understanding. And by labelling things you cut yourself off from tomorrow's spiritual possibilities, tomorrow's spiritual understanding.

To describe God ...my goodness what a task to describe God... to describe the *role* of God! Interestingly, fascinatingly, I have to say that God has no role. I have to say that God has no purpose as you understand 'purpose'. I have to say that **God IS.** God doesn't *exist*, even, because 'exist' implies work: 'I have to exist. I have to do *this* in order to exist. I have to do *that* in order to exist.' God exists... (there: earthly terms again – so difficult) ...God IS without existing.

God was before physical existence existed. God is apart from physical existence and yet God is *within* physical existence, and so – by that logic – you do not exist. What I mean by that is that you do not have to exist if you trust in God. You do not have to seek existence – existence is yours by right; consciousness is yours by right. And, by trusting in God, you cease to exist and you start to *live*. You start to create, you start to expand and you start to have an effect on the people around you.

If you would look for God, look in the mirror. If you would look for God – look up, look down, to your right, to your left, feel the chair under you, feel the carpet under your feet, take hold of the person's hand next to you – there is God. **There is God!**

Where is God not?

....God is not within the *beliefs* of the Field.

God exists outside of the Field but you exist within the Field, and so you have to reach outside of the Field to experience God, to not be surrounded by this dampening area of vibration that seeks to convince you that everything is going wrong in your life: 'You are growing old; you are infirm; you need ...you need ...you need ...take from everyone else!' Reach beyond the Field, through your heart-mind, to discover God without labels.

We, who are evolving as you are evolving, have not reached a point where we can understand all about God and, as far as our understanding goes, we believe that we will *never* reach that point. Does that mean that we will stop our evolution? No, our evolution is infinite but the ability to understand God expands with our experience, and God expands with our experience. So, the target is always moving and there are greater glories ...and greater glories ...and greater glories to understand as we evolve further up the steps of spiritual evolution.

God is a feeling. God is a warmth. God is Love. And what is Love? Love is harmony. And so, in your terms, seek harmony. Is there harmony in the terms that you are looking at, in the movements that you are part of? If there isn't, forget them – they are part of the Field. If there is – *there* is God ...or a small reflection of God.

Again, an expansion of the question and back to it – have I answered your question?

Heather: Yes, thank you.

Joseph: Thank you. Another question, please!

Des O'Neill: You have said this evening in different ways some of the important things are: our awareness of the Field and moving our 'parliament' from our head down into our inner stillness – things that are truly important. Where do our day-to-day lives come into this in terms of whether we are a baker, a builder, a teacher, a doctor? In terms of time and energy where should we be focusing?

Joseph: When you focus on God ...the sun shines in the morning, the curtains are drawn back and the first thing you should do is focus on the God-within. The first thing you should do is dedicate your tasks along that day's path to God and then you become God's baker, God's candlestick-maker. In the things that you do – take God with you, infuse them with God-energy and you will transform them.

There is, of course, a belief that if you follow the path of God, if you follow the path of spirituality, you must set aside what you are doing during the day; you must set aside the materialistic aspects of life ...and you cannot do that *at this time*. You have to, as someone once said, 'Pay unto Caesar what is Caesar's.'

And so you have to, within society as it exists at the moment, earn enough to continue to exist within society as it is at the moment.

But that does not mean that you cannot infuse your actions with God-Light. If you are a baker and you infuse your actions with God-Light: you give out bread that gives out Love that feeds the hearts and souls of those who eat it. If you are a furniture-maker and you infuse that furniture with God-Love: you make furniture that, for some strange reason, welcomes people home, makes them feel happy when they sit on it or eat from it. And you begin to transform the people who work around you and the people that you work for.

We are inviting you to become 'soldiers' for the Light, and you are going *daily* into enemy lines, into enemy territory. You do not fight with guns or weapons of destruction, you fight with Light, and you will find whatever you do – baker, candlestick-maker, furniture-maker, surgeon – whatever you do that during your day, as well as infusing the things that you touch and you create with Love, you will also touch the people around you. And they will say to you: 'I don't know why I am talking to you but I feel I can. I have this problem; I don't know who can help but this is happening to me...' And you will know what to say because you can draw, from within yourself, the God-vibration, the God-speech, the God-intent on behalf of that person.

It is fine to shut yourself away, if you so choose, to communicate with your God for a lifetime and do nothing else; but at the end of that lifetime some souls find that, in the review of their life, they have to ask themselves the question: 'Why did I spend so much time by myself and for myself and not for anyone else?' You have to see the whole of your life as a God-experience, as a God-adventure, as an adventure of the soul.

If you are in a work-situation you don't like, infuse it with God-Love from the start of each day to the end of each day and see it transformed. And if it does not transform you will be placed in a situation where you are happier because your vibration will raise and, if the vibration that you have raised cannot harmonise with the vibration around you, it will seek out a similar vibration, so you will be placed with other people who feel as you do, who create as you do, who work as you do, who bless people as you do.

Before the Fall you were creative. You are creative *now* – it is just unfortunate that you cannot remember that fact and you produce, as a result of your creation, more negative energy for the Field. Before the Fall you were creative angels; you created your own landscapes; you fashioned the surface of this planet with your thoughts channelled from God. You channelled God-Love into form. You did that *then* – you are capable of doing that *now* ...it is simply a matter of realising that.

It is unfortunate that you have to suffer in occupations that take up, as you have said, so much of your time but the way out of that is not to turn your back on those occupations but to *transform* them. You will be surprised, if enough of you do this, at the changes that happen in your work, at the new ways of thought that come into your life, at the better conditions you get in your work, at what you get out of your work and at the satisfaction levels of your work. And then there will come a time when the only work you will need to do, as souls, is to repair the damage that has been done thus far, and create a new 'whatever you wish to create'.

Doesn't that sound wonderful?

...But you have to start *now* working within the society that holds you, the restraints that hold you, and in putting God-energy into those restraints you will find that the shackles fall away and the restraints aren't there any longer.

Is that a sufficient answer?

Des: Yes, thank you.

Joseph: Another question, please!

Female member of the audience: Can I ask you about rainbows? You know when a lot of rainbows come in towards you... is it God or your loved ones that have sent them?

Joseph: The whole of Creation – when you take away the effects of the Field – is a conversation with God. It is simply that society at the moment (again because of the effects of the Field) blots out that aspect of your life. So, constantly, as a background to the busy, physical, material life that you have, there are messages. The messages can come to you in many different ways. They can come to you as light, as you have just said. They can come to you as someone who will, on a day when you need help, deliver that help and say to you *exactly* what you need to hear without you having to prompt them. They can come to you in the form of a series of signs and symbols, on a particular day, that point you in a certain direction.

You see, conventionally you believe that God should speak to you as a voice or as an action according to what you want, but God brings you messages all the time in many different ways according to what you *need*. So, if you need the upliftment of a rainbow ...it is there for you. If you need the encouragement of people who have passed on before you into the spiritual realms you will have that encouragement – very often in your head as something that they would say that moves you to tears, and you will think, 'That is just what they would say.' ...That *is* just what they would say because they are reaching out to you.

You need, in order to understand God's messages to you, to observe more keenly than you do at the moment what is happening around you. You will see things that you think are coincidence, but they will lead to another coincidence and another until you will build up a picture of what God is saying to you.

And God *always* says something to you.

How could God not say something to you when He is a part of you? The conversation is two-way – it is just that you do not understand how to pick up the information. So, watch for things. Be as you were before the Fall: which is as a child. As a child you look at the world with wonder; as a child there are no confines to what you believe and what you can imagine. In order to understand the God-message to you *personally* on a daily basis do not look for it in complexity; do not look for it in the rush, in the clamour and the noise of this physical world. Look for it in the silence. Look for it where you least expect it ...and *expect* it!

Expect God to speak to you and you open that channel.

And whether God speaks to you through a rainbow, or through a voice in your mind, or through someone who shows you the way by telling you exactly what you need to hear at this point in your life, He will speak to you. He cannot help but speak to you. Begin to pick up God-messages; begin to see the wonder in that rainbow; begin to see the wonder in the natural world; become attuned to the background to this natural world – to what is *beyond* the Field.

What is beyond the Field is your 'greater self' and the greater self of everyone that you will ever meet. Beyond the Field is God-Creation and God-Creation punches holes in the Field, and the Field looks and thinks: 'There is a hole here, I must stop it!' ...and stops you believing in certain things or clouds your information from God.

Always stick to that childlike belief that God is instructing you, that God is showing you things, that God is allowing you communication with those people who have moved on from this plane – people you have loved and *still* love – and you will get that information, you will get that contact always, always, always, always! **God never lets you down.** The Field draws curtains across the God-message but God never, ever lets you down.

THE JOSEPH COMMUNICATIONS: TRANCE MISSION

Does that answer the question?

Questioner: Yes, thank you.

Joseph: Another question, please!

Ed Morrison: If we didn't choose to come back, if in this lifetime, we could understand that we have learnt our lessons and that when we cross over we are as inner peace, if all of us were to stay across then other people couldn't exist because no one would be coming back to create it again.

Joseph: That is absolutely right ...I have to expand on the effects of the Fall.

The effect of the Fall on each soul means that that soul has to go through (and this is such an inadequate word) a 'cleansing' process in order to get out of the effects of the Fall. It is widely believed in spiritual circles that there are a certain number of levels beyond this Earth that lead back to God, that lead back to Infinity. What I want to do is to change that concept, to turn that concept on its head and say, yes, there are a number of levels, or zones, or dimensions, or areas of reality beyond the Earth plane, but they are *cleansing* levels that are there as an effect of the Fall.

Each soul who moves on from this world and chooses not to come back begins a journey (and this is a relative word) 'upwards' away from the effects of the Earth plane to refine his or her vibrations once again, step by step through journeying through increasingly beautiful and rare and etheric landscapes and spheres until you reach your 'start point' again ...the point at which you came down to Earth originally. And I tell you at that point you are an angelic being. It is amusing to see angels and humans being differentiated, being put apart: '*We* are human souls – *these* are angelic souls.'

I tell you, each of you is an angelic soul encased in matter as a result of the Fall.

Each of you is an angel that does not realise it as a result of the Fall. Each of you will not *become* an angel again but *is* an angel now. Each of you will reach a time when you will understand again that you are an angel. But you are an angel, you are angelic, you are one of God's angelic children *now*.

It is absolutely correct that if all souls chose not to come back then the Field would collapse. Unfortunately – and this is another grave point – the Field, because it draws not on God-energy but on energy created from the souls that live within it, *is already collapsing* ...but not in the way that we want it to collapse. We actually want it to *change*. We want it to go back to its original state when it was a Field of creative energy that was linked to God-energy ...God-energy that wasn't polluted.

The Field is a finite Field of energy and the Field at present can be seen to be running out of its energy. Isn't it true to say that the world is becoming a more violent place? Isn't it true to say that the world is becoming a faster and faster place with no time to be quiet, no time to reach the God-within? Isn't it true that there are natural physical and material disasters taking place with increasing frequency?

The Field irritates the Earth. You at your present time of evolution as, I have to say, 'participants' (but I don't mean that as a cruel word) in the Field, prove to be an irritation to the Earth. How often do people in the street thank the Earth for being under their feet, the skies for being above them, the oxygen that goes into their lungs and is passed out again so that someone else can use the atmosphere? How often is that world thanked for what it does? Instead the world is wounded, the world is polluted, the world is disregarded as an effect of your belief – or most of the Earth's belief – that the Earth is not important.

The Earth is vitally important!

The Earth is alive. The Earth is one of God's 'children'. The Earth should be held in the highest respect because the Earth allows you to undertake this phase of your journey.

Without the Earth where would you be?

So, the Field is already collapsing. It is like an oil field that is running out of oil. This is why it is so vital that people like you, who are spiritually-minded, pour into the Field God-Light, discover the God-within for yourselves and pour Light into everything that you do. You then begin to change the Field; you then begin to banish the shadows; you then begin to *illuminate* the Field of energy so that you can see clearly who you are; so that you can see clearly that you need to put aside violence, need to put aside pollution of the Earth, corruption of the Earth, the savaging of the Earth, the savaging of animals, the savaging of each other.

We ...I am not really allowed to say this ('allowed' is the wrong word) – I *shouldn't* be saying this, but if the world continues as it is at the moment, if the Field continues in its destruction of anything that it sees as being other than reliant on itself, then the Field has a probable lifespan left of between seventy-five to eighty-five years.

That is a sobering thought, but I would not come back *if* it were not possible to change things by what we do now ...today! Now ...tonight!

And what we do now – *today* and now – *tonight* is to love unconditionally; is to remember in our prayers not just ourselves and our families but, in our prayer for Light, to send out Light to *every* aspect of this world. Not just the ones that are easy to love, not just the people who are working for the Light but the people ...*especially the people*... who are working *against* the Light. **You cannot change darkness by sending out more darkness.** You have to send Light out; you have to change people by illuminating them and you have to put aside that very difficult bias that you have, as physical beings on a material level, that says: 'I don't like this person.'

Let me tell you something – you don't have to like someone in order to *love* them.

You don't have to like someone in order to *change* them.

You change them by directing Light to them, by saying: 'Accept this as my gift. Others hate you. Others hate what you do. I don't agree with what you do but I know I can change you. I know I can lift you. I know I can make you aware of who you are by sending Light to you – and that is what I do to you day and night.'

If enough of you do that – and this is a global movement – then the effects of the Field will be turned around and society will reset itself. You won't harm yourselves any more; you won't kill each other any more; you won't fear each other any more ...it is down to you. This is the message that is *difficult* to get across:

It is down to you.

It is not down to a priest. It is not down to us... We can advise you but, because of free will, we cannot do it for you – we can only stress the urgency of doing it and doing it right now. And we ask in all that you do that the word 'selfish' does not come into it and the words 'for everyone else' do. You sit for yourself and for everyone else. You send Light into the world for yourself and for everyone else, because when you help everyone else you help yourself. It cannot be otherwise.

So, yes, we are working towards a time when all souls are extricated from the Field but, with duality of purpose, we are also working towards a time (in what *time* is left as we see it) when the Field can be regenerated, can become the positive, creative Field of mankind that it once was.

You cannot change things on a material level *alone*.

You have to work always to change things on a material level, yes, but you have to understand that there has to be an *underlying* force and it is that force that must come first – **first the Light and then you change things**. Hand-in-hand with the Light you change things but you have to have enough *power* to change things. Light is power – God-power – and you have to have enough power in all situations to turn things around or your endeavours will come to nothing. How many endeavours, that are started just on this level in order to help people, peter out or become corrupted because they don't have the Light in them? They need the Light as life-force to sustain them, to give them longevity.

Always the Light! Now the Light! And yes, please, when you get back say: 'I don't want to go back, thank you very much. It is rather nice here. I think I will have a look around *here* instead. I think I can do without the beer. I prefer what you have here and I understand that there are greater glories and wonders ahead for me. Why would I go back?'

Why would you?

Does that answer your question?

Ed: Thank you.

Joseph: Thank you.

Eilish Doyle: How do you know if we have come back *why* we have come back? How do you know why someone you are speaking to has come back?

Joseph: It is not for you – except if it is of benefit to you and the people around you – to see their soul path but you will understand, from the vibrations that are given out by a soul, whether that soul is an older soul or whether that soul is here to bring Light into the world and to teach others.

We are all old souls. I love the term 'old soul' – I see it bandied about so often on Earth: 'This person is an old soul!' Yes [*smiling*] but that doesn't necessarily mean they have learnt anything! They can be an old soul because they have come back ...and come back ...and come back ...and come back for one more ride on the 'merry-go-round' without *ever* appreciating that they are part of God and that there is a greater purpose to their mission.

The Earth-destiny of souls is held secret by the Lords of Karma because you have free will in everything, and one of the attributes of free will is that you are allowed your dignity and privacy except from those who are helping you to evolve as a soul. If we wish to look specifically at the soul-route of a specific soul we have to ask permission. We have to open the 'book' as it were, having been given that permission, and see what route that soul is taking, but also see how the route of that soul interconnects and ties up with the souls around that soul – not just the souls that that soul has met up until that point in his or her life, but the souls that that soul *will* meet in five years' time, in ten years' time, and the effect that that soul will have on the other souls based on their present period of learning and their present evolution as a soul.

You should not ask to see the soul-path of another except where that soul-path is given to you clairvoyantly as an aid to helping that soul, or that soul-path is given to you in a flash so that you can heal that soul.

Every soul is an 'old soul' because we all go back – you and I – to that time when we visited this region of Creation, of being, to play ...and forgot how to play or began to play very badly. I include myself and the soul group that I am a part of because we are evolving, we are cleansing ourselves, but we have a greater view than you do. That is not meant as an arrogant statement –

it is simply a fact. We have evolved to a certain level and can see the path more clearly than you can because we have turned our backs, in a sense, on physicality and have progressed as a result of that. But we come back because we understand the *connection* of each soul to every other soul, and we understand that everyone has to get out of this current situation before we can all go 'home' and start again – before we can have new 'toys' to play with.

So, we can tell, when we have permission, the state of a soul. The guides of that soul – the spirits who have elected to help that soul along its path – can tell *instantly* because they are linked to the karmic path of that soul as advisors. You – those of you who are spiritually aware, who are clairvoyant, who are clairaudient, who are clairsentient – when you *feel* something special from a soul it is not necessarily age... it is evolution. So, if you feel a wonderful vibration from a soul, it is because that soul has harmonised with God to a greater degree than most souls have at this time. And you should accept that for what it is – a wonderful connection – and not seek the background of that soul. That background of that soul is private to that soul and to that soul's advisors.

And all souls – whether you have this wonderful burst of marvellous energy from them or whether they treat you with aggression, disrespect and a total disregard – should be treated equally by you. Of course, you have to avoid those souls that would immerse you deeper in the Field but you can still love them, you can still send out Light to them. And you should not, by the same token, be in awe of the soul that gives out a wonderful, *heavenly* vibration. Be in awe of the fact that they are not [*in the higher realms*] but they wouldn't want you to be in awe of them. We are all equal. We are evolving on different levels and at different rates but we are all equal **because we are all the same thing.**

Look for the vibrations around souls, yes. Be thankful for them but you will not be able to – or be allowed to – see into their vibrations *except* if, in your work on their behalf, it is crucial that you do so. Does that make sense?

Eilish: I was just wondering if it wasn't terribly important to know your own state – where *you* are.

Joseph: Of course it is, but you must understand that you are dealing with a physical mind; you are dealing with a heart-mind; and you have taken on many personas during your existence as a soul. You have gone through many situations; you have faced many challenges. But the challenges are not important – the effects of the challenges on you *are*. And in the work that we are advising you to do – *suggesting* that you do – we are asking you, not to look at yourself, but to look at what you can channel on behalf of *others*.

There is a trap you see: there are many people who become so involved in their physical mind as to who they are and where they are that **they forget that each day they should send the Light out.** And the Field loves these little traps. The Fields loves to say: 'Who are you? Think about it! Who are you? Channel your energies into it. What point are you at? Channel your energies into that! Go on a great quest! Find this out! Find that out! Study it! Sit in contemplation!' And it becomes a circle of energy that detracts from your *real* purpose.

And your real purpose is so *simple*.

...Your real purpose is to remember who you are and then be joyous in who you are, accept the Light that comes to you, allow it to transform your challenges and your view of life, and allow it, by sending it out, to transform the challenges and views of life of others.

Do you see that?

[*Pause*]

Do you see that?

Eilish: Yes, I think so.

Joseph: Thank you. God bless! Thank you. Another question, please!

Jane: Joseph, could we make this the last question so you don't over tire Michael?

Joseph: I must at this point just tell you about Michael. ...Where is Michael?

Where is Michael? He is perfectly safe. He is cocooned. He is, in fact, *safer* during the time that I communicate with you than he is on a day-to-day basis because we surround him with energies that keep him from straying off; we surround him with energies that allow him some peace and a view of *his* life that ordinarily he would not have. And that energy, unfortunately, when he is pulled back into his body is blinkered from him, he cannot see it but it has gone into his subconscious.

So, Michael is, at this point, being ushered back towards his own body, which is as it should be. I always overrun him but I promise not to do so tonight, so one last question, please!

Pauline Byrne: When we come in as a soul, we also bring in the sins of our forefathers of seven generations back – can you just talk about that a little bit?

Joseph: I can indeed! Do you know, I hate the numbers that are bandied about on the Earth plane – I am sorry, but I do! I see some souls who say: 'There are seven levels above you. There are eleven levels above you. There is a council of a certain number talking to you. There is *this* number. There is *that* number.'

As far as I am concerned that is *not* the case. For example, the levels above this one (and 'above' is such a limiting word) ...the levels that exist *beyond* this one but also *within* this one (Complicated isn't it?) are not segregated into a number of levels. They are segregated, via the soul's heightening of vibration, gradually into new landscapes and new vistas.

The 'sins of the fathers'...

...the Field is the sins of the fathers.

The Field is the sins of the fathers. The Field is the culmination of the thoughts and beliefs of generation, after generation, after generation of souls. And, yes, there is a cause and effect by dint of certain situations. And, yes, for certain souls it is actually 'the sins' (in inverted comas) that can be seen as the fathers because the souls come back to revisit those same 'sins' – in other words those same errors, those same areas that prevent them from moving on. They are drawn back into the same situation so in that sense the 'sins' *are* the fathers of the soul that comes back to experience more of the sins of the fathers. It is a cycle. The souls come back to experience more of the same thing, more of the same *error* – not a sin.

The Fall was not a sin. The Fall was a misjudgement, and so you are suffering from a misjudgement. And God does not judge you and we do not judge you ...**you judge yourself, ultimately.**

The only judgement that goes on is: **is this action beneficial to mankind or upsetting to mankind?**

Does it pull mankind down?

Does it elevate mankind?

If it elevates mankind then it is from God, it comes from the heart-centre and it expands God-consciousness within the Field. If it is against mankind then the soul has to learn that that is not the way to go *if* it wants to elevate itself and others – always *if it* **wants to elevate itself and others.** You see, you all have free will, which is why we come back to say: 'We suggest... We only *suggest* that it would be a good idea not to come back here again.' We can only suggest. We can't make you; we can't force you – we wouldn't want to force you.

So, certain souls, by their own free will, revisit challenges that bring them pain, that bring others pain. If God cannot get through to you via me speaking or your own heart-mind then He will use the materials at hand. He will use the challenges of your life to bring you up to a dead-end, to a brick wall, to a closed door so that you turn round and think: 'I have learnt from that. I don't want to revisit that area, that 'sin', that set of circumstances again.' And you move on and upwards.

So, my feeling is: I hate the word 'sin'. I hate the word 'sin' and Michael is reminding me (because he is coming quite close now) of a dear, dear friend of his [*reference to Joan, his teacher*] who was once accused of being a miserable sinner, to which she replied: 'I am not miserable – I quite enjoy it.'

[*Audience laughter*]

And that is what I would like to leave you with: my love, God's Love – no judgement; just a need for change. We look forward to a time where you stop punishing yourselves; where you understand once again your potential to create on a daily basis, to create either negativity or positivity, your ability to channel God into every life, into every moment, to make such a difference. We don't want to see the world as it is – we want to see the world as it *was*. We want to see you as you *were*. We want to welcome you back into your spiritual family, but we cannot do it for you.

So, I ask... as I must move sideways to let Michael back in... [*smiling*] he is knocking at the door of his own consciousness... must move sideways... we ask that you take some of this on board and examine it, look at it; look at the *only* way there really is to change the world ...and I won't have to come back again.

Chapter Nine

Joseph Trance Demonstration – 1st September, 2010
The Sanctuary of Healing, Lancashire, UK

Spiritual topics discussed:

Aliens.

The artificial prolonging of life through modern medicine.

The reason for natural disasters.

Inner guidance.

Spiritual distractions.

The reasons why souls reincarnate back to the Earth plane.

The effect of increased spirituality on the physical body.

We are spiritual beings having human experience.

Advice about simple meditation without ritual.

The ego.

Joseph: It's good to be here ...**but where is here?**

Here **is wherever you choose it to be** because *here* is a state of consciousness, a state of mind; *here* is the passing parade of experience that is brought to you in order that you might return 'home'; *here* is where we both are; *here* is my position in the hierarchy of evolution and *here* is also your position. There is no separation – the only separation takes place in your minds and in your attitudes; in my mind and in my attitude. And so, to be *here* I simply have to think of being with friends; I simply have to think of being with other aspects of myself ...**and here I am.**

And you may think that it would be wonderful to be in 'my here' and it is my job tonight to take you to 'my here', and I do that by changing your perception or by changing those parts of you which you no longer need so that you change your own perception and link with my sphere and the spheres beyond. And you can do that at any time: you can be *here* – which is 'your here'; you can be *here* which is 'my here'; you can be *here* which is 'God's here' ...according to how you think, according to what you believe, according to how you act. It is as simple as that!

I come to 'this here' and I see a world that is in turmoil; I see a world that is violent, a world that is uncaring, a world that is self-centred. But I also see a glorious world, a world of Light, and that Light is here – **is here** *now* – it is simply a matter of turning your attention towards it. I hope in some small measure that, this evening, I can help you to turn your attention towards it. Changing the world is simply a matter of turning your attention away from the violence, away from the seeming darkness, away from the upset, away from the depravity towards the Light, towards another *here*, a different *here* ...a *here* that has been here all the time, waiting for you to rediscover it.

I am not here to lecture (I *love* to lecture) ...I am here to listen. I am here to listen to your questions. I am here, hopefully, in the name of God and in the willingness of God to flow through me, to answer your questions. So, *Joseph* for a while will shut up now and ask for the first question please.

Grayling Barraclough: Joseph, from your perspective do what we refer to as 'aliens' (i.e. non-human beings) exist and, if so, what part do they play in human affairs? And if the world as we know it is going to come to an end – as you have said it could well do in the next eighty years or so – how would they be affected?

Joseph: It is again a matter of *here*. You say, 'aliens' but you also say 'aliens' to those who are not of your race. Aliens everywhere! Aliens in other countries, aliens on other planets and in other star systems. The universe is teaming with life because there is nothing other than life in the universe *except* in our minds, except in the *darkness* of our minds. **Everything is alive** and so, yes, within that restrictive term there are other beings on other worlds. The worlds *themselves* are 'other beings' but there is a greater and more complex question that needs to be answered here and that concerns *this* area of space.

This area of space – the Earth and the planets within the solar system exist within a bubble of negative vibration that was caused at the time of the Fall. Because of that enveloping of vibration that was brought onto man by man himself, by his own volition, the glories of the greater universe and *universes* are shut off, are concealed, are hidden for the time being. It is, in a very real sense, as if the Earth and this area of space is out of sync. with the rest of this particular physical universe.

All evolved life is aware of other aspects of evolved life at some conscious level. There are certain beings that are aware of your plight but are not allowed to and can do nothing about it. Why? Because you have to come out of this situation *yourself* – **this is the law of free will.** Millennia ago you placed yourselves in this situation, and we and other sentient beings, other intelligent beings, are waiting for the time when you decide to come out of it. We cannot interfere according to the law of free will. We have to wait until you find us, you look at us, you remember us, you come back into the family. We can suggest ...we can bring Light ...we can hope ...we can teach ...**but ultimately the decision to change things has to be yours.**

It is extremely insular to say that there is no other life in the universe; it is extremely insular to use the word 'universe', *singular*; it is extremely enlightened to use the word 'universes', *plural*. And running through the different levels of physical matter is spiritual matter, and it does not matter where you evolve from – whether it is from this planet's lessons or from the lessons of other planets in other star systems – you ultimately return to the Godhead in order to evolve the Godhead and also to return yourself into some level of matter.

But we are not concerned this evening with beings on other planets and on other worlds. We are concerned with beings on *this* world and how 'being' on this world needs to be different, needs to be enlightened, needs to be Light-enriched. And then at that point and **not before that point** – *if* you survive in your current civilisational form – you will become aware of other beings on other worlds and they will be *allowed* to contact you.

You often look for beings in metal spaceships and vehicles. Consider that there are *far more* spiritual states of existence on other worlds, that there are states of existence that rely on *refined* physical matter. This is why you cannot see them. And that that type of existence allows those beings to be in contact with you *instantly* when the time is right – not in spaceships, not in metal – but to manifest, to connect, to contact ...but not yet, and, if things do not go according to plan, not for a great deal of time.

Is that a sufficient answer?

Grayling: Yes, thank you.

Joseph: Another question, please!

Susan Leach: I have a question, Joseph. I was interested in the question at the last trance meeting about euthanasia [*reference to the August, 2009 demonstration*] and I would like to go to the other side of it where we have preservation of life at all costs and people can be kept alive with mental and physical deformities – are we here for a certain number of days and are we extending those days, or would that body die if the time was right?

Joseph: You must have seen instances where your loved ones, your friends, have been in a situation where they have been kept alive (or so it seems) but the spirit has all but vacated the physical body and the physical body shows signs of still being here because it is *of this planet* but the spirit appears to have left. **The spirit *has*, in fact, left.**

It is a delicate balance and would that you could see the spirit doctors that try to sit with physical doctors (doctors in earthly matter, in an earthly body) to influence them, to say, 'The time has come!' And would that you could see the spirits that stand around those who should have departed to try and disengage them from a physical body that is still being maintained; and the difficulties that those spirits have in detaching themselves from the physical because of the drugs that they have been given, because of the machines that they are hooked up to and, very often, because of the *hope* of the people around them that they will continue to exist on a physical level.

Again it is down to a matter of seeing and knowing. You have certain tribes on Earth, who know when it is time to die, who know when it is time to move on and prepare for that date, and are always correct in when that date is coming. And they move easily, peacefully, comfortably from this world to the next world.

You have to come to a time when that knowledge is part of the medical facility, to a point where that knowledge is built into those who are training to become doctors and nurses, so that they operate, yes, on a physical level but are also *psychically* aware enough to know when a patient has had enough, when a patient is being pulled back to the spiritual realms, when a patient has to sever those ties between the physical and the spiritual.

Your medicine is based almost totally on maintenance of the physical – **maintenance of the physical at *any cost*.** And yet the physical – because of its reliance on the energies from the Field, which is set to negative – the physical is constantly breaking down, is constantly becoming less than it was yesterday; tomorrow it will be less than it was today, and so on. And there comes a time when it is no longer feasible for the spirit to be housed in a physical shell, because all the spirit is doing at that point, if the physical shell is maintained, *is helping to maintain that physical shell.* And consciousness suffers and there is much pain – not physical pain but spiritual pain – pain that results from knowing in the subconscious that it is time to leave, pain that results from knowing in the subconscious that it is time to return to spiritual family.

Isn't it a strange balance? On the one hand you have to let the span of days play themselves out; on the other hand you haven't to maintain the body to the point where the spirit is trapped.

How can you strike this balance?

You strike this balance (again back to the centre, back to the dot-within-the-circle) by expanding consciousness to the point where you know, where the patient knows, where the doctor knows, where the nurse knows the state of the patient ...not physically (Why worry about the physical?), and not particularly mentally, but certainly *spiritually*. **Where is that patient at within that arc of days?** Is it the end of days and the beginning of new days somewhere else? If so, then the machines need to be unhooked, the drugs need to be withdrawn and the body needs to be returned to the Earth so it can be refashioned as another body, as something else, as another shell for another 'visitor'.

Is that a sufficient answer?

Susan: Yes, thank you very much.

Joseph: Another question, please!

Rosalyn: Yes, I would like to ask a question – is there a planetary guardian for every solar system?

Joseph: 'Guardian' is such a delicate word because 'guardian' infers that those who are being guarded are aware of that guardianship and benefit from it. The solar system, the planet, each of you, has guardians; each of you has guides, but those guardians and those guides cannot prevent you from putting yourself in harm's way if you so choose, if you so wish.

It is the same for the Earth because **the Earth itself is its *own* guardian.** The Earth guards itself but the Earth so loves its inhabitants that often it stifles its own miseries (when it could end them instantly) in order to overlook the trespasses of its surface.

The Earth guards itself *ultimately* by the type of actions that you see around you on your news programmes – by the floods, by the earthquakes, by the tornadoes, by the so-called 'freak weather' because these things are, in fact, erupting at points around the Earth's surface where it can no longer bear the pain, no longer hold itself together; where the thoughts of men and women have damaged it to such an extent that it has to rip apart; it has to vent those vibrations; it has to try and get rid of them, to 'scratch the itch', to get rid of the pain.

But the Earth does this reluctantly. God does this not at all. Man does this often. There is Love, and millions of souls are aware of the plight of souls on Earth and the plight of the solar system. But we can only guard, we can only protect, those who *wish* to be guarded and who *wish* to be protected – again we are down to that universal law of free will.

And as long as souls wish to immerse themselves in violence, in materialism, in suffering, in pain, in ignorance …then we are powerless to guard. All we can do is what we are doing – what I am doing, what those who are stood around me are doing tonight – all we can do is pinpoint Light to those who are ready to accept it. Pinpoint Light and say: 'Take this Light out! Share it with people. Change their minds. Change their viewpoints. Let in the guardianship. Let in the Light.' And as a result of that we can guard, we can guide …'guard' and 'guide' are very close together as words… guardian and guide. We seek to guide, we seek to guard **but we cannot protect you from yourselves – only you can do that.**

And, in order to do that, you have to change your mind.

There are great guardians of nature – the devas. There are great fabricators of the universe – the angels. There is a great Love that permeates everything that you see and cannot see, everything you can imagine and things that you cannot imagine. That, of course, is the guardianship and guidance of the God that you are a part of.

The theme tonight seems to be (and I am glad it is) to point out that man and woman turned their backs on the Light; and that to restore guidance, to restore guardianship, to restore *inner* guidance **all souls have to do, on Earth, is to turn their heads back to the Light.**

It is as simple as that!

Remember that the Field makes it complicated; the Field makes it seem complex and says to you: 'You can't do anything! You can't stop a war. You can't heal a person. You can't sort out a family rift. You can't forgive. You can't love. You can't go around with your head in the clouds and change things!'

…Far better you went around with your head in the clouds than buried in the effects of the Field!

The future is simple! A future ... *if you want a future...* is simple. It is simply a matter of turning away from what is happening on Earth at the moment and saying: 'That is not part of my world-view. That is not part of how I think. That is not part of how I act!' And time and again the Field will attempt to convince you that it *is* part of the way that you feel and act. But you must hold up your beacon, your torch of Light, and say: 'No! My world is different! My world is guided. My world is guarded. I am guided. I am guarded!'

...And you will be, and others will be because, little by little, you begin to illuminate others because you are chasing away the Field, you are chasing away the darkness.

Don't I talk a lot!

[*Audience laughter*]

I would far rather *listen* and that is the second part of the answer I must give you:

I would far rather listen.

Listen to what?

Listen, yes, to my companions where I live, where I exist, where I choose to be my 'here'. But also listen to the God within me, because the God-within talks to me, and the God-within talks to you. And that is another 'fast-track' to salvation, to guidance, to guardianship – **to listen to what the God-within is saying.** Not the Field, don't go out there – go in here [*pointing to the heart-centre*]. Your universe is also in here. And you push away the Field and you say: 'No, I am becoming quiet, I am going in here and I am going to listen.' And *in listening* you discover Light ...and *in listening* you discover purpose ...and *in listening* you discover what to do next.

On Monday God says: 'Do nothing!'

On Tuesday God says: 'Pick up the phone and talk to a certain person.'

On Wednesday God says: 'Go into this organisation and become a part of it.'

On Thursday God says: 'Go out and simply be a companion to this person or that person.'

On Friday God says: 'Here are some thoughts. Here is another way to view My universe. Take them on board; think about them; accept them if you will, please. They are your thoughts. They are Mine but they are yours – I want you to remember them.'

And in listening you change the world; in turning away from the Field you change the world and then you will have no need of guidance. You will simply be part of the process of Creation (as you are now but masked and hidden), part of the joy and bliss of Creation, the joy and bliss of being in different worlds, in different ways, in different lifetimes, in different spiritual spheres. And all the time transmitting back that joy to your God who sent you there in the first place to experience, to be happy, to be blissful, to discover yourselves, to discover the rich joy of others …that aren't 'others' at all but are actually part of *you*.

I have wandered! Has that answered your question?

Rosalyn: Thank you very much.

Joseph: Thank you. Another question, please!

Steven Riding: Joseph, is the world going to end in cataclysm and the re-emergence of Atlantis?

Joseph [*smiling*]: Am I coming home? Are you calling me back?

I am amused by your newsstands; I am amused by your bookshelves. But I am also, at times, horrified by these things because I see a lot of distraction: I see many titles and many themes that take you off course. They tell you that *this* is going to happen; they tell you that *that* is going to happen; they tell you you're going to be invaded; they tell you that you *have been* invaded; they tell you that this stone will help you ...or this poem will help you ...or this light will help you ...or *that* will help you ...and they pull you in, very often, to the middle of a 'fenced off area'. An area that will delight you for a time, but has no substance – except that it delights the Field *even more* than it delights you.

And there are many, many theories going around regarding Atlantis, regarding aliens, regarding what you should do to make yourself feel better, to elevate yourself. There are many theories going around that say at a certain point, on a certain day, you will 'sprout wings' and elevate to the spiritual spheres!

These things – to my mind and to the minds of the people who work with me, my colleagues – are *dangerous* because they take you off the road; they take you off the focus, off the target. And the target (to come back to your original question) is that **there isn't much time left in which to be on target.**

There isn't much time left to change your mind. There isn't much time left to put down the books, to put down the areas that call to you and appear to be an inspiration. Again I must say to you, 'Go within!' If you read a book, or watch a programme, or talk to a group and what they are saying, what the book is saying, what you are watching seems plausible – go within. Take that concept in, become quiet, shut out the Field, fence yourself in with God, and then ask God – *the God-within* – whether these things resonate positively with you. If they do then they are right for you. If they don't – if there is some niggle, if there is some question, if there is some doubt, if there is some feeling from within you that things are not right – be brave, let them go and search for the things that *do* feel right inside.

There isn't much time left *if* you don't change; *if* you don't change your mind.

If you change your mind there is all the time in the world and more, because at the point that many, many souls change their minds about how creation operates, change their minds about how the Earth should be ...then the Earth changes, then the path of cataclysm is avoided, then the Earth begins to restore itself. And the spirits – you – living on the Earth restore to themselves their sacred memories, their ancient memories of *who they really are*.

I see great complexity in many works, in many books, in many theories. Great complexity! And if you are on the cusp of wondering whether something is right for you or not, if you go within and cannot make up your mind, view the area that you are excited and enticed by through your *physical mind* and think:

'Is it complex? ...Is it complicated? ...Does it go round in circles? ...Are there a lot of big words? ...Do I have to understand great swathes of material in order to absorb and take on board this material?'

If the answer is 'yes' – then throw it out!

...If the answer is 'yes' then throw it out because the answer to the future of your world, the answer to the future of spiritual evolution on Earth, is simple. So, *so* simple! It is the dot-within-the-circle, and the dot-within-the-circle is saying: 'I am God. You are God. Remember! I am God. You are God. Remember!' ...Nothing more complex than that!

And, at the point that that is taken on board, everything else makes sense; and the scales fall away and you do what is necessary to change the world, to expand the amount of time that this Earth has left *in its present form*. 'In its present form' because, again, there is an arrogance that society has that considers that the Earth will go if you go. No, the Earth is stronger than that; the Earth has guardians; the Earth guards itself. You will go but the Earth will continue. The Earth will be re-shaped.

Unfortunately, it will be re-shaped so that souls can come back **to experience at the same point at which they left.** It has to be so – spiritual law, God's law, universal law. So, the Earth will prepare itself for millennia and back we will come ...back we will come, innocent after a long sleep!

Innocent after a long sleep but with the same *tendencies* built into our souls. And it matters not whether there is another Atlantis, or another civilisation, or skyscrapers, or cities, or villages, or mud-huts ...people will be people at the point at which they left this Earth by causing cataclysms. And they will have to take up the journey again because *only they* can rid themselves of the past – of the controlling, enveloping and constricting effects of the past ...and that goes back to the Fall.

And the only way to get rid of those constricting memories and constricting tendencies is to change your mind about them – not this mind [*pointing to the head-centre*] but this one [*pointing to the heart-centre*] – is to say: 'I let them go now!' In letting them go, you let the whole scenario go, you weaken the Field around you, you weaken the Field around others and you extend the life for *you* on this planet.

Is that a sufficient answer, please?

Steven: Thank you.

Joseph: Thank you. Another question, please!

Rosalyn: Could I ask a question? Have human beings reincarnated on Earth from a previous universe and, if so, what is their purpose in this universe?

Joseph: I will let you all into a secret: you are all from a previous universe; you are all from *every* universe because you are all from God. It is only your perception that boxes you in.

An excellent question and thank you!

But you see how your perception boxes you in? It boxes you in, in terms of: **is there life outside the solar system?** It boxes you in terms of: **is there life outside of this universe ...is there a previous universe ...is there a universe to come?**

And, yes, there have been many universes but you have been a part of them all because you are visitors, you are guests, you are children playing in realms of physicality, but you cannot remember that you came from beyond those realms of physicality. So when this particular physical universe began to expand, you were not dependent on its expansion in order to exist. You existed outside of it, despite it, apart from it, and what is also exciting is *that you still do.*

Part of spiritual evolution, part of spiritual awakening, will be an expansion of your ability to perceive. The effects of 'the Fall' – terrible to always bracket it like that – the outcome of the time when certain spirits got it wrong, for right reasons, initially, they got it wrong, the effects limit your perception. Is it not true that dogs can hear on levels that humans can't? Is it not true that they are discovering bands of light that are beyond human perception? Why? Because those things exist beyond the matrix of perception of the human being, but *once* you were privy to those extra dimensions. And you were able to, not only perceive them but use them as your tools in order to create the worlds that you wished to live in, in order to experience, in order to take that experience back to God, and in order to share your experiences with others ...at the same time knowing that 'others' are also yourself and that God is yourself.

So, souls are at present, with regard to the Earth, incarnating directly from the 'levels' as you would have it – this is another blocking off of the mind – incarnating from the levels directly above this one because they *wish* to come back, or from higher levels – and we have discussed this and we have highlighted this in other talks [*reference to* **Your Life After Death** *and to other trance demonstrations*]. But always, in *my* experience, the souls – the brilliant points of Light who are incarnating now in an attempt to shift consciousness before it is too late – are incarnating from the cleansing levels that exist (and here is a relative term) 'around' this Earth, around this area of space ...**never from beyond** because beyond is too refined a place.

That sounds terrible: 'too refined a place' but it is compared to where you are existing at the moment, locked within the boundaries and fences of the Field. The spheres above the cleansing spheres are too brilliant to have an impact on the Earth at this time, on the consciousness of mankind at this time, on the Field certainly at this time. So beings are sent, spirits are sent – like you, like me (however they are clothed) – are sent from the higher cleansing spheres. They take the decision to incarnate – as do you all – but for a *different* reason.

Many people come back for one more trip, one more ride, one more thrill to do it all again. The spirits from the higher levels of the cleansing spheres come back because they love you so much that they cannot rest, they cannot go on, until they have made a point, until they have presented something for you to accept or to reject **but to look at and consider.**

Would that we could convince people not to reincarnate! Oh, would that we could! Sometimes we can; sometimes we can't – very often we can't. They are blinkered, they are hell-bent (because you are coming back into a hellish situation) on coming back to re-experience and to take up the reins exactly where they left off in their past life. Would that we could convince them otherwise to go on, to cleanse themselves, to evolve through the spheres and then to escape back into Infinity ...back to God ...back to the created playground that you all came from originally. **And that is why highly evolved spirits incarnate.**

I had the choice [*smiling*] – I am sharing with you *secrets* tonight – I had the choice to come back and I took one look and said: '...NO!'

[*Audience laughter*]

...But seriously, I felt that I could, on this occasion, do more good by channelling information directly from what you would regard as a high sphere. But others from my group have and do decide to come back; and our hearts go out to those spirits because they are taking on a great deal. It is not as though they can simply come back into physical bodies and remember who they are and teach. As they come back into the dampening effect of the Field that portion of their memory that links them to where they have come from is wiped, and they have to re-discover it via the channelling of Light to them from our sphere and higher spheres.

They are in danger for every second of their incarnation, and we feel for them, and we weep for them, and we bite our 'nails', as it were, for them until they are restored to us. The danger is that they will forget during that incarnation *totally* who they are, and that the mission that they set off on with such zeal will never come to pass because they cannot remember it, because the Field *loves* highly evolved spirits. It eats them for lunch ...and dinner ...and tea ... and supper because of the Light that they give out. Remember that the Field needs energy; the Field is a negative Field of energy – no better source than, 'Ooh, the Light is strong in this one!' So, the spirits who come are in danger.

I have gone out of my way again and around the houses, and we have talked about universes and spirits. Does that answer your question?

Rosalyn: It does.

Joseph: Thank you.

Doreen Marr: I would like to ask one, Joseph. Previously you have spoken to us about being compressed, but with decompression coming from spirituality is there a danger of an adverse physical reaction to this increased opening in communication with the spirit?

Joseph: That is a very interesting question. Very interesting question!

As you evolve spiritually, the 'matrix' (if that is a good enough word) of your soul becomes enlightened – not enlightened as in: 'I now see' (although that also applies) but enlightened as in its construction. Its creative molecules, governed by you as a soul within them and the God within you, become lighter and there are certain changes to the physical body.

The physical body itself becomes lighter, not that it weighs any less, but it becomes more susceptible to the thoughts and the intentions of others, more susceptible to attacks from the Field and certainly more sensitive. And *sensitivity* is a paradox here because sensitivity is what we are trying to bring to you, but sensitivity can be hell, can be frustrating because you pick up the intentions of others and you *see through* the intentions of others. **You see how the world works and that changes you forever.**

But you are not left unguarded and unguided on this journey, and there are certain things that you can do to protect yourself:

1) **Is to walk within the sphere of God-Light that surrounds you every day.** And to pull it on as a mantel in the morning and to pull it around you at night as you go to sleep, and know that nothing can harm you. Remember the things that you see in sharp focus as you evolve spiritually have no power over you except that you give them power. And so you have to pull on this mantel of glorious white shimmering Light and say: 'I exist within a bubble of God-consciousness, within a world that I have made and the outer world cannot get in to me.'

2) This is always controversial because **you should put aside the eating of meat.**

Why?

...Two reasons:

First of all, when you eat more refined, more spiritual food you help to stimulate those higher atoms and you remain in contact longer with your spiritual side and with those who wish to contact you from that spiritual side.

Secondly, when you eat meat you are ingesting – 'in-gesting' ...letting into that world that you have just 'sealed' – terror, fear, disease. On a physical level your animals are stimulated by drugs, by poisons. On a mental and physical level they are abused and are killed, not humanely at all, but in terror. And that terror – that powerful vibration that resonates at the same vibration as the Field around it – is held within the physical body of the animal at the time of death ...**and then you eat it.**

With your advanced spiritual senses you eat it, and so you are picking up – not only from around you as a highly advanced spirit, as someone on a spiritual path, as someone who is opening up, but you are also picking up from *inside* of you: 'What is going on inside of me? What is going on inside of me? Yes, there's the God ...there's the lunch that I ate ...oh, there's the terror that *by volition* I have eaten.'

So, you have to be careful what you put into your mind. What you *should* put into your physical mind and spiritual mind is God-Light constantly to protect you; and you have to be careful what you put into your stomach.

Remember that there are many gateways into your soul; your soul picks up on so many levels. Your soul knows whether it is hot or cold. Your soul knows whether the person that you are talking to is happy or sad, is attacking you or loves you. But your soul also knows what is going on within the physical body. And the physical body knows too, and transmits those signals to you and absorbs vibration – just as, before you discovered the effects of the Field, you absorbed vibrations from the Field: you became worried for no reason, you became upset for no reason, you became ill for no reason. Now you have shut that out, you have to be careful what you take into yourself.

So, yes, of course there are effects. There is a change that comes to a person as that person advances spiritually, as that person becomes 're-aware' spiritually, but I have to tell you that the benefits far outweigh the side-effects of becoming more spiritually aware.

And also remember that, even if you have a difficult time on Earth (and who doesn't have a difficult time on Earth? I have a difficult time on Earth just by visiting it) you have distanced yourself, to some extent, from that difficult time by your thoughts and beliefs and changing spiritual focus. And, **more important than anything**, you have earned the right to stand on the spirit side of life, to look back at your life, to fold your arms and say, 'No way am I doing that again!' To then turn round and to progress through the ever more refined spheres that lead back to bliss and to 'home'. Is that a sufficient answer?

Doreen: No, not quite, because I feel that the cells you are awakening, and you might call them protons and neutrons or something (I am not a scientist), but what I am saying is that these cells become more activated and your nervous system starts to get more active the more sensitive you become, and I can't find anything that stops that if there is a weakness in the body. I am not saying it wasn't there before, but perhaps I was strong enough or protected sufficiently that I didn't feel the weakness until I started to develop.

Joseph: Recognition is what stops the effects. Recognise that you *will* feel different and recognise that, if you place yourself in a situation where you feel debilitated after you have supposedly opened up to spiritual development, then that situation is not right for you.

Doreen: It isn't quite like that, sorry.

Joseph: It is difficult to work spiritually because you are pulling against the effects of the Field, but remember that you can re-program, as I have said, within your God-bubble of Light, how you *wish* each day to be. And on day one your perception will say to you: 'I still feel weak.' On day two your perception will say: 'I still feel weak.' And on day three ...on day four ...on day five ...but to counter that from your soul and in your meditation you should be saying: 'Nonsense! I cannot feel weak – I am a child of God. That is an illusion! That is a lie – off you go!' And there will come a time when you counter your *perceived* negative effects of advancing spiritually with your creation (because you have advanced spiritually) of the world that you want and the way that you want to feel. Do you see that?

Doreen: ...I do.

Joseph [*smiling*]: That was a very tentative 'I do'.

[*Audience laughter*]

You see there is only one way I can present things to you; I can only say to you the secret to everything, to how you want to be externally and internally, is down to you.

It's down to you!

...The illness you want to fight is down to you; the place you want to live in is down to you; the world that you want is down to you because you are the co-creator of all these things.

And part of your spiritual journey is, yes, to feel the effects of (how you described it) the cells becoming 'different' on an earthly level (when they are not actually on an earthly level – they are becoming different, more awakened and aware on a spiritual level), but part of your journey is to realise that you then create and have *always* created (even before you felt you were spiritually aware) the world that you want around yourself. Maybe you did it subconsciously before, but now you have the glorious and golden opportunity to do it *consciously* and to say: 'Away with you! I feel fine – I am part of God. How can I feel otherwise?'

And it is difficult! It is difficult – you have millennia of conditioning on this planet that says it cannot be so ...and yet it is. **Yet it is!** You create what you want to create today – no matter how you feel.

What do you want to create?

Then go and create it!

And you will. And you have to fight against the effects of the Field until you have proved for yourself, time and again, that you are the creator. You are the creator of your circumstance, of your world, of your wellbeing, of your spirituality and of your perception. The greatest gift you have got is that it is placed into your hands, [*turning to the rest of the room*] and your hands, and your hands and into everyone's hands.

Escape from this planet is in your hands; conversion of this planet is in your hands; how you feel, how you look, how you are, what you think is in your hands – no one else's. Society will tell you otherwise but society is wrong.

Are we any clearer?

Doreen: Yes, that comes back to what you believe to be true.

Joseph: Exactly but isn't that a simple statement?

Doreen: It's simple, yes.

Joseph: And have we talked about complexity?

Doreen: Yes.

Joseph: Complexity is the destroyer, the masker, the container – it takes away truth.

Truth is simple: you are what *you* decide to be.

You always were because before you fell – I fell – **we were what we decided to be,** but linked to that knowledge and linked to a knowledge that we are a part of God. We are each creators, and so each test, each challenge that comes along in life, viewed with spirituality, becomes an *opportunity* – an opportunity to prove to yourself that you are the creator, that you are in charge of a situation – the situation is not in charge of you.

It's that simple. I wish (well, I don't wish) ... in a way of speaking I 'wish' I could make it complex but I can't. I can only present a simple message because the message is simple, and the message being complicated over millennia produced this world. Prior to that, the message being simple produced Eden – a beautiful world, a beautiful part of a vibrant universe that you cannot perceive now because it is closed off – not by God, not by anyone else, but by us ...and we have to unlock the door.

Thank you for your question. I must invite another.

Floris Tomasini: Can I ask a question? It is just to get some clarification, O.K. I heard something really quite beautiful (and it is on my wall): we are not human beings having a spiritual experience but spiritual beings having a human experience, and if you remember that we are spiritual we can actually create anything. Is that sort of what you are saying?

Joseph: That is exactly, *exactly* what I am saying!

You never were physical beings. You aren't physical beings. You are, unfortunately, told that you are physical beings; you are told that you are mental beings. Society is set up in such a way that it addresses your physicality, it addresses your mentality but it ignores your spirituality. And your religions, for the most part, regard your spirituality as something that is tacked on when you leave this Earth.

There is no difference at this moment between me and you. The only difference is one that doesn't really exist, is one of perception because you believe, for the most part, that you are physical beings, and then one day you are released and you become spiritual beings and you traverse certain spiritual heavens.

You have always, always, always, always **been** ...but you have not always, always, always, always been physical beings. You have always, always, always, always been *spiritual* beings – part of God. 'Reflection' is a bad word – it is so difficult to describe the process of donning a 'suit of clothes' in order to perceive yourself as separate from God. It is such a complex way of words...

...What happens is that there is **GOD** – and then there is **God that is God** but there is also *God that is you*. And *God that is you* plays and creates as **God that is God** plays and creates, but **God that is God** and *God that is you* remembers that **God that is God** and *God that is you* is also **GOD**.

The problem occurs when **God that is God** and *God that is you* believe that **GOD** is **GOD** and you are you – and the two are *separate*. And that occurred in this instance through a bending of creation, a twisting of creation, undertaken by **God that is God** and *God that is you* initially in order to say to **God that is God**: 'Look what **God that is God** and *God that is me* has done in order to glorify **God that is God**'. But we ...you ...I got it wrong and encased and encapsulated ourselves in matter to the extent that we forgot who we were.

So, the lovely poem on your wall is perfect, and I can go home.

[*Audience laughter*]

Perfect! Thank you. Does that answer the question?

Floris: Yes, thank you.

Joseph: Thank you

Grayling Barraclough: Joseph, you have talked about doing meditations, sending out Light to people, sending out Light to the world. Are there any words or symbols that you could recommend as part of that practice? For example, people talk about the 'true word for God' and that kind of thing...?

Joseph: Again this brings me back to complexity, to rigidity. In your meditations for the world you will find that if you allow the **God that is God** *within* you to dictate the course of the meditation (having sealed yourself in a bubble of **God that is God**) then on different days your meditations will take different forms.

Sometimes you will have such Love for people that that is all you want to send out, that you want to embrace them, to hold them, to hug them and to make them better in that way. Sometimes you will be taken to an area of landscape in your inner-vision and think, 'Why have I come here?' ...Because that area of landscape needs that same Love, needs that same infusion of Light; and so it is your duty on that day to send out Light into the trees and the landscapes you see in order to heal them. Sometimes you will find in your meditation that you touch on the sadness of souls; and it is your duty on that day to reach in, in your inner-vision, to their hearts and to try and illuminate the Light within their hearts so that their despondency, their depression, their misery is taken away from them because you have re-ignited that fire within them.

I am not one for ritual. I am not one for key words. I am not one for specific names and secrets. I am not one for conspiracies. I am one for (please, God) *the truth* as I see it and the truth as my companions see it. And I also feel that by investing power (remember that whatever you perceive to be true you invest power into) into names, and symbols, and secret societies and half-truths then your power goes into those things rather than into what you really want to do.

And what you really want to do is to change things, help people, love the world, shape the world in God's image again. And so, I am wary of anything that holds itself to itself and says: 'This is the way – by using this symbol, by using this name, by using this incantation.'

I am wary of those things. I am *terrified* of those things! I prefer instead to say: 'Father, what do You want me to do today in my meditation? Take me where You will in my inner-vision and give me the insight, the power and the strength to do what must be done.' And if nothing happens then you do nothing that day. If you are taken somewhere then give always of your Love – not of the ['true'] name of God, because the Love within you *is* the name of God ...is the *only* name of God. I don't mean the actual word 'Love', I mean the power, the energy, the peace that you give out as a human being. That is the name of God. That is the word of God. **The word of God is Love and nothing else.** Does that make sense?

Grayling: Yes. Just one more thing, Joseph. Would it be OK if we turned the light on perhaps because of the cameras? It is quite dark. [*The room had become dark because of the fading evening light*] Would that affect you in any way?

Joseph [*smiling*]: Are you seeing my best side?

[*Audience laughter*]

Grayling: I can't see at all!

Joseph: It will not disturb me.

Jane: Joseph, could you make this the last question, please, so we don't over tire Michael?

Sarah Sarginson: I have a question. To sit and say that I will do God's will, where does our ego fit into this?

Joseph: Ah, the ego! Ah, the pretension! Ah, the ego that says to you: 'I hurt ...I need this ...I need that ...I need to be in this group ...I need to be in this position ...I need ...I want ...I'm hungry ...I'm thirsty ...I'm this ...I'm that ...I need to survive!'

Sarah [*laughing*]: Yeah, that ego!

Joseph: That ego! That ego! In discovering God, in discovering enlightenment and spiritual knowledge through meditation, many people feel that they will lose the ego: 'I may lose myself.'

And my answer to that is: 'Good! *Good* – lose yourself!'

But you will find in losing the ego that is of the Field – the protective element of the Field that you feel you need in order to survive – you will discover your *greater self*. You will be more of yourself than you have ever been. You will experience life more richly, more sensitively, more colourfully, more excitingly than you ever have – not from the point of view of the physical ego but from the point of view of the I AM ...from the point of view of the **I AM GOD**. I am God – I am me, but I am also God.

So, the physical ego fits nowhere. The physical ego exists to help you survive, to help you survive on a *physical* level but it gets out of hand. It makes you the centre of the universe (which you are) but it makes you the centre of the universe in a strange way by saying: 'I am *not* the centre of the universe – talk to me! Comfort me! Look at me! Feed me! Love me! Understand me! Counsel me!' ...And you are not the centre of the universe.

When you let go of those things in meditation, you realise that you don't *become* the centre of the universe but you *are* the centre of the universe – and I don't mean this physicality; I mean the universal creative force that is God. And you realise that everyone else is the centre of the universe too, and that also helps you with your physical ego because when you are encountering someone else, you look at them from the point of view of them being you and you being them. So how can you harm them? How can you hurt them? How can you say anything about them? How can you upset them in any way? How can you feel less than them or more than them ...bigger than them ...smaller than them? **You are them – they are you.**

So, in meditation, in expanding spiritually, you lose the physical ego and you gain yourself – the self that, when this personality has been shed, will *still* be there – the greater self, the self that can look back over life, after life, after life and say: 'I finally got it right this time. I don't need another suit of clothes. I am going this way – not that way.'

Chapter Ten

Joseph Trance Demonstration – 6th October, 2010
The Larkhill Centre, Timperley, UK

Spiritual topics discussed:

Creation, energy and God.

The illusion of separation from God.

Co-creation and God's intention in creating all life.

2012 and other spiritual distractions.

The nature of time.

Whether God already knows the fate of our planet.

The law of cause and effect.

The Fall.

The Bible.

Angels.

The afterlife and reincarnation.

Michael's observations: The questions raised during this meeting were given to a spokesperson who put them to Joseph on behalf of the group, hence the lack of individual names in this particular transcript.

We also experienced phenomena – an 'attack' on the proceedings – during this demonstration, which took the form of a loud screeching emanating from the lighting system that momentarily caused a break in the communication. Joseph became silent and stood completely still until the noises had subsided, subsequently noting and dismissing the disturbance and continuing with his delivery. The point of interference is referred to in the transcription below.

The disturbance, which we later discovered had also resulted in the (new) transformer linked to our camcorder ceasing to function, putting an end to our visual record of the evening from that point onwards.

Joseph: I promised Michael that I would begin this session with something humorous, and so [*smiling*] I have to say, in introduction, that Michael has now 'taken leave of his senses'. He has taken leave of *his* senses so that I can take control of them for a short time in order to talk with you. And I know that sometimes Michael wishes it was someone else who is doing this *...and it is.*

I come back because there is an urgency for change in this world; there is an urgency for change within your personal worlds; there is an urgency for change every minute, every day, at the moment. And I have to say that we are not getting through as we wish to; that there are points of Light around the world that are having *difficulty* establishing themselves; that there are many distractions, many walls that are put up, many barriers that are put up. And many souls, who reincarnate in order to teach **in order to expand consciousness**, become, as it were, 'lost in the fog'. And each time I come through I feel that there is a *greater* urgency to shout, to wave my hands about, to somehow make the people that I am talking to *see*.

That sounds very harsh. I don't mean it to sound harsh – I mean it to sound *urgent*. I mean it to sound like I have something that I can see, that I can do, that you don't *yet* have, and I desperately, desperately want you to have it.

And what I wish to share with you is simple – **very, very simple** – but it gives you the way home, the way back, the memory that links you back into who you really are, why you are really here and what *you* can do to encourage others to find themselves and to find the way back. You are not supposed to be here lifetime, after lifetime, after lifetime. It has been your choice, but it is now time to make a different choice ...to choose better ...to choose a more evolved path ...to choose the way back home to your family – your *spiritual* family – and to your God.

I don't come to preach – I come to answer questions. I ask for questions, please. A question, someone!

Spokeswoman for the group: Scientifically we are taught that energy cannot be created nor destroyed but simply changes from one form to another – does this apply to all creation?

Joseph: Creation is a bringing forth, from Oneness, of opportunity. Creation is a bringing forth, from Oneness, of illusion – *illusion* in order that different perspectives, different points of view, can be examined and enjoyed.

We have to bring into the equation the word that I have to *sneak* into these meetings ...and that word is 'God'. I have to sneak the word *God* into meetings, at present, unfortunately. There is a lot of resistance to that word, but in order to explain energy, I have to first explain the *source* of all energy **and the source of all energy is God.**

God sends forth from Himself (...Itself ...Herself) expressions into physicality, facets of Himself, and those facets are there to enjoy different perspectives and bring those perspectives back to the Godhead to enrich the Godhead. God constantly seeks to be more than He is at this moment; and he seeks to be more than He is at this moment through *you*. In order to distinguish yourself – *in illusion only* – from the Godhead, you have to have somewhere to express yourself, and that somewhere is a physical universe.

Energy is simply the time between something 'not being' and something 'being' according to God's will and according to your will.

When you perceive of something in your mind's eye, you harness energy – **you *create*.** You begin the moment that you conceive of something to create that something – whether it be a solid something, whether it be an emotional something, whether it be a state of being that you wish to enter into – you create it the moment you believe in it, the moment you turn your mind to it. And then you draw out of the pool of 'no-thing' – *nothing* ...'some-thing'. You begin to shape your dreams, and the conversion from the *no-thing* into the *some-thing* is what you describe as 'energy'.

Energy is a movement.

God is still.

You are still at your heart, at your soul, but you have to perceive God and you have to perceive a universe in which to exist at this present time. You create that universe, second by second, by pulling from the pool of energy, pool of what is not...

[*Break in the communication because of disturbance from the overhead lighting emitting a loud screeching noise*]

Energy disrupts. Energy disrupts – we are creating our link to God here this evening and energy disrupted that link momentarily. I apologise.

When you create something in thought or with your hands, you pull from the pool of 'what is not' – the creative molecules of 'what will be'. And that pull and that shaping, as a sculptor would shape a sculpture, is what you call 'energy'. Does that answer your question?

Spokeswoman: Can we change form?

Joseph: You can change thought into form. You *constantly* change thought into form. You can change your form according to your belief in how you are. You can change your form with regard to illness, for example. You can banish illness by drawing into yourself White Light, by transmuting the molecules of your physical body.

If you are asking, can you change form from one form of physical life into another, I have to ask: why would you wish to? *Why would you wish to?* In the measure that you believe – you can, but the problem is you don't believe.

And, *if* you believed to such an extent, would you not use your time – instead of changing from one form into another – in changing one heart into a different heart; in changing this planet into a different planet; in changing each soul so that each soul can see what you now see? That is *true* transformation into spiritual energy. Do you understand that?

Spokeswoman: Yes, thank you.

Joseph [*smiling*]: Another question, please, but without the noises!

Spokeswoman: Would you not think that we are all part of God's energy here and now?

Joseph: Absolutely! But you must understand the distinction that I have made here between energy and God. **We are all, each of us ...I am ...you are ...everything is ...this room is ...this world is – part of God.**

But life expresses itself through change and change comes through dreaming on a physical level, through imagining, through wanting, through desiring, through creating. And that transmission of energy from the pool of God – that transmission of purpose, of intention from the pool of God – is what we call energy. But very definitely we are all One. There is one organism in this room; there is one organism across the world; there is one organism across the universe.

There is only God.

You are a reflection of God, a facet of God, God looking back at God so that God experiences you and you experience God. But it is only an illusion, as in a mirror – it is a reflection. You are sent out, as part of God, to experience, as part of God, and to share that experience with every other 'reflection' and also with the Godhead, **but there is, in truth, no separation.**

The illusion of separation came a long time ago, came at the time of – how I, and many people on this side, in my soul group, describe it as – 'the Fall'. At the time of the Fall there was a shift in consciousness. Until that time each of you, each of us, realised that we were part of God. That was the natural state of things. And then there was a change in thinking – a 'separation' ...but the separation is illusion. The separation comes from the minds of men and women, comes from a history of thinking in a certain way.

And we, and you, are here to remove that, to make people aware of the fact that they and God are One. A difficult task because that awareness can only come from *within*; can only come from shutting out the layers of illusion and sitting *within* yourself; contacting the God *within* yourself and feeling, knowing, living, experiencing that 're-connection' ...or connection that has always been there but has been forgotten. Is that sufficient?

Spokeswoman: Yes.

Joseph: Another question, please!

Spokeswoman: When the Creator created all life, what was His plan?

Joseph: Ah, the small questions. [*Smiling*] The small questions!

[*Audience laughter*]

'Plan' is a human word. Plan implies a point A to a point B. With God, as *we* understand Him – and remember that we, too, are evolving and, although we have access to more knowledge than you, we do not have access to *all* knowledge at this time, but as we perceive God (and there are groups of us who sit to contemplate God), as we perceive God: **God simply exists to express.**

Expression is not a plan – expression is a joy in being. And so if you were to try and define 'plan' in God's terms, the plan is **for every part of God to experience the joy that God experiences.**

Now 'every part of God' means: everything on a physical level, everything on a spiritual level, everything in all the zones that (again an earthly term) 'lead back' to God.

So, I am suggesting to you that in an ideal world (and it is an ideal world that we are, please God, working towards) your sofa at home, which is alive, would be as joyous as you would be at that ideal point. Your connections with other people would not be the connections that other people have for the most part *now* on Earth – a maelstrom of fear and mistrust, and a *little* joy and a *little* delight, and anger and violence. Your connections would be joy. You would re-explore – having regained your knowledge of your true creative ability as part of God – you would re-explore the *potentials* of creation.

You share in creation at this very moment; it is not something you have to work towards. You do not *become* a co-creator with God ...**you** *are* **a co-creator with God.**

And, unfortunately, because you are free to think however you want to think and to do whatever you want to do, God supplies (via the A and B points we talked about earlier – that energy-flow between A and B) whatever you as a co-creator decide to co-create. Therefore, if you decide, consciously or sub-consciously, to create anger ...anger is what is delivered as energy to your door. If you decide to create depression – depression is what is delivered to your door.

You are a co-creator now.

It is God's... again if I say God's wish, 'wish' is the wrong word ...it is God's harmony; it is God's ...even 'intention' is the wrong word ...it is God's *state* for you to exist in a vibration of harmony and creativity with Him.

It is at the human stage that the plan (if 'plan' is the right word, and it isn't) – that the intention goes wrong. It becomes an intention to protect your corner; it becomes an intention to take in power; it becomes an intention to become more important, when *God's intention* energy-wise, ideally, is to provide you simply with joy, and for you to connect with everyone else around this planet (as you *do*) and to also provide them with joy; and to reach out to the animal forms around you, and provide them with joy; and to 'Christ' the planet – to change the planet; to make the planet a harmonious, creative sphere. Where at the moment you are in a creative sphere, but – because of the field of consciousness around the Earth that you link into, which I call 'the Field' – it is a negative creative sphere; it is a struggle; it is a violence; it is an agitated sphere.

So, God's intention is for you to experience Him as He originally created you – in joy ...free from suffering ...free from anger ...free from the loneliness that comes from believing that you are separated from God – and then wouldn't life be wonderful? Wouldn't life be wonderful!

Is that a sufficient answer?

Spokeswoman: Yes, thank you very much.

Joseph: Another question, please!

Spokeswoman: Would you comment on the prophecies that have been put forward for 2012.

Joseph: I would indeed. I would indeed!

I shouldn't be an angry man – I am not *really* an angry man; anger is something that I left behind a long time ago, but frustration is something that I am an expert at. And I see so many blossoming terms, so many blossoming circumstances or proposed circumstances, and I feel – **I know** (I cannot convince you of that, but I *know*) that many of these circumstances, many of these prophecies, many of these suppositions spiritually are what I would call 'an attack' by the Field of consciousness. There is no greater way to divert a soul from the *true* course of spiritual evolution than by involving them in something that takes their mind and heart off the true purpose.

As I have said in other meetings, if you are expecting a burnt cinder on the 1st of January, 2012 **you must look to your heart but not to your skies.**

You are simply moving out of one period of 'agitation of molecules of vibration' into another 'period of agitation of molecules of vibration' – a *potential*, not a certainty – **a potential.** In other words, the elements around you will present to you the *opportunity* for change *if* you want to take up that change, but that does not mean that the structure of the Earth will come tearing down on the 1st of January. It will be a very gradual change. In fact, *unless* people respond to the difference of vibration around them that will take some years to set in, there will be no change.

It worries me (to expand a little) as to the many areas that are investigated currently in the name of spirituality. It is true that you can harmonise with crystals – you can harmonise with *anything*. It is true that you can harmonise to the soul within and to the God within and around you, through sound. It is true that you can heal – of course you can heal *spiritually* – you can restore people with all kinds of malady. But you have to be cautious and you have to be careful that these 'labelled' areas of spirituality do not become the be-all and end-all for you.

And it is great, it is right to say, 'What about 2012?' But then, having asked the question, it is time to sit down; it is time to go *within*; it is time to go within the chamber of the heart and say, 'What do *You* think, Father? What do *I* think, Father?' And between the two of 'You' – responding to that feeling of positive or negative from the heart-centre, or from perhaps direct instruction from the soul – you will know whether there is any truth to 2012 or to any prophecy. And you will know the value of such things within your *own* spiritual sphere of progress.

And I would ask you here to be brave – to appreciate the crystals, to appreciate the sounds, the gongs, the chanting, the different labels of healing ...to appreciate all those things because, at their heart, they have spiritual value – but I would ask you to be discerning enough and quiet enough to hear from here [*pointing to the heart-centre*]. And if, from here, what you hear is, 'Not for you,' then dispense with those areas that you have attached yourself to.

There is *one* goal at the moment: the goal is to reconnect with God; the goal is to bring Light to this world; the goal is to end what has been happening for centuries – end the violence, end the cruelty, end the inequality.

And how do you do that?

You do that in such a *simple* way. You do that by sitting quietly in your corner with your God; you do that by switching off the physical mind and linking instead to the spiritual heart, and you listen and you act.

I am glad you asked that question because it leads to 'complexity' and it leads to the human mind loving complexity – loving things to be involved and convoluted and complex. That is the work of the human mind operating on energy pulled in from the Field, which is set to negative. The way to God, the way to understand anything is so simple. So simple! Would that the members of my group soul and I could stand hand-to-hand in a ring around this world, and reach out and shake the planet until all the complexities fell away ...and keep shaking and keep getting rid of the complexity ...till all that is left is Light and simplicity, **because in Light and simplicity you see clearly.**

And what we want you to see clearly is yourself and your connection to God ...all else then follows.

I know this has been a circuitous route, but ask yourselves the question in all areas of spirituality: does this make sense? Is this right for *me* – not for anyone else, but for me? And is it too complex for me? And allow yourself some 'simple time' each day – some 'simple time' each evening when you shut out the demands of the physical world and the demands of the physical mind. And instead you listen to the gentle entreaties of the spiritual heart that will feed you, re-awaken you and put you on a completely different path.

Does that answer the question?

Spokeswoman: Yes, thank you.

Joseph: Thank you. Another question, please!

Spokeswoman: Can you speak about time, and I know we are not supposed to have time in spirit, but if all this is supposed to be raising the vibration of the Earth and getting everyone on a different wavelength, does God already know the outcome and is there sort of a timeline in our time?

Joseph: As to whether God knows the outcome – God knows the *potential* of His children. And God knows that, minute by minute, the decisions that His children make illustrate, build, create, to a lesser or a greater degree, a certain set of circumstances. But minute by minute those circumstances are changing (...'minute by minute' – time again. Time again!).

I would like to rub out – if I could put on a blackboard the word 'time' – I would like to rub it out, and I would like to write instead 'experience'. The passage of time, as you see it, is in reality opportunity to experience, freedom to experience ...to experience *whatever* you want ...to experience a terrible world ...to experience a wonderful world.

You experience it linearly, but I would like to suggest that, if I look to the back of this room, I have a panoramic view of the back of this room, but if I concentrate I can pick out certain objects and obliterate, in my mind, the others. **Time is like that.**

Personal time is like that. Personal time, in reality, is experience that takes you back to God and experience that you choose to look at in a certain way. You focus on today, but that does not exclude tomorrow except in your own mind. You are all 'time-travellers' because you all go backwards and forwards in time in the spirit, do you not, every day of your lives? You are reliving the holiday from fifteen years ago; you are anticipating the retirement; you are wondering what is for tea this evening. You are travelling backwards and forwards in time *all the time*. You are making selective choices about which aspect of your total existence you zero in on at any time.

With regard to time, with the urgency that we have with the world at the moment, there is a certain set of circumstances that is building up, and that set of circumstances is building up because the *majority* of human beings have turned their back on their spiritual core, and instead are concentrating on materiality – materiality that is drawn from the Field of consciousness around the Earth and not from God-energy. That Field of consciousness is finite. That energy is finite, and so relying, believing in only that energy and shutting out the God-*within* and *without*, the human race is extinguishing its possibilities minute by minute.

We come back so that, minute by minute, as many souls as possible can be guided into re-establishing the flame-within, the God-within, the Light-within, so that we can re-establish that Light in humankind, so that they can send it out to the planet and change things again ...re-experience the Earth as the Earth was millennia ago.

I have to be very careful here. I would love to say, 'It's working!' I would hate to say, 'It's not working!' All I can say is that the opportunity to experience this world in Light is, at present, drawing to a conclusion.

The reason I talk to you, the reason I commandeer Michael, is to re-ignite the spark in as many souls as I can – not in the hope but in the *knowledge* that, if I re-ignite enough souls, if the people like me who are working around the world re-ignite a certain quantity of souls – then this world will begin to change, and that perceived end of current experience will be withdrawn from.

I gave a number of years at a past meeting. That number of years, as a *potential* if the Earth does not change, if mankind does not change its thinking, is at the present time around eighty **...around eighty!**

And I think that brings home the *seriousness* of why we come through to communicate with you. Eighty years ...but I do not want you, under any circumstances, to take that number out with you as an absolute. As I have said, it changes minute by minute dependent on what souls put into the Field of consciousness around the Earth.

If enough of you thought in the right way, rediscovered your heritage, understood that the best thing – the *only* thing – that you can do to change things is to give out Light, is to bathe situations and the planet in Light. If enough of you did that, that cataclysmic end to a 'certain potential' that is being delivered at the moment would never come. **Would *never* come!** The Earth would change, its viewpoint would change, its perspective would change and it would be a far *different* world – not just in how you react to each other but in the way that it looked – to the planet that you have *now*.

So, time is a difficult one to explain. In my sphere, for example, I can step out of one set of circumstances, put them, as it were, 'on hold', visit you, talk to you and re-establish my existence, my experience, my consciousness on that level at the exact same moment that I left it when I get back. And yet part of me is also experiencing that aspect of my existence without break. It is not that I have split myself; it is that I can change my focuses – 'focuses', plural. And that really is the nature of time – a very *difficult* subject.

A very difficult subject because you are in a linearity, because you look at your lives and your bodies and say they are subject to the ravages of time. They are at the moment, but they needn't be. And that is what we are working towards – a different consciousness so that you can repair yourselves, repair others, repair the world.

A complex subject, but have I given it *some* meaning?

Spokeswoman: Yes, thank you.

Joseph: Are you sure?

Spokeswoman: Yes, thank you.

Joseph: Thank you, [*smiling*] ...am I sure? Yes I am.

Another question, please!

Spokeswoman: What are the Creator's rules or laws regarding life?

Joseph: The Creator's simple rule is: **to be.**

TO BE.

There is no restriction on what you do. However, there are *consequences* to what you do. If you live life in a harmonious way then that harmony comes back at you. If you live life in a destructive way then you suffer. But that is not God's wish for you; that is not God's rule for you – it is simply a learning experience that comes to you as a spirit, which you would call 'cause and effect'.

You see, God is not a teacher. God is not a controller. God is not a restrictor. God is a lover. God is the greatest Love in your life ... and then some. God is the greatest Love you can ever, ever experience, because at soul-level there is only God-Love.

So, God ...'separates' is the wrong word, God ...'distances' is the wrong word, ...God gently pushes out part of Himself so that that part can look back and experience Him – and Him experience that part, and says, 'Go and do! Go and be! Go and experience!'

If – as has happened on this planet and has happened for millennia – that experience then hardens and crystallises vibration; that experience, those choices then distance, coagulate, solidify the perceived distance between the individual and the group and God.

Does God mourn for that child that is out? God simply perceives that child as being at a point in its infinite existence where experience is coming to it that maintains the distance, the illusion, between God and the individual. And He sends His Love, He sends His Higher Vibrations *always* to encapsulate that soul, so that that soul in the fullness of 'time' begins to realise that certain ways to act result in separation, as it were, from God and certain ways to act result in a closeness to God.

God makes no rules regarding your life – no matter what you do. If you now take a machine gun and take against me and everyone else in this room and kill them – **God makes no judgement.**

God is infinite patience because God has the whole picture. God knows that eventually you will remember. God knows that eventually you will turn back to Him inwardly and outwardly. God knows that you *will* come Home.

The consequences that you see around the world at this time are caused not by God, but by a set of circumstances that happened a great deal of time, a great deal of perception, ago. To encapsulate them, I will try – but it is a subject that will be examined at greater length in coming years [*reference to the book on the Fall*]. But, to encapsulate them: there was a decision made long ago – long before this civilisation walked the Earth – by another civilisation that there was a different way of vibration that could be harnessed. That instead of working with the natural ways of creation, a certain small distortion would result in a better world and a happier God (although God was and is as happy as He was then ...HAPPY).

The result of that altered vibration (which to understand you would have to understand that, at that point in creation, the civilisation that existed was more aware of its God-creative abilities than you are now)... the result of that vibration was to trap mankind within a Field of consciousness, was to solidify the illusion of separation from God, was to instil in mankind a *supposed* need for power, for material things, for food at the expense of other beings, and that is what you are experiencing now. The present conditions on Earth – the poverty, the violence, the anger, the illness – are *all* as a result, not of any rule from God, but of a decision that mankind made a long while ago.

And you will think, 'What has that got to do with me?'

It has to do with you ...and you ...and you ...and you ...and *me* because we were there, because we were part of the race, the civilisation at that time that – I will not say got it 'wrong' – but *skewed* reality. In order to appreciate that, as I say, you have to understand that at that time you were closer to 'God-men' than to men and women; that you (...we – I...) encapsulated yourselves, limited yourselves, cut yourselves off as a belief, which you then perpetuated, which you then made a solid thing, a concrete belief.

And we have to – having learnt that there is a different way, having remembered, having escaped from that bubble of illusion – we have to *convince* you that there is a different way; that you do not need to be ill; you do not need to be violent; you don't need to have lack; you don't need much of the material things that you build around yourselves. It is time to let them go and create new things.

You don't need to have a world that is running out of resources. All you need is your memory of who you were before the Fall; that memory that brings the link of Light between God and yourself back – restores it so that you infuse yourself with God-Light and infuse others with God-Light, and you make the change and you tear down the walls that were put up so long ago.

You had a greater hand in creation than you know – a far *greater* hand. Today you take a chair, and paint it, and put a nice cushion on, and say, 'I have created that – isn't it fantastic!' ... And it is – it's wonderful. But originally, in the civilisation that you were each a part of so long ago, to create a chair would simply have been a matter of thinking of a chair, and thinking of a pattern, and thinking of a colour, and having it in front of you. And then, when you didn't need it any longer, saying: 'I don't need the chair now – thank you.' And the chair would go back into creative molecules to be used by someone else.

But none of this is to do with God making rules – it is rather to do with mankind perpetuating mistruths, believing them to the extent that they envelop you, restrict you and *seemingly* separate you from spiritual truth.

Is that a sufficient answer?

Spokeswoman: Yes, thank you.

Joseph: Thank you. Another question, please!

Spokeswoman: There is documentation in the Bible, I am thinking about in Genesis, where it explains that there were Gods that came down from the sky and that they loved the daughters of mankind and co-created with them a cross-breed called the Anunnaki [*reference to the Nephilim*], and I am wondering how true or how much of what it says in the Bible is actually the word of God?

Joseph: There is a problem with so many spiritual books ...a problem with so many spiritual books! If I were to ask you, word for word, to write down *now* the sentences that you have just delivered to me, there would be mistakes. If you were then to mass-produce those sentences there would be further mistakes. If you were to present those sentences to certain political and religious factions throughout different ages, they would alter those mistakes – that are already based on mistakes – in order to satisfy their own needs, their own aims, their own agendas.

So many spiritual books are quoted chapter and verse and word for word. And again I would say with these books that the truth lies not in written words **but in what you feel within.**

There is an element of truth, of course, in many spiritual books; and you will say: 'Well, Joseph, you've written a book ...you've written two books ...you are about to write a third book. How dare you tell me that the spiritual books have no value?'

And I would say: 'What you should take out of a book is the *essence* of it; the words behind the words; the feeling behind the words, and take those words within yourself.' And again, as I have said earlier, examine whether or not those words are true for you.

One of the greatest gifts you have been given as part of God is the ability to reason. Unfortunately, with society as it is at the moment, you very often forego that ability to reason to ask someone else and to invest in what the other person says. So, very often the doctor becomes God, or the solicitor becomes God, or the politician becomes God ...because it is *easier* to invest in what they say than taking into yourself those aspects of life that trouble you that you are seeking answers for.

It is the same with many of the spiritual books. If you invest in those, they allow you to get on with life without having to make certain decisions. As moral decisions come to you: 'It says in my spiritual book *such and such* – that is the answer. That's what it says. The 't' is crossed and the 'i' is dotted – how can it be *other* than the word of God?'

The word of God is a living thing. The word of God depends on what you need at any given time. **The word of God comes from within,** and in dictating my books that is *all* I want to say to you, that – and please **to send Light into the world.**

I am asked at many meetings about Indians [*mystics*], about DNA, about where super-beings came from ...I want to share a secret with you (but if you have read the books you know it's not a secret) ...you are all super-beings. And it amuses me to see much discussion about angels these days – the angel who will choose my new set of clothes; the angel who will park my car; the angel who will tell me what to do with my boyfriend, what to do with my house, what to do with my money – there is *always* an angel with me.

And, yes, there is!

There is an angel much closer to you than you can ever imagine because you ...and you ...and you ...and you ...and me – **each of us is an angel.**

We came to this place originally in very different form – *very different form*. We came as co-creators, we came as 'children' to enjoy the experiences of this planet and this solar system and, unfortunately, we got things skewed, we got things wrong.

And there is a *hint* (going back to your spiritual books) of this in many spiritual books ...there was a 'battle' in Heaven. No, there wasn't – there was a battle of wills. There was a battle of the outer will of the physical mind and the inner will of the spiritual heart, and as a result of that battle *for a time* the physical mind won and you lost your knowledge of who you really are.

And, because of the solidification, the contraction, the manipulation of matter that you created at that time, you lost your angelic form. It is still there; it is compressed; it is within you. You are an angel – you need to rediscover that. I am an angel – I am *presently* rediscovering that. And I look forward to the day when I can, as it were, open the 'hatch' of that top sphere, and throw it open and step out into the Infinity that once was and always will be mine – as who I once was and still am. But I'm having to, by degrees, cleanse myself of the lower vibrations that have clung to me for so very long – as are you.

So, there are great truths in your spiritual books. There are also great blunders, there are great manipulations and there is great *rigidity* in those books if you refer to them and not to yourself. My advice would be: read them, take the salient points within you, examine them and, if they offend you, throw them away. **Throw them away!** Don't let any written page, any written book restrict you. The moment you do that the shutters come down around you and you will not allow yourself to look at, to entertain anything that comes to you that is new and different.

You build barriers through religion. God doesn't exist within barriers. God is freedom. God is a connection that you already have.

Read the books ...absorb from the books ...take what you want from the books ... and *heresy* – throw the books away! They are *only* books. Have I have ranted for long enough on that question?

Spokeswoman: Yes, thank you, for the time being.

Joseph [*not hearing*]: I'm sorry?

Spokeswoman: For the time being!

Joseph [*smiling*]: For the time being! Yes, I will probably rant again. I will live to rant again – live to rant another day! Another question, please!

Jane: Joseph, could you make this the last question so we don't tire Michael?

Joseph: Is that a question?

Jane [*laughing*]: It's a command.

Joseph: The answer to that is, yes, I will. A question, please!

Spokeswoman: Can you tell us a bit about the afterlife and the time in between incarnations, and do we have to keep coming back?

Joseph: Excellent question! I know that Michael was in public relations; I think I want you to act as *my* public relations person, because I have just spent over a year with Michael dictating and channelling through information regarding the afterlife; and they are presently working on putting this into a form that you can read and then throw away!

[*Audience laughter*]

It is a very complex system that we have. There are a great many spheres and I *cannot* go into the entire book now, but I would say that we touch upon your ability to create being heightened when you pass over; your ability to attract similar vibrations being heightened when you pass over so that you will find yourself in a sphere very similar to the personal sphere that you have created whilst you were here.

You will find yourself with regard to reincarnation being, for all the world, *talked out of it* if we possibly can. **If we possibly can!** Now *there* is a turn around in thinking, because all the philosophies say that you are sent back; all the philosophies say that you have to come back; all the philosophies say that you are 'working something out' by coming back. I would say to you, *we* would say to you:

You don't have to come back if you don't want to.

I would say to you that you bring yourselves back. And that sounds impossible: you come to the end of a life on Earth and it's been heavy... and it's been sad ...and it's been painful ...and it's been cruel ...and it's been depressing ...and it's been poor – and then you *want* to come back!

But many souls have not invested enough time in the exploration of spiritual possibilities to understand much about the next life. And so when they arrive – as *inevitably* you all do – when they arrive on that far shore, they are unable, to a certain extent, to take in the possibilities that that shore offers to them.

They are used to a life without an afterlife ...but they *still* exist. They are used to a life that they have invested two hundred percent into – a life that they wanted to continue. And so, symbolically, there comes a time when they are around a table with a number of guiding influences, and those guiding influences say: 'It really isn't a good idea to go back.'

And many, many souls say: 'But this time I can get things right. This time a love affair won't end badly. This time I can sort out the business. This time I can be healthy when I am younger so that I will be healthy when I am older and I'll have a longer life. I *miss* things – I miss the television, I miss the food, I miss the arguments, I miss the physicality.'

And we say, 'Well, you are in a physicality now. Isn't the table you are leaning against solid?'

'Yes, it is but that's not 'real' physicality – it's back on the Earth that it's really physical.'

And it is pointed out to them that there is an easier way, that evolution can actually take place spiritually by evolving through, as I describe them, the 'cleansing spheres' that lead back to God. But no, ultimately because they have freedom and, ultimately because they have not divorced themselves from the ways of the Earth plane – they seek, they elect to come back.

Of course there are exceptions. There are exceptions in that certain people seek to come back for the very reasons we have been examining here tonight: for the reasons of bringing Light into the world, for the reasons of opening people's eyes so that they don't come back. And the reasons those souls do that is because, not until every soul has escaped this current illusion with its potential for so much pain and destruction, will they rest.

Again back to the Oneness. You and I are One. You and I and God are One. What would you have me leave behind, if I am escaping into Infinity? What should I leave behind – my finger, my foot, my knee? We are all One – the whole being has to move up.

So, it is a combination of many souls who come back because they want to, to relive something again for whatever purpose. And there are souls who come back because [*smiling*] they don't want them to do that! Because within a lifetime they *hope* that the effects of the Field will not smother them, so that they can get out the message of Light, so that they can provide illustration from without and within to change the way that souls look at this Earth. It is a beautiful place – but not at present. It is a place of wonderful potential – but not at present. And why would anyone want to come back here at present?

With regard to what happens next that is a *vast* subject. If I can condense, very briefly, I can say that the levels that exist 'above' (such a strange word 'above' – the levels that exist actually 'within' but on a different vibration to this one) exist to slowly eliminate, from the evolving and remembering soul, those molecules that tied it to the Earth, those conditions of thought, of emotion, of physicality that tied it to the Earth. So that by the time it reaches, as it were, the 'last step' it finds that that is the *first* step. And it goes through that 'hatch' into Infinity to take up its life again as an angelic being that can then explore other possibilities in other physicalities and other spiritualities – **and have fun with God.**

So, I would leave you with that thought, and I would leave you with the thought that it seems to be a very serious message – it *is* a very serious message, but there is reason to rejoice because you are part of God. And, if the potential that the Earth has at the moment comes to fruition, then *eventually* you will find yourself in a similar position, listening to someone else and this time you might make the choice that will bring you into the Light.

You cannot be destroyed, you cannot become extinct. You can put yourself in some very strange situations, but you are always, always, always part of God. You are always, always, always *totally* loved and there is always, always, always help. Help for me from above, help for you from me and the others, help for you from guiding influences around you.

And life is what we talked about earlier – life is God and God is JOY, and that is all we seek to restore. Tear up the books but please take out the word.

Chapter Eleven

Joseph Trance Demonstration – 20th November, 2010
Waterloo College, Seaforth, UK

Spiritual topics discussed:

Assessing the worth of channelled material.

The need for simplicity in spiritual matters.

The best preparation for children coming into the world.

Meditations to combat the negativity of the Field.

Karma.

What limits our ability to give spiritual healing?

How to effectively heal the world.

Why the Field of mankind became negatively charged.

Joseph: I told Michael that I would begin with the word 'awakenings' this afternoon, because there is much talk of *awakening* in spiritual areas today, as though one minute you are asleep, the next you are awake ...and off you go. If only it were so simple – if only it were so simple for you; if only it were so simple for me!

But it is simple. It *is* simple if you understand that it is not a matter of awakening – it is a matter of changing the 'dream', and the message that I and those who work with me on a spiritual level (those who are my colleagues in the soul group that I belong to) bring is concerned with changing the dream.

All experience is a dream. All experience is a projection from within of what you want, of what mankind wants, of what creation wants. And you will probably say: 'I don't want war. I don't want pain. I don't want suffering. I don't want misery. I don't want to be sad. I don't want to be alone.' ...But collectively, because of the effects of the Field of human consciousness on the individual, **you *do.***

So, you have to be strong, and my message is one of a request for strength. You have to be strong and say: 'I don't want it so I won't have it – I will *change* the dream. I am the dreamer – not what is outside of me. **I am the dreamer.** If I want harmony I can dream it. If I want health – I can dream it. If I want joy I can dream it ...not only for myself but for those who haven't yet changed the dream, because my dream – when I connect to the God-within – is stronger than theirs, is everlasting and cannot fail.'

Changing the dream every moment, every day!

What do you want spiritually; what do you *need* spiritually? What does the world want spiritually; what does the world *need* spiritually?

Dream it ...see it ...believe it ... breathe life into it ...and you *change* this world.

Then we see what you would describe as 'awakenings' ...a transition from dependency on the Field, from dependency on the world as it has been for so long – to dependency on the God-within. The *joy* of dependency on the God-within!

I changed my dream a few 'moments' ago (as you would understand it) to be here; I dreamed my way out of my level of consciousness and into yours. I came here to *hopefully* answer your questions, and so I ask you – what would you like to ask me? A question, please!

Grayling Barraclough: Joseph, there are other channellers out there – Abraham and Bashir, just to name a couple – and first of all, are you aware of these other kind of spiritual beings or whatever they are (one of them is claiming to be an alien) on the other side, so to speak? And why are these messages different and, in some cases, contradictory?

Joseph: I make no claim for myself; I claim only on behalf of a 'movement' that will change things. Those of you who have seen me, heard me talk before, know that I like basics – **I like simplicity**. I abhor complexity because complexity throws up a smokescreen.

And your judgement, as to whether channelled material is of worth to you, should be: 'Is this too complex? Does this say anything? If I follow the advice given through this channelled material will I change? Will my life change... and will it change for the better?'

If it changes only by becoming more *complex* then I suggest to you that that material is not coming from the right source. If it changes towards *simplicity*, makes your life easier and makes others able to understand the spiritual message from you, then you are on the right path.

Channelled material comes from *many* sources. During the course of a day you can channel at different levels: you can channel your own inner harmony, or you can choose to channel the complexity and the irrationality of the human Field. You can channel happiness, or you can channel sadness, you can channel loneliness, you can channel anger.

Channelled material doesn't *necessarily* come from the highest source. The highest source that you can reach is within your heart-centre, and channelled material has to resonate and harmonise with what you believe and what you *feel* within your heart. If it does not – throw it out!

I care not for labels. I care not for names. I come to you with a name that I had at one point in my past, but *only* so that you have a gathering point, only so that you can focus on one individual for the time that I am here in order to explain things to you. But I do not hold, in reality, with names or labels – *this* spirit or *that* spirit. I hold with *the message* and you should hold with **the message**.

Forget who the person says they are, where they have come from and how they have lived. What are they teaching you *now*? Is what they are teaching you now sound? Is what they are teaching you now of help to yourself and to others? Is what they are teaching you now able to make a difference in this world? If it is not, then I would *suggest* to you – I cannot force you – but I can suggest to you that you throw it out.

Seek always that which is simple. Seek always that which resonates within you and makes sense within you. Seek always that which, when put into practice, works! I pray to God before I come here that the words I give you are able to help you, that the exercises I give you, you are able to put into practice to prove for yourselves that the spiritual message that I bring you is the correct one.

You must be discerning.

Also remember that the Field wishes you to be immersed in complexity, and your human mind wishes you to be immersed in complexity because it is linked to the Field. 'Be ye as a little child if you wish to enter the Kingdom of Heaven' – this is what it means. The answers are simple, the spiritual message is simple but, unfortunately, humanity seeks complexity. Everything has to be overly difficult to understand, to explain and to pass on. **If it is difficult to explain and to pass on, it is not of God!**

Are there other channelled 'informations' coming through at this time? Of course there are! There is a great movement around your world to stop things getting worse *before* it is too late. But be careful, because you enter a minefield when you seek to discover more about yourself spiritually. The mind doesn't want you to, the Field doesn't want you to – only your heart wants you to. Be *aware* from the heart and, in doing so, you will discern whether the material that you are receiving is of use – or is of the Field.

Is that a sufficient answer?

Grayling: Yes. Just picking on something you were saying there: if there are all these other people or other energies around trying to get into the Earth, why aren't there more channels? Are you aware of trying to create other channels? I'm just trying to get an idea of how it works from your perspective.

Joseph: The group that I am a part of spends a measure of its conscious time, of its focussed time, directing vibrations of peace and of understanding towards the Earth. We have certain points to which we can send information. Some of those points are at a point where they simply pick us up as intuition. Some of those points are at a point where they can openly pass on the communication that we send to them.

We send Love and harmony to the Earth as a whole too but, unfortunately, the density of the Field prevents us from doing the good that we want to do. But wherever there is a group sitting for the right reasons, wherever there is an individual sitting for the right reasons, wherever there is an opportunity to get in ...then the energy that we direct *gets in...* to a lesser or a greater degree.

And there are other group souls involved in similar exercises at this time; they may present the messages that come through slightly differently, but the underlying message is *identical*. And the underlying message is that you need to change now, you need to love now, you need to be in harmony with each other now, and you need to dream (as I said at the beginning) a *different* dream on behalf of humanity. Does that make sense?

Grayling: Yes, thank you.

Joseph: A further question, please!

Maria Cass: Hello, Joseph, my name is Maria.

Joseph: Hello, Maria.

Maria: I have become interested in alternative therapies and a 'different way' over recent months, and since then I have had the unexpected but pleasant surprise to find myself expecting a baby, and I am just interested in your views of children coming into the world at this time.

Joseph: Life seeks to express itself through life. Each soul that comes here comes for a purpose, and your child comes for a purpose. And the purpose that we instil in the children that are being born at this time is to further the spiritual message, and turn humanity away from its materialism and away from its lower instincts of violence and power-seeking. What specifically do you want me to answer with regard to children?

Maria: Well, to me – I don't know if this is connected – I'm interested in this new way of life and now I find I am bringing a baby into the world I have that thought: this baby has a special purpose.

Joseph: By becoming aware, by opening your spiritual heart-mind to the promptings of greater spiritual evolution, you pass on to the child that is coming to you those values and that vibration so that your child is born already open to spiritual awareness.

It is an excellent example of what *should be* done at the moment, because *all* mothers pass on their predominant beliefs and thoughts to their child. The vibration flows between mother and child – not just physically – but also psychically and spiritually. It is meant to be that way, and the child is placed by the Lords of Karma with a certain mother and a certain father so that their vibrational contribution to that child should help it on life's path to find and discover its own spiritual evolution.

And so it is vitally important that spiritually-aware mothers retain that openness to the Light of God and to the harmony of the spirit worlds. And, in doing so during their time of pregnancy, they pass on that vibration to the child; they surround it with a protective Light. And the child, until the point that it is born, is *active...* is active within you but is also active in that it talks to its advisors, it talks to angels, it talks to God and it talks to itself.

And were more mothers spiritually aware until the time of birth, their children would go on to do great things spiritually because they would have been cushioned from the Field for the full course of that pregnancy. Unfortunately, with many mothers the thought is of what the baby should wear; where the baby is going to school; should the baby be in a better house now; should the baby be able to drive a better car when it grows up. And all these worries, pre-occupations and *material* considerations are then passed on to the child, and the encroachment of the Field takes place earlier on in that child's development – in the womb in fact.

When, if the mother were to spend a portion of each day linking into the God-Light within, praying for direction for herself and the child, then the Field is kept at bay and the child has a greater chance of passing on spiritual information and spiritual help when it is actually born into a physical world, because the effects of the Field have been kept out for as long as possible. And that child has been able to take advice from the spiritual worlds and from the God-within right until the last moment. It strengthens the link; it helps the child once it is born to communicate with higher spheres of being.

So, yes, your child is placed with you for a reason. Each child is placed for a reason and each child is given the opportunity to grow. The generation that is coming now is also given the opportunity to teach. And it is important to talk to your child; it is important to establish that spiritual communication and to say: 'I surround you with Love and with Light. I surround you with God's freedom. I acknowledge God's purpose in you' – to strengthen that link between yourself and the child, and to strengthen that child's ability to go forwards that much more quickly in physical life **and to make a difference**.

We have closed down for generations the intuition that children have. At a certain point you tell them they can't see the person in the room; you tell them they shouldn't be listening to voices; you tell them that is nonsense; you tell them that is imagination …and that is *exactly* what the Field wants you to do. And the spiritual facilities become masked and there is, around the child as the child grows, the hardness and the impermeability of the Field so that their original mission is, many times, clouded at best and knocked out of them at worst. And it takes so many years for them, if they are spiritually-minded, to chip away at that outer layer before they can receive communication. Whereas, if they were encouraged to believe *that it is normal* – to see someone from another realm is normal, to hear voices from another realm is normal – then that child is able to go about its mission at a much earlier age. So many wasted years and so many wasted opportunities! We have to dream a different dream for our children, too. Does that make sense?

Maria: It does, it makes a lot of sense.

Joseph: Does that answer your question?

Maria: It does. The phrase that pops into my head often is, 'This baby is here to make a difference', and you have said that exact phrase.

Joseph: The child is here to make a difference, and I have to tell you that your child is listening to what is happening now, because that child is unfettered by the beliefs of a physical world. That child is a delightful spirit that knows it is a delightful spirit, and is happy to listen to the musings of the soul group and to listen to the spirits that are here this afternoon.

A further question, please!

Yvonne: I have a question. Hello, my name is Yvonne.

Joseph: Hello, Yvonne.

Yvonne: The question I have is – I'm aware at times that the strength of the Field is such that it is like you're stuck to it like glue. What I do in my life is, of a morning, I have a routine that I do because I find that my mind wakes up connected to the Field sometimes before my physical body wakes. And I have a ritual that I do that brings back the simplicity that helps me function in a way that I'd like to. And I'm also aware at times – especially at this time of the year – the power of the Field becomes so intense with the material realms of Christmas being a shopping expedition. You spoke earlier about the fact that there were techniques and exercises that you could speak to us about with regards to staying connected to the simplicity, which is the beauty of it all. And I was just wondering if you could maybe discuss some of those simple techniques for us, please?

Joseph: Yes. First of all, the time of year: you are turning into the darkness, you are turning into the winter months, the Earth is turning into the winter months and everything in life is an illustration of what is wrong. Everything in life, everything that

331

the Earth brings you, everything that your lives bring you, are promptings from a higher source – from the Creator – to say that things are *not as they should be*. And the intention of plunging you into darkness for half of the year is to make you appreciate the light – to take you into the darkness and out into the light to show you that **what you need is balance**.

But it is true at this time, unfortunately, the Field (if you will forgive the pun) has 'a field-day' because people, as spirits, *need* light; they respond to light; they thrive in light because Light is Love, Light is God, and when that light is diminished for a time they begin to feel below standard, they begin to feel ill, and that is *exactly* what the Field would wish for them. And the Field says on dark mornings: 'Yes, you are ill. Yes, you are lonely. Yes, it is difficult to get out of bed. Yes, it is difficult to be cheerful. Yes, it is depressing. Yes, it is sad.' And if you respond to that then you are giving your energies to the Field, which is what the Field wants, and the Field is donating to you its collective belief, its collective suggestion that things are *not very good* indeed.

The technique is simple: the technique is to surround yourself inside and outside with Light. The technique is to sit quietly and to say *literally* to the day: 'Go away! Go away – this is my time to connect to God.' And you can use whatever analogy, whatever images strike you as being appropriate. You could, for example, imagine that there is, coming from your heart-centre, a flex or wire that leads to a plug and there is a special socket in your home that connects – not to the ordinary electricity supply that you have – but to a supply of Light from God, a supply of Light that comes down through your roof and down into the wall and, whenever you connect with it, there is a brilliance of White Light that flows from that plug and along that flex into your heart **and illuminates you**. You can imagine that you are sitting in your chair and a cylinder of Light comes down from the ceiling and surrounds you so that, all may be dark around you, but within that cylinder of Light you feel power ...you feel restored ...you feel health.

The God-within is *always* within.

The God-within doesn't fly south for the winter.

The God-within is *always* accessible, and it is a matter of connecting – not with your physical mind (your physical mind will never make you feel better) – it is a matter of connecting with your spiritual heart.

Again, you can use imagery in order to reach the spiritual heart. You can imagine (if you are a very head-centred person) that there is an image of yourself inside your head *here* and you step into a lift, you step into an elevator, and the lift, the elevator, goes down into your heart, and when the doors open you find yourself in a chamber of Light and of warmth and of peace. You can imagine that you are in a different house and that, whenever you sit down in meditation, you are taken to an exact replica of the house that you are living in now, but a house that is on another plane altogether – a higher plane, a plane of Light – and sit there allowing the Light to be absorbed by your body.

But once you reach the heart-chamber you will *know* because you will find an increase in your joy levels; you will find that instantly you become peaceful, instantly you feel that connection that says: 'I'm not alone. My worries have melted away because they are of the Field and nothing to do with me. I can ask any question here and receive an answer. I can take any challenge into this Light and know that a solution will manifest during my daily life.'

And the more that you do this, the lesser will be the effect of the dark months and the dark days on you, because you will see that *you* are not dark; and you will see that *everyone* else around you is not, in reality, dark. Every soul in this room this afternoon is made of Light. Every soul this afternoon in this room is an angelic form. I repeat that – I have said that many times: you were not *once* angels – **you *are* angels!**

You are angels who, through misguidance, descended into a heavier form of reality. But you are still who you were, and it is a matter of contacting who you were and bringing that out into who you are, realising that in every challenge in your life – whether that challenge be illness or perceived poverty or problems relating to people – *every* challenge can be solved by bringing out who you *were* into who you are ...**realising again who you are.**

That brilliance is a Light that never needs batteries, that never needs recharging, that you can take with you throughout each day to eliminate your problems and to eliminate the problems of others. And when you visit the heart-chamber, when you recognise who you are (who you were – who you are) again, your worries become like television series – something you can watch but don't have to take part in. They will still be there for a time, but you will have distanced yourself from them and they won't matter.

And when they don't matter ...they don't *create matter*.

You are not putting energy into them to continue creating them and to continue giving them substance. So, you distance yourself from them, you go into the heart and, in going into the heart, those problems aren't 'matter' – they are not there. And, over the days and weeks as you meditate, they will melt away.

And if they don't melt away – if certain of them are there to teach you a karmic lesson – then that lesson will be so much easier for you; you will know what to do; you will know how to tackle them; you will know how to challenge them; you will know how to move through them.

The best advice I can give you, the God-advice I can give you, the *good* advice I can give you – is to come in here [*pointing to the heart-centre*] to revisit yourself, and to ignore what the Field is saying to you – whether it is saying it to you through people, through situations, through challenges, through what you see on the news, through what you read in the newspapers... ignore it. Ignore it! Go within daily, charge yourself *daily* with Light and you will see that you are changing your dream and able then to change the dreams of others.

Is that a coherent answer?

Yvonne: Yes, thank you. Interestingly, I'm a beekeeper and the light of the beehive in the summer is very easy to see, but they have now proven that during the winter months when bees hibernate, it is actually the busiest time for the bees – it is just that they do it all inside the hive. So, it looks on the surface as if the hive is in darkness in the winter months, but actually the light and the energy of the hive is on the inside. As you were speaking then the thought that just kept coming into my mind all the time is that the bees show us that it isn't that it is darkness, but it is that the light is inside at that time – that's all. I love the fact that you said to say to the day to go away. Thank you very much – that is a lovely gift, thank you.

Joseph: That is a beautiful analogy. I know that you have seen the hive connection in the bees and I know that you have seen the unification of mind there, and it is a beautiful analogy because, again, you are being given an illustration through other aspects of Creation as to how we relate because we are all part of a 'hive'. We are all individuals but we are all connected as part of a hive, and it takes the 'strong bees' to direct the other bees to the honey. You have to be one of the strong bees, you have to do the 'dance' that leads the other bees to Light and then you change – as the bees recognise that you are bringing Light, that you are bringing better 'honey' – you change the other bees, you change the hive-mind. And, by changing the hive-mind, you change the nature of reality so that that brightness that is *within* is suddenly *without* and the darkness is gone.

Another question, please!

Maureen Michniewicz: Can I ask about karma? When things happen to your family we are told that is bad karma from a previous life. What is your take on that?

Joseph: My take on karma is that much is said about it without too much being understood about it. Again, from the point of view of the Earth, karma often looks like a dire punishment because of something that, as you say, you did wrong so long ago – something you can't remember, and your hands are tied and here you are being punished because of it.

I use the word 'nonsense' quite a lot and I shouldn't really but – nonsense! [*Laughing*] **Nonsense! Karma is not that at all.**

Karma is a process whereby, in any person's life, there is quite a straight path and quite a crooked path. The straight path is the one that the spirit doing the travelling (the person on Earth) is urged to take: the straight path, the spiritually easy path. In other words, to recognise and remember who you are and to do something about it – not to concentrate on the desires of the Field, but to concentrate instead on getting the 'hive-mind' right and on getting your own mind right.

Certain instances in your past (your past in this life and your past in other lives) have meant, because of how you have tackled them, that your vibrationary rate has stayed at a certain level. Now, in order to evolve or in order to visit and experience the spiritual realms one after another …after another …after another …after another – your vibration has to be capable of recognising those realms. In other words, it has to vibrate at some point at the same rate of vibration as those realms – each individual realm – or you cannot see that realm and you cannot enter that realm. So, your karma is designed to increase your vibrationary rate *spiritually* (not physically – things are fast enough physically as it is – but spiritually) to increase your vibrationary rate through the experiences that come to you.

Karma is a matter of recognising something that leads to an increase in vibrationary rate. Unfortunately, because of the effects of the Field and because of the desires of the individual based on past life experience to this point, sometimes those signposts are not recognised easily. Sometimes the individual going through the challenge wants to repeat the challenge: 'I got it wrong last time – I'll get it right this time!' ...'Whoops, I have got it wrong this time again – I'll get it right next time!'

Then the relatively smooth path of individual spiritual evolution becomes a crooked and a jagged path, because the God-within seeks to elevate the individual during the passage of *one* lifetime as much as He/She/It can. Therefore, if a spirit will not recognise the Light, the only tools available to the Lords of Karma and to the God-within are the tools of the material world. So, aspects of the material world are drawn to the spirit so that the spirit can work out what is necessary and what is not necessary for that spirit's evolution, for the heightening, the speeding up of that spirit's vibrationary rate.

So, karma is not a cruel thing; it is the world as it is that is a cruel thing. And karma is not a debt – karma is a point. Karma is a point on a 'graph' that says: 'This particular individual has not reached this point and still believes in the principles below this point and, because of that, the vibrationary rate (it sounds very mathematical) is only up to this level. Therefore they can only experience, when they come back to the spirit worlds, anything to this level. What we must try and do with all our hearts and minds is to get them up to *this* level at least whilst they are on Earth. It will seem difficult for them, because they are locked within an illusion that lasts, for them, a lifetime and seems to be ever such a long time. But, nevertheless, we have to try and bring them to a different way of thinking by allowing them to come up against circumstances that they can then judge for themselves ...whether those circumstances are detrimental to their spiritual progress or beneficial to their spiritual progress.'

Karma, then, is a marker: it is a marker of the soul's evolution or re-emergence. 'Evolution' suggests that that soul has not been up to that point before, when in fact it has. In fact, each of us – each of *you* – came down from a point *far above* that point in order to experience the Earth plane as was. It was the effects of the Fall that necessitated that spirits needed to find their way out through experience.

So, karma is a set of experiences designed to elevate you, to liberate you, to free you.

I do not hold with the wagging of a finger and saying, 'That is your karma because of something you did wrong in the past.' We all got it wrong. I got it wrong. The soul group got it wrong. We didn't intend to get it wrong – we thought we were doing something right. **It went wrong.** Because of that we were blinkered and, unless we are evolved enough to respond daily (minute by minute, second by second) to the promptings of the God-within, we have to learn with the tools that are at our disposal at this time: the tools of the physical world. And the tools of the physical world group themselves around us so that we can progress from that physical world into the spiritual realms where we came from, once again.

You might say: 'Well, what is the Field doing whilst all this is going on?' Well, of course, the Field is making it harder for that karma to be experienced, because, as you perhaps take the rugged road, the rocky road, the bent and twisting road, and you come up against circumstances which are challenging, the Field convinces you that they are *more* challenging than they are. The Field convinces you that you are a thoroughly bad lot, and have 'sinned' against God and against the Field in the past ...and adds weight to those karmic lessons.

Again it is a matter, in all challenges in life, of going within and of seeking the advice of God. That is one of the points of karma – to turn you from the outside to the inside; to seek your 'help to yourself'; to seek the help that you can give to yourself to elevate your vibration; to seek God and to see that *there* is a centre that is immovable and cannot be degraded or damaged by the effects of the Field.

Gosh, we have gone a long way! Does that make sense?

Maureen: It does very much, thank you.

Joseph: Thank you. Another question please!

Ian Tumilty: Can I ask if there is a limit on the ability of our healing that we can deliver?

Joseph: The only limit on your healing ability is the limit that your physical mind places on the healing and the limit that the person or situation that you are trying to heal also puts on the healing. You – *we* – are creative beings. We were designed by God – we are children of God – to be *as creative* as Him. **As creative as Him!** And God does not sit by a bedside and say, 'I wonder if I can heal this person?' God says, 'This person has nothing to heal!'

It is only the *physical* that appears to need healing; it is the person's point of view that needs to change; it is the person's 'dreaming' that needs to change. It is important, in healing communities and individuals, to again establish your link with God and to push outside of yourself, to one side of yourself, that recognition of yourself as being a finite physical being, and to push aside your *desires* for the healing, because the desires, very often, come from the physical body and the physical mind and not from the spiritual mind – from the heart-mind.

So, you push those things to one side, you connect with God and then you say: 'Father, I exist as a healing channel and nothing more. Take over – *You* do the healing!'

And then you accept that the healing has been done.

This is most important because, immediately you close down after healing, there is a tendency to question *just how much* healing has been given. Is the person healed twenty percent or forty percent? Or did the healing take place or did it not take place?

And the physical mind again puts mantraps between you and the healing you wish to give out. So, you have to accept that, the minute that you ask for something from God in order to make someone more harmonious, then that energy has been given. So, it is best to heal and then set about doing something different *entirely* that takes the physical mind off the fact that you have acted as a channel for God-Light.

What you then have to consider is: how much does the person believe in healing and (a very grave question but one that has to be asked) *does the person want to be healed?*

Very often illness is an opportunity. Yes, it is an opportunity to learn and to evolve, but it is also an opportunity for many poor souls to shine in a way, to receive attention, to receive a level of interest from others that they would not normally have were they not ill. That sounds a terrible thing to say but, nevertheless, in *many* cases (not in all cases) it is true. And so the best way to heal someone is by sneaking up on them, is by healing them and *not telling them*, is by seeing the Light that you are sending out from God enveloping them, changing them and wiping away the symptoms.

What we are doing, the reason that I come back to communicate, is to bring healing… **as you change the world you are healing it.** You have to heal at base level, and you also have to understand that God understands what is wrong with that person. And very often what you see as being wrong with that person *today* is something that is deep-rooted in *yesterday* – is a belief, is a wound, is a recognition of self in a skewed way that is nothing to do with what is happening today other than it has caused it. It might be that the arm that is giving a problem relates to a feeling that 'I cannot give' that goes back to childhood or to a past life.

So, healing is a very complex series of events... but not to God. God knows *exactly* what to do, and the best healing is a matter of faith, is a matter of tuning in, is a matter of saying: 'Thank you, God, it is done!' ...And then a matter of taking your mind off the subject.

Is that sufficient?

Ian: It is. The sneaking-up approach is something I do with my father and I find it does work. I don't want to sound evangelical, but how do we spread – because we are all like-minded souls here – how do we spread the 'word' as it were? How do you get the message across to people who don't want to listen because they are too engrossed in the Field? How do you do that?

Joseph: Sneaking up is a great way to do this as well. Not to tell anyone, and to, each day, spend a portion of your time – be it a minute or five minutes – seeing the world that you want, and seeing the world that those souls who will not change at this time *really* want.

Because here is another revelation: those souls do not want the violence that they instigate; they do not want the pain that they instigate; they do not want the illness they instigate – *not at core* but on the surface. They feel that they want those things; they feel the need to survive and the need for power on a mental level, on a physical, emotional level but not at a God-level, not at the level of what they *really* are.

So you have to appeal spirit to spirit to what people *really* are and, therefore, you have to send Light into their hearts and say: 'I recognise you as who you really are.' Because who they really are is far stronger than *who they think they are* – far stronger than the prejudices; far stronger than the violence; far stronger than the tendency towards depression, and sadness, and anger, and anxiety; far stronger because everything else is an illusion. So, point to point, you have to send Light out to the world, and sneak into that soul and say, 'I recognise you.' Not, 'I recognise your mind – I recognise the problems in your personality.' But, 'I recognise you *heart to heart.*' ...**And heart to heart is where the change takes place.**

You also have to send out, to believe, to live in your own view of how the world should be. Now you each do this because you are, each of you, creators so every minute of every day you are creating around you what you believe to be true and what you expect from life. So, you have to generate your individual world *outwards*. You have to be strong enough to say to yourself: 'I live in a world that is peaceful. I live in a world that is loving. I live in a world that is understanding, that is harmonious. I live in a world that is charged by God-energy and not by the limited negative energies of the Field.' And you have to live in that world. Just as you live in the world that you have created day by day, you have to live in *that* world, and by living in that world you become a beacon for others who wish to live in such a world, and you become an inspiration to those who wish to uplift their lives.

There will always be the stragglers and they are the most difficult to reach, but the message that I bring through – the message that *we* bring through – is that, if *enough* of you join together heart ...to heart ...to heart ...to heart ...to heart, then there is no power left in the Field to mask those who are left – those who want to cling on to the physical power; those who want to cling on to the hurts that don't really exist; those who want to cling on to notions of taking land and manipulating people and collecting material things. If enough of you join together (and remember we join to you – God joins to us, joins to you, to each other) then you won't have to worry about those who are stragglers because there won't be enough negative power for them to invest in any longer. And at that point they, too, *inevitably* remember who they are, and your world vision of

Light and peace becomes *every* world vision of Light and peace **...and the world becomes *once again* a vision of Light and peace.**

This world was such an exquisite place. An *exquisite* place! A place to visit and then to move on from; a place to revel in the different aspects of creation: the Light that was in each life, the Light that was in every blade of grass, in every area of the Earth, in the mountains, in the seas and the skies – such an exquisite place! And slowly, because of the effects of the Field and because of the effects of the Fall, that vision of reality has become encased in a hard shell of darkness, a hard shell of dependency on a Field that purports to give but in effect *takes*.

What we have to do is to reach in to that inner vision of the Earth, which is still there – compressed but still there (just as you are still an angelic being – compressed but still there) and say: 'I recognise that vision – not the vision that comes through my window, comes through my television screen, comes through my newspapers.' And then you amplify the power of inner vision and you change things.

Again it is a simple, simple, *simple* thing and it is so important that, along the way, you do not become entangled in the complexities that tell you that they are here spiritually. Always go within; always test what you are being given, and if it comes up short, if it is too complex, if it does not contribute to a change in global experience for the *better*, throw it out. Is that a sufficient answer?

Ian: It is, yes. I will carry on sneaking up on people.

[Audience laughter]

Joseph: I try it all the time. I sometimes try to influence people – just, I suppose, out of what you would describe as 'ego' – to sneak up on people, as it were, and to say: 'How is this for a thought?' as they are immersed in their newspaper and thinking that things are *ever so bad*, or sitting in front of the television screen listening to and absorbing and believing everything that is said to them. I sometimes just touch them on the shoulder and say, 'How about this for a *different* way of thinking?'

Oh dear, I should know better. Sometimes with a child you get through, sometimes with a dog you get through, but very often there is so much going on, there is so much speed, there are so many layers of complexity on this physical level that that Light – whilst being absorbed by the inner-core of the person and doing some good *there* – does not come up to the surface. Such a pity! But for now we are here to change things, *you* are here to change things ...**and change things you will!**

Another question, please!

Jane: Could we make this the last question so we don't overtire Michael?

Denise Wood: Can I ask a question about the Field? When you talk about it, I almost get the impression of a kind of external malevolent force, but I know that isn't the right understanding. Could you explain what it is?

Joseph: Yes, this goes back ...and back ...and back ...and back ... further than the dinosaurs ...further than this present civilization ...further than the civilisation that was there *before* the dinosaurs – to a time when this world was a co-creation between God and between the angels. And at that time there was (and *still is*) a creative... ('hive' again is perhaps a word I should use) ...a creative 'hive-energy' that was used to shape certain concepts: not concepts as you would see them now, not shaping a new fridge or a new car, but shaping certain concepts in order to experience them, and in order to experience the differences and the similarities between each angelic form.

At the time of the Fall, things became not the straight path but the crooked path, and, as a result of that, mankind separated itself in thought *but not in reality* from the God-within. There was a movement away from the God-within and a reliance on each other and not the God-within. As a result the actions of the Fall (and these are actions that will be described in the coming months to Michael [*reference to the book on the Fall*] – if I don't 'overrun' him) made things *denser*. And this area of being became a trap, became somewhere that spirits wanted to visit ... and visit ...and visit ...and visit ...and visit, believing that *this* was the centre of Creation and that God wasn't – God was outside of that.

Also as a result of those moves, the Field of energy that circled and permeated the Earth and permeated each person – **each angel** – on Earth at that time became heavier. The Field is part of Creation – it is sentient and is aware, and it was fed from the time of the Fall onwards by the insecurities and anxieties of the people on Earth rather than the bliss that fed it before the Fall. As a result of that the Field became *itself* anxious, became *itself* insecure, and sought, as a collective thought-field, to draw on similar energies from the people who were living on Earth at that time. It sought to make them dependent on it, fearing that, if they were not dependent on it, it would not exist – which is a fallacy.

And so the Fall generated a different *spin* into the Field of energy that permeates and surrounds the Earth. And, as a result of that, the Field at any time is seeking to be recognised like a small child, to be recognised by the people that live within it. Unfortunately, it is drawing on their energies and they are not drawing on God-energies to feed it a new directive.

The Field is therefore finite, and this is why it is so important that we change things at this time. We have to inject and re-introduce into the Field its original vibration that was not one of fear; that was not one of illness; that was not one of sadness, of lack, of intolerance – but was one of high creativity. We can only do that by seeing that Light in the Field; by going against the wishes of the Field; by being the person who is strong enough to say: 'I am not ill today – I am not having that today! I am not going to be angry today. I am not going to be hateful today. I am not going to be prejudiced today. I am going to live as I want to live and that is the energy that I want to give out.'

By changing your views you change the energy that you give out and, little by little, you infuse the Field with its *original* vibration. The Field needs to remember too. Just as you need to remember who you are – the Field needs to remember who it is, and then it will stop being the 'frightened child in the dark' and will come out again into the Light. And the world will change back into what it was – a sphere that is fed by God-energy and angelic-energy. And a Field of creativity around the Earth will once again be fed by that God-energy rather than by draining the energies of the people who incarnate again, and again, and again seeking the same experiences; and live shorter lives than they should in physicality because their energies are drained, as they become older, by the Field.

It is a *vast* subject and it is one that we hope to explain in the next book, but is far too vast and will take more than just myself to explain it.

Does that make *any* sense to you?

Denise: Yes, absolutely!

Joseph: O.K.

I wish to just close by talking very briefly (as Michael pushes to get back inside his own body) about Christmas, which is coming up and to talk about just the *Christ* part of that word 'Christmas' – the Christos, the Light that you are trying to bring into the world.

And this Christmas it is right – it is completely and utterly right – to enjoy each other's company; it is right to give presents to say *I appreciate you*; it is right to eat nice things; it is right to drink nice things; it is right to visit those people that you don't see at other times of the year.

But it is also right and necessary to inject Light into the world as part of your Christmas, as part of your celebrations. Celebrate what is *possible*. Celebrate what is within you, what is within each person that you meet. And, as you hold their hand at Christmas, put Light into their body and into their soul. As you think of them at night before you go to sleep, give them the Light that they need. As you talk to them on the telephone talk about what you will, but at the same time pour Light into their lives and into their souls.

And see the world this Christmas as you wish it to be in the name of God and in the name of **who you really are** ...and give the world the greatest gift that you possibly can.

Chapter Twelve

Joseph Trance Demonstration – 11th March, 2011
The Sanctuary of Healing, Lancashire, UK

Spiritual topics discussed:

The probability of the end of the world.

Children who are being born to help save the world.

Combating the effects of the Field.

How we bring Light into the Field.

The effect of the consumption of meat.

Is our life shown in advance of us incarnating?

Do animals choose to incarnate?

How to deal with someone like Colonel Gaddafi.

How to avoid returning the Earth plane.

The eternal love-link and the meeting of loved ones in sleep state.

Do elevated souls returning to teach slow down their own progress?

Joseph: My first impression on entering this sphere is similar to trying to catch a speeding train. The haste with which you consume your lives is frightening as a vibration when you re-enter it, and it is not something that I would do if I didn't *have to* do it. And the reason I do it is to:

1) Hope to slow you down by what we say to you.

2) Quicken your vibrations.

There's a contrast, *there's* a paradox! I liken this life to a speeding express train and yet I ask you to quicken your vibrations... **the two are not the same thing.** The speed with which you live your lives has no place in it for God, has no place in it for spirituality, has no place in it for reflection; and your 'vibration' or personal signature is trapped within the speed of your lives. As you evolve as souls, your vibration quickens but your *perspective* slows down. You realise that life is not about the next appointment, the next holiday, the next car, the next conversation, the next fix for your senses. You realise that life is about the ALL; is about the perspective from the spiritual side; the perspective that says to you: 'There is all the time in the world to explore who I am, all the time in the world to explore how I relate to others, all the time in the world to examine the creative abilities that are placed at my fingertips.'

Unfortunately, on Earth at the moment – the Earth-life that is like an express train – there isn't all the time in the world. Your opportunities to examine that spirituality, to slow down and discover yourself, to slow down and discover how you *should* relate to each other and to the Earth – those opportunities are becoming more and more rare.

My message is a serious one, my reason for coming is a serious one, and yet I hope tonight we can look at it with a *light* heart – with a heart filled with Light – because, only by viewing the spiritual options open to you with a heart filled with Light, can you open yourself up, can you increase the rate of your vibration and, in doing so, slow down this reckless train that you are speeding towards cataclysm in.

Grave words but words that I hope will be flavoured with some other points of view tonight, because I bring with me colleagues from my area of living or 'dimension', if you like, my reality, my perspective, and together we hope to change *your* perspective just a little ...just a little.

Is there a question, please?

Grayling Barraclough: Joseph, you have said on a number of occasions that if things don't change (which at the moment doesn't look all that likely) the world could come to an end in around eighty to a hundred years' time or so. Could you just tell us, in your view, how that will actually come about because it is difficult to envisage it at the moment happening – how do you think it will come about exactly?

Joseph: If I were to say the world will end in a fireball; if I were to say the world will end because of plague; if I were to say that the Earth will end because of earthquakes and tidal waves – I have, at that moment, placed in your creative mind *the ability to contribute to that end.*

If I can take you to my dimension, it is *as though* (and these are words and concepts that don't really apply but they are the closest that I can approximate to what happens) we have a 'viewing wall' or a dimension that shows us *probability*, that shows us what will happen if point 'A' meets with point 'B'. At the moment there are many point 'A's travelling towards a single point 'B' and not many point 'A's travelling towards point 'C' – which is spiritual enlightenment. We know how, if it comes, the end will come but if I share that information with you, you then hasten *that end* because of your fear, which contributes to the power of the Field – the creative mental Field of mankind – and you actually *co-create that end.* Do you see that?

Grayling: Yes.

Joseph: Therefore I cannot, in view of what I want to get across and in view of the change that we wish to come, say: 'It will be on such a day; it will be in such a manner.' And always there are, connecting on this wall that we look at and this plan that shows us what is likely to happen, there are new connections being made – connections that add to or subtract from the conclusion that we see at the moment. That conclusion is etched on the wall ...but is not etched in stone. This is why we come back. If it were pointless to come back, we would not come back. We would allow cataclysm to take place; we would allow renewal to take place so then we would lecture and talk to the new generations and new civilisation coming up, which, in effect, is the old civilisation that has put itself to sleep and has then been renewed.

So, the fact that I have caught this 'express train' this evening should indicate that **there is still hope;** there is still the ability to change the connections to the extent that the cataclysm, at worst, is pushed away for a time – a time during which people can look at things with a different perspective – or, at best, is pushed away to the point where it is eliminated. That is a huge task – *a huge task* but not beyond the limits of our vision and not beyond the limits of your capability as creative spirits.

So, we come to say: 'Yes, all the indications are at the moment that it will happen. Yes, *we* know all the indications indicate that it will happen in a certain manner, **but there is *still* time.'** Whilst you still walk this Earth there is *still* time; whilst you still draw breath there is *still* time. And as each person changes there is a force for the good there; a force that can anchor this world in Light rather than in darkness; a force that can change things and a force that can eliminate ultimately that coming cataclysm. Does that make sense to you?

Grayling: Yes, that makes sense.

Joseph: I wish I could show you the wall. I wish I could show you the points that we connect as we view this particular area of 'what may be' – what is *likely* to be. We want to change it into 'what won't be' ...and 'what will be' is a new way of living – a renewal without the need for civilisation to end itself in its current form, to be placed in stasis for many centuries and then to come back only to repeat the same mistakes again.

Another question, please!

Shirley Hayhurst: Could I ask you, Joseph, following on from that, we are told that there are many souls coming to the Earth at the present time to help to bring Light to the Earth – many children are being born who are more enlightened and they are coming to help to save the Earth at this time. Do you know anything about that?

Joseph: I know everything about that!

[*Audience laughter*]

I know everything about that! There are many brave souls and they *are* brave souls, who are old souls (in the sense of 'old souls' from the spiritual side of things and not old souls who simply repeat the same process again, and again, and again) who have chosen at this time – because of their *love* for their brothers and sisters, because of their love of the Earth and because of their knowledge of the 'big picture' – to try and change things.

Unfortunately, it is an indication of the state of things here that more and more of these spirits are being born at this time. It is an indication of the need to change quickly that these children are being born. And you can recognise these children psychically by their aura, by the impression they give off that they have been here before, by the impression they give off that there is a wisdom even when they say nothing, that they know what to do, that there is a contemplation; and you will also see with these children a *stillness* that you do not see with many young people today.

They should be nurtured; they should be given the opportunity to blossom. I describe them as 'brave souls' because once they come here, the Field of mankind, which is set to negative and seeks to renew itself constantly in a negative form, sees their Light and seizes on their Light. And seeks to put in front of them and around them, and around their parents, so many *distractions* that the child cannot emerge from its earthly programming to do the spiritual job that it is supposed to do. **It is important that you pray for these children.** It is important that you pray for these workers for the Light, and it is important that you pray that they do not become polluted by the Field, that they are protected at all times, that their guard is never let down and that they are never let down in their mission.

Many come back tired, defeated and sometimes totally believing that they are the personality that they have had during their latest incarnation. That personality has been so overwhelmed by the *overwhelming* desire of the Field of mankind to put a lid on anything other than the current viewpoint, which is chaos. It is important that groups of Light are formed around these people once they are discovered – once you are *certain* that here is someone who is here to teach, to enlighten, to open minds and to open hearts. And it needs dedication from the groups around them *constantly* so that at some point in your day you pray for the people you know are here to make a difference. You pray for their security; you pray for their vision to be a constant one; and you pray that they are led to the situations that are right for them in order that they might expand other minds.

So, yes, many, many souls are coming back and many old, old, *old* souls are coming back, and the problem is: **they have done so before.** This point has been reached in civilisation previously. This point where souls rush in to try and make the difference before things become so locked in negativity that there is no option but to shut down the operation and to start the business again ... the business of experience ...the business of discovery ...the business of linking to God and realising that each of you is a part of God, each of you has a different way to live, which – if you embrace it – will lead you out of the darkness this time. **But we want it to be *this time* and not *next time*.**

Look after the children who come in Light; look after the souls who want to teach you a different way. Always test them, of course. Always check that what they are saying is sound but – having established that what they say is sound, having felt in here [*pointing to the heart-centre*] that what they are saying is sound – protect them, help them, become the modern equivalent of 'disciples' to give them the energy they need, to give them the rest they need, to give them the vision they need to continue their work.

Is that a sufficient answer?

Shirley: It is, yes, thank you, Joseph and I suppose the Field will want to stop them, won't it, and so they probably have a lot more dangers around them than normal children?

Joseph [*smiling*]: I have to tell you that the Field is panicking; I have to tell you that the Field is afraid; and I have to tell you that the Field should not be looked upon as something that is an enemy.

The Field is a 'child' misunderstood by itself. The Field, after all, was an extension on an earthly level of everything that you think and say and do, and (in the same way that I mentioned earlier that if you fear the cataclysm, you help to create it) if you fear the Field then you bring it closer to you because it *thrives* on the fear that you generate. It is better to say: 'Naughty child! Never mind, you cannot do anything to me today, but I can do *something* to you – I can show you a different way of life; I can show you a different way of thinking; I can show you a different way of feeling.' And to bless the Field – the Field doesn't like that, I'm afraid. Blessing the Field actually puts a protective barrier between you and the effects of the Field. Also understand that on an earthly level – not on a spiritual level but on an earthly level – the Field is part of you. So you are, in effect, fighting part of yourself and **if you fight part of yourself you cannot win.**

Which half of you wins?

What you have to determine is that you are the *stronger* element of the two halves and to, therefore, embrace the other half in Light and say: 'You don't understand today but I pray that you will understand tomorrow. Bless you! May you be at peace and may you be open to the Light that I (and we) are pouring into you.' Then you start to – not diminish the Field – but change the Field to the point where it once was, where the Field was benevolent, where the Field was a contributor to and a co-creator of the good things in life.

That is what we are trying to re-establish – a Field that re-links itself with the God-within and the God-without, so that you are not drawing for your life-energies on a Field of negative energy, but on a Field of God-energy that is linked to greater God-energy that feeds you and sustains you, that projects your future as a future evolution in front of you, and acts as it was supposed to act in the beginning (and by 'in the beginning' I mean in the beginning for this *particular* planet) as a manifestor of your desires.

But the desires then were not desires as they are now – the desires then were to examine possibilities in the name of God to see *what could be*, to see what could be for the good of all. At the moment the desire of the Field is to manifest chaos so that the Field can be fed. But the Field, ultimately, in manifesting chaos, is putting an end to its reign because, in manifesting chaos and in helping individuals to believe in chaos and co-create chaos, there comes a point where the 'operation' (as I have called it this evening) has to be shut down and where the Field has nothing to sustain it ...**and the Field then also goes into stasis.**

Isn't that amazing? You go into stasis as a species and the Field goes into stasis. The problem is when you come back (because you have to come back and you have to go through the same 'moves' to build up understanding again) **the Field comes out of stasis with you.** You have an opportunity at a point of new civilisation to decide whether you wish to revisit the discrepancies of the past or whether you wish to enlighten yourselves, but you are also 'encoded' (because you have to become a physical being in part again) with the discrepancies of the past. Deep down there is that desire and so it is such a difficult cycle to break.

You have to break it now! You have to break the Field's grip now! You have to put Light into it and Light into everyone you meet. And then on that 'wall' that cataclysm will have moved away and have been eliminated, and there will be another set of circumstances for us to communicate with you about.

Another question, please!

Margaret Scanlan: Leading on from that, is there anything you can advise to help us give that Light out and just spread it about a little bit more?

Joseph: Yes. I would go back to my analogy of coming into this world, of stepping onto a speeding express train. In order to come here I have to sort of step onto that 'train' whilst it is still moving. And unfortunately, at this point in earthly creation, you find yourselves in a society and an environment that is constantly moving – you have noise; you have vision; you have pressures. And many souls find that they *cannot* get off that express train; that they always have to have that accompaniment of cacophony – daily, minute by minute, second by second. The only time when they escape is when they sleep. And even then there is no escape, because their desires are linked into that society that wishes them to move so quickly that they anchor themselves close to the Earth plane, and cannot escape fully as spirit people to review what they are doing and to review their earthly life from a different perspective.

My advice, therefore, and the advice of the people who are around you (although you cannot see them) and of the circle that is above you, through you and around you at the moment, is to *be still* – and that is such a simple thing to say: 'Be still!'

BE STILL!

...I have said it in this room; I have said it in other rooms [*reference to other trance demonstrations*]; I have said it in the books we have written. So seldom are those two words appreciated and *understood* – **be still** – in modern parlance: 'Yeah. Right ...Whatever!'

The secret of generating Light is not complex. You will not find it in archaic terms; you will not find it in vast books that invite you to change radically your thinking and involve yourselves in certain rituals. **The secret of generating Light is to be still.** The Field is moving at the same vibration as that 'express train', and when you become still, you get off the train – maybe only for a few minutes each day, but you get off the train. And when you get off the train wonderful things happen to you ... **you become aware**. And you will say: 'Well, I *am* aware – I've been here for ten years ...twenty years ...thirty years ...forty years. Of course I am aware!'

No, you are not!

You are *involved* – you are not *aware*.

'Being aware' means, in the stillness, allowing your spiritual perception and your spiritual desires to come to the surface. 'Being aware' means that you can, in stillness, *connect* with whatever your concept of Divinity is and become, at that point, EVERYTHING – **because you *are* EVERYTHING.**

Your individualisation is a smokescreen; it is a mask; it is not the truth. You are individual, yes, in the way that you look at the universe and that is a blessed thing, but you cannot be detached from the rest of the universe because **you *are* the rest of the universe.** When you become still you become aware of that, and you become the most powerful point on Earth at that moment. Letting go of the 'express train', letting go of the worries, letting go of the desires, letting go of the fears, letting go of the pre-conceptions about how life will be **you discover *you* and you fill, as a vessel, with Light.** And then you say: 'I am All, thank you Father. I bless All, thank you Father. I illuminate All, thank you, Father.'

And the physical mind *initially* will say to you: 'That cannot be. You haven't made a difference. You haven't hurried here or hurried there. You haven't knelt in a certain way. You haven't said certain prayers.'

Forget the prayers! Forget the kneeling in a certain way! Forget the need in your physical mind to go here and to go there. **Be still and you touch ALL.** And in touching ALL you are the most powerful force for good in this region of reality, this area of dimensionality. Do you see that?

Margaret: Yes.

Joseph: I wish that I could say to you: 'Come with me to my area of living. Come with me and see how *we* live.' We are capable – *as you are* – of wonderful creation; we are capable – *as you are* – of building tremendous artefacts, tremendous realities and tremendous vistas for the good of all and for the good of the ALL – for the good of the Divinity. But we do these things by simply accepting that we can do them, not by attaching to them a complexity. It is difficult because you are in the complexity and the complexity tears at you and rips at you, and wants you to believe that it is true. 'Be ye as a little child if you want to enter the Kingdom of Heaven' – what does that mean? Be still, be simple – not simple in that you ignore the world – but simple in that you have the power to change the world. Does that make things any clearer?

Margaret: Yes.

Joseph: Has that answered your question?

Margaret: Thank you, Joseph

Joseph: Another question, please!

Pamela: I've got a question. Do you think it is important for us to stop eating the flesh of animals because we are putting violence into the Field by actually creating murder in another living creature?

Joseph: You have a problem here in that your animal bodies that you consume are packaged, are desensitised and are presented to you as the *norm*, and the cruelty with which those animals are despatched is the norm. It is desensitised, you are not aware of it, and that is exactly how the Field wants it to be, because the animal forms that are terminated in order that you might eat meat are done so with fear in their hearts and in their minds, with pain in their hearts and in their minds, and the fear and the pain from that slaughter actually feeds the Field... **feeds the Field** with more of what it wants to keep you exactly where it wants you to be.

I belonged, at one time, to a civilisation that revered all forms of life; a civilisation that would pray over vegetables before they were consumed. And I have to take you back, further than that, to a civilisation that existed in parallel with other forms of life on this Earth and consumed – not living flesh, not vegetable matter – but *Light* ...**consumed Light and gave out Light.**

You are not capable of doing that *at this point*, so you have to consume the condensed matter around you in some form in order to release that Light within you to continue your existence on Earth. However, there are different forms of life, there are different forms of sentience and, as you approach the vegetable matter and plant life, there is a looser bond of sentience flowing through that type of matter.

You also make the mistake of assuming that animal life is not intelligent life. **Animal life is far more intelligent than you** *at this stage* because animal life can see us, animal life can see into other realities and other dimensions, and animal life can remember a time collectively – through the devas that give form to the animal life – when you were different than you are now and when you lived in harmony with them. Did you know that animals can speak? Did you know that animals can communicate with you through thought?

And did you know that each animal soul is held in *equal* **reverence to Divinity to you?** Isn't that shocking? Many people will say that that is shocking:

'Is the water vole as important as me?'

Yes!

'Is the gazelle as important as me?'

Yes!

'Is the mouse as important as me?'

Yes!

'Is the bee as important as me?'

Yes!

'Why?'

...Because you are all the *same* **thing.**

When you harm something, when you kill something, **you harm and kill a part of yourself** and, as I have said, you release into the Field the fear that the Field needs to feed on.

Also consider that when you consume animal matter you absorb (because you are psychic, because you are spirits, because you are linked to that animal) the fear of that animal, the dread of that animal, the shock of that animal being displaced into the spirit world from one second to the next. And also you are not designed *ultimately* (and I will get back to this in a moment) to consume heavy matter. As the angels that you once were, you consumed the lightest form of matter which is White Light.

You do yourselves harm by consuming the heavy matter of animal flesh. You consume it ...it makes you ill ...it slows you down ...it corrupts you bodily and corrupts you physically, and then you say: 'Why am I ill? Why has God made me ill?'

Also, by consuming lighter matter, you *elevate* your vibrations above the everyday vibrations of the Earth and that allows you to communicate with the higher realms.

I wish to get back to an argument that I have seen which amuses me: 'We have canine teeth – we are *designed* to eat meat.' You are designed to eat meat because as a civilisation you evolved yourselves *yet again* from stasis, carrying on your back like a heavy weight the effects of the Field from the last civilisation; the effects of the Field that says, 'Create fear in others! Create violence in others! Eat animal flesh!' ...And you evolved in heavy matter accordingly.

You have canine teeth today, but it doesn't mean that you *have* to eat meat tomorrow.

Does that answer the question?

Pamela: It does. Thank you very much.

Joseph: Another question, please!

Shirley Hayhurst: I'd like to ask you something, Joseph. We have been told previously (not by you) that, before we come here to the Earth, our life is shown to us and we agree to come and live that life. Then, before we come here, all that memory is taken away so that we can then experience what we are meant to experience whilst here. Do you think that this is true?

Joseph: You return to the spirit world, and **our duty then is to convince you not to come back**:

'Don't go back! Do you remember the pain in your elbow? Do you remember how painful it was when your first love left you? Do you remember the grief that you felt when members of your family passed away and you didn't believe there was anything else? Do you remember what it was like growing older and running out of energy because you were running on the energy of the Field and not on God-energy? Do you remember what a terrible time you have just had lying in a hospital bed for weeks? And now you come over and we say to you, "Please do not go back!" What is your answer?'

...And you say: 'I want to go back.'

And we say: '*Why* would you like to go back?'

And you say: 'Because I have unfinished business and because I think that *this time* I can be successful at the business; *this time* I can be successful in love; *this time* I can get it right!'

And we say: 'You can get it right on this side. **You can get it right on this side!** You can get it 'righter' on this side without going through the agonies of the Earth-life.'

'I want to go back!'

'But the people that you have loved, part of your soul-family, are on this side – only certain of them are returning to the Earth.'

'I want to go back!'

'There are wonderful things to experience here; there are wonderful dimensions that you can step into; there are wonderful things that you can create; there are wonderful things that you can be. You will discover so much about yourself.'

'I want to go back!'

...And so the person, in effect, is put into stasis (much as people will be if the end comes) and is 'shelved' as an individual for a while. And it is worked out on behalf of that individual what can happen to them, if things go according to plan, to awaken their spiritual senses *this* time around. And there are certain milestones placed along the path **and those milestones are inevitable.**

Those milestones are *inevitable* and are placed there with Divine consent. However, the soul can meander between those milestones; it can do exactly what it wants. And the soul, when it reaches those milestones, can also do exactly what it wants. It can draw, from those experiences, an enlightenment or it can draw, from those experiences, a sense of bitterness that such things have happened to it; and move on again to meander to the next milestone.

So, the life is not planned in that it is pointed out to the person: you will meet point 'A' ...point 'B' ...point 'C' ...point 'D'. Nor is it said to the person: you are going to accomplish this, that and the other – except in cases where the soul is a returning soul hoping to put Light into the Earth plane. And *those* souls say, 'I don't want to go back, *but...*' That is the difference – the souls in stasis say, 'I *want* to go back,' but the other souls say, 'I *don't* want to go back but, in good conscience, I can't do otherwise because I need to help, because I need to change things.'

So, what is pointed out to the soul is not what will happen to it in life *except* to replay past experiences and to say: 'If you go back and if you want to experience 'A', 'B' and 'C' – you will experience 'A', 'B' and 'C' *perhaps* but you will also experience the problems that you had with 'A', 'B' and 'C' last time because those problems are still attached to the earthly part of you.'

When you come back into physical matter you pick up, as it were, the 'old suit of clothes' – not the old personalities but the vibrations that surround you within the Field that bring to you certain results inevitably. **Inevitably!** So that is what we say to souls: 'You will meet 'A', 'B' and 'C' but you will also have the effects of 'A', 'B' and 'C' from your past life.'

If only I could expand your vision this evening, I could show you an unfolding universe that is not what your scientists say it is, but part of a greater unfolding universe, a greater number of dimensions than you can ever conceive of with your earthly mind, and those dimensions are glorious and you will not die. You don't die when you come to the spirit world and you don't die as you elevate yourself through the various cleansing spheres and you emerge one day in full creativity and knowledge of what you once were.

...And what you once were and what you are now is an angelic being.

An angelic being! God did not make the angels and then make mankind. God dreamt the angels and the angels were a reflection of Him, were a reflection of what He desired in terms of feedback from the universes that He and they were capable of creating. There is no need to then go on to create human beings. You are condensed; you are masked; you are cloaked; you are wearing a suit and it is of your own making originally.

But given that opportunity – I want to go back into the 'suit' or I want to become the angelic being and delight in creation and delight in the wonders of the dimensions that are around me that are ever changing and ever more evolving, which choice do I want to make?

...'I want to go back!'

Ah... if I had teeth I would grind them [*audience laughter*] and I would have ulcers. Does that answer the question?

Shirley: Yes, it does, and why do the animals want to come here? They suffer a lot more than we do.

Joseph: The animals are drawn into creation. It is a different pathway and we must talk about devas (as we are about to talk to Michael, in terms of the information that we bring through to him on the Fall [*reference to Joseph's fourth book*]) and devas are, if you like, an angelic representation that is able to fragment itself into myriad life forms. Unfortunately, when you became trapped within your own perception of how things should be and in your own perception of how the cycle of life should be millennia ago, you also trapped the devas and you trapped the animal forms.

This is a movement; the reason I am here this evening is to bring you a 'movement' – to bring you not a club, not a religion, but a 'movement' **and the movement is away from this place.** And the movement is for *every* trapped form of life to open the 'hatch', to emerge into the 'sunshine' and to realise what it really is.

The animal life forms *do* realise what they are, but there is an allegiance that goes back to the Fall between the devas and the angelic beings that have condensed into the human form, that links them one to the other. So, you are linked one to the other, and the intention is to bring everyone and everything out, to then cleanse this level of reality and to start again. Not with a new civilisation that is skewed from the point of view of having a Field waiting there to pollute it from day one, but from the point of view of repopulating this reality *in knowledge* of it being 'reality' only as a playground in which to experience each other, in which to experience God and in which to experience creative capability within this particular set of vibrations.

Gosh, I go on!

[*Audience laughter*]

Does that make sense to you?

Shirley: Yes. So even the devas are trying to help us to escape?

Joseph: The plan is to escape. The fragmentation of life is again something that I wish to discuss and to report on at length at a 'later date' (as you would see things), but life was not originally fragmented – life was one. We are going into complexities here that you do not have the time to listen to and I do not have the time to report on, but there is a reason why you see male and female, and there is a reason why you see the human being and the animal forms.

How do I condense this into a little pocket of information? Briefly there is one intelligence around the world and there are different viewpoints of that intelligence – which are you. You are the spirits that see things in a slightly different way from your viewpoint. Originally there was a more cohesive form of life on Earth. Your angelic form is not masculine; your angelic form is not feminine; your angelic form is not a human being; your angelic form is not a tree ...it is not a gazelle ...it is not a pig ...it is not a cat ...and yet it is *all of those things* encapsulated in one greater point of view.

It is, if you like, a 'super you' – a super vision of what you are capable of and, above all, it is a *harmonic* version of yourself. Harmonic in that it has married together male and female; harmonic in that it has married together different viewpoints – not just of human life but of animal life too; harmonic in that it knows that it is a part of the Whole and everything else, but maintains its own viewpoint in order that it can report back to the Godhead and to others in a unique way.

You have such a journey ahead of you, such a journey of rediscovery. **Re-discovery!** Everything that I am saying to you is known: is known within your soul, is known within those moments when you *be still*. It is not new knowledge. Gosh, my words are not new knowledge. They are not new – they are original and what the world needs is original knowledge. You look at a programme or you listen to a record and you say, 'That's original!' I don't mean it in that way. This is the original way of things; this is the original message; this is the *origin* of what you are, what I am and what everything is.

Your viewpoint on Earth is so limited. That is not a disrespectful thing to say – it is a fact. It is so limited because you are condensed, you [*smiling*] are put into a 'jam jar' and the lid is put on, you are placed on a shelf, someone exits from the room and closes the door behind them... and through that door is EVERYTHING. What do you see through that door? It is difficult for you to see through the glass; it is impossible for you to get off the shelf; it is impossible for you to shake yourself off the shelf, end up on the table, roll onto the floor, roll over to the door and open it. You see the complexity of what is surrounding you? What you are perceiving tonight is only a small fraction of what you are, what you once were and what you shall be again – whether it is today or, in terms of earthly time, in a million years' time.

Does that make sense?

Shirley: Yes, it does.

Joseph: Good. It makes no sense to me whatsoever!

[*Audience laughter*]

Shirley: Especially the jam jar!

Joseph: Another question, please now that I have answered that one successfully!

Yvonne Ball: Joseph, in your dimension how do you look at and deal with someone like Gaddafi?

Joseph: There is no one like Gaddafi in my dimension, first of all, because the vibration of that poor soul cannot exist in the atmosphere within which I, and the members of my group soul, live. That is not an arrogant thing to say; it is simply a fact.

You have touched here on a very important point because the Earth, the world, perpetuates itself. It perpetuates its state of war; it perpetuates its state of dictatorship; it perpetuates its state of violence. And part of the reason *why* it perpetuates its state of violence is that when such a soul rises into prominence, the hatred of people reacting to what that soul does **fuels that soul to do more of what it is doing.**

You have been told throughout the ages to love one another and to love *especially* those who seek to do harm to you. This is not soft love. This is hard love because, when you bombard a soul with enough Light, you neutralise the negative aspects of that soul and you neutralise what that soul is doing. **You can never neutralise violence with violence.** And when you think of someone in a violent way (remember that you are a spiritual being) you send violent beams to them; you send anger; you send sharp instruments; you send cutting edges; you send harsh, sharp vibrations. And those harsh and sharp vibrations are exactly what is surrounding that person at this time. **You make them stronger by your anger.**

And you will say with the earthly mind: 'Well, how can we love such people?' And I have to say to you: 'How can you *not* love such people?' In order to restore the balance, in order to see the world that you need and that you want, you cannot just pay that world lip-service. You have to love.

Love is the only transforming solution.

If enough of you love a person such as Gaddafi – you change that person, you break down the barriers, you ignite and restore to strength the God-spark within that heart, and that person changes from *within*. Never, ever will someone change from outside: 'I will make you do this!' No. You won't! It has to be: 'I will make you do this because I am now showing you a different way; I am showing you a better way; I am showing you that you have been mistaken; I am showing you that you wish to change.'

There is another question here about what happens to some souls, because many people on Earth *wish* retribution for such souls. **Wish retribution for such souls!** We do not wish retribution for *any* soul. It is enough, at this stage of evolution, to say that that soul brings retribution to itself, but not retribution that is a judgement from God – retribution that is a means of freeing that soul from the mindset that it has adopted. Retribution that says: 'If I cannot teach you and change you from within, I will surround you with more of yourself until such time as you recognise that the 'yourself' you are being surrounded by is not the self you wish to be.'

We love all souls. There were times when we didn't. There were times when I didn't; there were times when my colleagues didn't, but we love all souls. We love each other and, in loving each other, we see only the good – *the God* – in people.

And you will say, 'Well, he has killed people!' But has he? He has caused violence that has taken away the physical existence, but those people are still alive. And those people, if they are elevated souls, and once they regain their spiritual memories, are the *first* – **are the first** – to send direct Love back to that soul that took their life, because they see such a waste of opportunity, they see such a waste of spiritual talent, and they see the need to change.

There is a final coda to this question, and it goes back ...and back ...and back ...and back to a time when things were sent askew and when the life-force was shattered, when the aspects of the Whole and the individual as a Whole were sent to the four winds. There were certain souls at that time who began with a very good idea, as they saw it, and began with an idea that they thought would glorify God and God's 'stage-set'. By that I mean the Earth plane, and by 'God's' I mean an area or dimension that was created by you as angels in order that you might experience the different levels of reality that you are capable of creating. But at that time those certain souls thought that they had a great idea for advancing things, for making a good idea even better ...and it went terribly wrong.

And those souls are trapped, and those souls still surface and still have (because of what we have discussed earlier) with them, as they re-incarnate, the coding of the Field that surrounds them and makes them act in a similar manner *each time* they come back here. And the souls that emerge and seem to wreak so much havoc are most times the... 'instigators' is the wrong word ...the 'members of the committee' that originally got things askew. **They are to be pitied.** They are to be pitied because, ironically, if you hate them, in a way, you follow them because there links, from you to that soul, a vibration that is similar to their vibration and tugs you along to some extent as they continue their malpractice on Earth. Does that make sense?

Yvonne [*smiling*]: Eventually it might do. Yes, thank you, Joseph.

[*Audience laughter*]

Joseph [smiling]: There are concepts that I am working on in my dimension and I feel that eventually those will make sense as well.

[*Audience laughter*]

Everything that I say to you is simple. It becomes complicated when I have to explain it in terms of what happened to the Earth.

Also the information that I am bringing through (I and my colleagues) has to be presented correctly, has to be presented stage ...by stage ...by stage ...by stage so that it will make sense [*reference to the book on the Fall*]. So when you ask me a question that relates back to the Fall, I have to take only a part of that to answer that question. The whole of the Fall, as a report that I am giving at the moment, will make sense. I can't say, 'I promise you,' because there will always be those who say, 'I want to go back!'

[*Audience laughter*]

There was another question.

Karen Toft: Could I ask a question, please, Joseph? If we keep our lives simple, then, and live in Love and Light, now that we are becoming more aware of your message and send out the Light to the world, is that enough that, when we do eventually pass over, we won't ask *can we come back*? How do we safeguard against not having to come back?

Joseph: The fact that you are asking that question at this point means that you have made the judgement and you have seen that there is an option. Having seen that there is an option, you take that option with you when you depart this life. And, as you continue to work spiritually, *you* distance yourself (no one else does it for you) from the chaos of this world. You wake up in the morning and you say: 'Yes, I will put Light into the Earth but, as the Earth is at the moment, I do not wish to be a part of that aspect of earthly life.' You realise that what is happening to you is a passing parade, you are not an integral part of it and that the experiences that come to you from dawn 'til dusk on a daily basis are actually that ...experiences. They are not the solid things that you think they are; they are not the be-all and end-all that you anchor your life-energies into.

So, each day becomes an adventure, but an adventure that you can increasingly retreat from by becoming still, and you begin to see holes appear in the illusion. I do not mean that you will see a ragged curtain instead of the back wall of this room, but what I do mean is that you will have moments of clarity where you will view a person operating in a certain way and saying certain things; you will view a situation on Earth; you will view your own life ...the house you are living in ...the car you drive ...the holidays you go on ...the work road that you travel every day ...the work that you do – you will view them for what they are: **things that bring you experience.** Each soul should be seeking to take to the next level the experiences of the Earth and not the materiality of the Earth. You cannot drag the house with you, you cannot drag the car with you or the holiday with you ...**but you can take with you the *effects* of those experiences on your immortal soul.**

Ask questions! Ask questions of what I say. Ask questions of what is brought to the table spiritually. And what attracts you – accept for that time; what repels you – dispense with. And understand that, as you go through life spiritually, your views will constantly be changing. You will constantly be flexible as someone who is looking at the spiritual way of life. That doesn't happen in your earthly life – not very often – you see life as a road, you see it as a journey, you see inevitability in what will happen to you in certain points in your life. But the spiritual aspects of your vision will say: 'No, that is not the case – I reject that. I see only opportunities to grow, to become who I was and to influence people as I used to when I was an angelic being.'

That mindset, because it is a spiritual mindset and is a heart mindset, does not leave you when you make the transition from this dimension into the next stage of your infinite existence. That is not wiped, but first you have to have it. And there are many souls who have it deep down but it is masked, and they are so immersed in the minutia of this earthly life that when they make the transition **that is all they see.** They miss – not the experience – but the materiality. That is *all* they see. They have not elevated their senses above that materiality. That is what you must do and, in asking that question, you have already done so. Do you see that?

Karen: I do, Joseph, but if you are in a soul group and – say – you have lost your partner or your mum or your dad or somebody like that, and they didn't have the advantage of the knowledge that we have now got ...it just seems a bit unfair sometimes that they might be disadvantaged. Could you help them... if you pass to the same soul group when you pass over, could you help them not to come back?

Joseph: The love-link is eternal. The love-link binds one to another – if they truly love each other on whatever level – **forever**, and ultimately the love-link is between all of us. That love-link has been lost between all of us, and that desire to be with certain people extends to *everyone* as you elevate yourself through the various cleansing dimensions.

You cannot lose the people that you feel you have lost on an earthly level. You cannot lose them because they cannot lose themselves. They are eternal, immortal beings. You also have to think, not within the dimensions of the Earth plane, but remember that when you sleep (if you are sufficiently aware) you 'travel', as it were, and you change your perspective so that you visit certain regions within the higher dimensions. You can, for example, visit those people who you feel during your earthly life that you have lost. You talk to them and you also recognise them *spirit-to-spirit* – so you recognise them as mum, or dad, or as a brother, or a sister, or as a dog ...but you also recognise them **as who they *truly* are.** So, you have wonderful conversations with them, wonderful harmony with them when you escape this level of consciousness during your sleeping hours. The problem is when you return to this level of consciousness those memories are most often masked. And they are masked by the effects of the Field, because you are immersing yourself again in heavy matter; you are immersing yourself in a world that believes that it loses people.

I am not being harsh here. I am not taking away the pain that goes with losing someone, and it is right that that pain should exist to make you realise how important that person was. What I am saying is that you haven't really lost that person and that there is connection with them, not only when you make the transition and are reunited with them, but *now*. There is connection with them during your sleeping hours, if you are of sufficient mind to be able to escape your physical body.

Those people cannot be harmed. They *cannot* be harmed. They cannot die. It is their physical presence that you miss, but imagine seeing them once again, as that physical presence, with that physical presence perfected according to how they view themselves – in other words, they are young again, they are vital again, they are whole again. There is that physical presence that you remember, united with the lights from their soul that they have acquired to this point in their spiritual existence. And so you see the mother, you see the father as who they *were* but also as **who they *are***, and you think: 'Isn't that wonderful! They are so much more than I believed. They are so much more free than I remember them being. And they are forever mine and I am forever theirs because we are a part of each other.' And as long as that volition to connect is there – **it is there**. It is as simple as that. Do you see that?

Karen: I do, Joseph. It is just a matter of if that person wanted to come back to Earth and, if we in this room have the knowledge that will help us when we pass over not to come back, but somebody that doesn't have this knowledge in the same soul group might *want* to come back.

Joseph: Two observations on that. First of all, with what I have just said, you must look at people and say: 'I don't really know that person. I know an *aspect* of them but I don't know their total motivation, so it is not up to me, with my earthly mind, to say that the person is going to choose to come back.' You don't know that. You would have to see the entire spectrum of that

375

person's existence before you could say: 'Well, they are going to come back.' You can't say that – you can't judge.

And the second thing is, if the person does choose to come back, again look at what I have just said regarding meeting that person in sleep state. You are not losing that person. Yes, you will worry. Yes, you will be anxious because they have made a potentially dangerous decision to come back here, but because of that love-link you will be able to connect to them and to advise them as to what they do next in their earthly life. So, in effect, if that person does choose to come back, *you* will be one of the people to convince that person not to come back *next time*.

Also remember that the earthly life, from your point of view, is a long journey, but from our point of view is a 'blink of an eye'. And I want to tell you that you will actually spend *more time* in the spiritual realms even when you are incarnated on Earth than you do on Earth – more time because your existence is not confined to this 'mask', and the times that you spend at night can be vast sessions of teaching, and learning, and listening, and reconciliation, and reunification before you come back.

Does that help?

Karen: Yes, that's wonderful. Thank you.

Mike Sly: Can I just ask...

Jane: Can this be the last question? Thank you.

Mike Sly: I just wondered a little bit more about the discussion we had earlier this evening about the souls who are currently choosing to return to the Earth in relatively large numbers to try to actively influence the prospect of what you have described as a 'closing down of operations'. Your perception there was that those souls clearly had, I suppose, very high motives, but paradoxically they find their own spiritual development being intermittent or in some way slowed down by that decision, and that strikes me as a really difficult paradox.

Joseph: It is a difficult paradox but it is also an example of the love that we are each capable of. They understand that they might be taken off course – and yet they come. They understand that the people around them might seek to shut down that ability with them – and yet they come because they come praying and connected to the Divine **in the hope that they will make a difference.**

It is not a Divine judgement that someone should come here and be absorbed and influenced by the Field to the extent that they cannot function as to their original mission. It is the effect of this area of reality on a soul according to free will – this Earth, this reality, acts as it does according to free will. All messengers can do is ...be a 'messenger' and pray that at this time they will have the strength to get the message out.

Believe me when I say that every effort is made to make sure that those messengers return to their rightful place. And you must understand that it is far easier for a soul that has been on our side of reality for some time – it is far easier for *that* soul – to retain and regain its soul memories than it is for someone who is steeped in the way of life of the Earth plane to the extent that they reject anything spiritual.

So, they come in, they do what they can and then they go back to where they came from – actually they go back to somewhere a little higher than where they came from when they return to the 'Lighter' side of life, and I mean the side of life that currently has more Light in it.

You have to forgive me because I am about the extract myself from Michael; I have over-run him once again. I thank you for your consideration of my words and hope that you will consider them in the future – in *your* future.

Chapter Thirteen

Joseph Trance Demonstration – 7th September, 2011
The Sanctuary of Healing, Lancashire, UK

Spiritual topics discussed:

Does each incarnation aid a soul's progression?

The cleansing spheres.

Are some souls forced to reincarnate?

The Earth's original purpose.

Advanced souls who return to Earth to help.

The reason for natural disasters.

The limitation of words.

What is the next spiritual phase for mankind?

Is the date of the 21st December, 2012 significant?

Assessing the truth of spiritual concepts.

Using God-power.

Free will.

The Fall.

Who created God?

Joseph's previous lives.

Joseph: To begin with I would like to talk about travelling for a little while. Have I travelled to get here? ...Yes and no.

I have travelled by thinking myself into this state, into this projection, into this illusion but I haven't actually gone anywhere ...and yet I am travelling. I am travelling onwards in evolution; I am travelling onwards in understanding – **as are you.** You sit in a room – or so you think – but each day you are travelling. *Now* you are travelling. And along the path of each day you pick up 'souvenirs', you pick up trinkets, you pick up mementoes of your journey and you put them in the invisible 'suitcase' that you carry with you every day. **Every day!**

And then you bring them back to show your God. What is in that suitcase? Have you brought back fine works of art? Or have you brought back something that is mass-produced for the market? Have you brought back something that you will be proud to display within your 'home' – within your aura? Or have you brought back something that is broken and chipped because it wasn't of real worth anyway?

You cannot *help* **but travel.** When you are asleep – you travel. When you are sitting in front of the television – you travel. Always you are travelling. Always you are picking up souvenirs, and one day you have to show those souvenirs to Divinity.

My point is that the souvenirs you pick up should be of the best quality every day of your lives. Will the things that you are bringing *with* you enhance you? Will they help you to evolve? Or will they, as in the case of many human beings, be something that you drag behind you, something that becomes so heavy that your advancement is slowed down?

Please – a little plea before we begin – each day, choose your souvenirs carefully! Choose your souvenirs wisely, and then, when you open that invisible suitcase on the day that you present your 'souvenirs' at the 'customs station' on our side of life, there will be a tick on the suitcase – and through you go, which is what we want.

You haven't come to hear me talk about souvenirs. You have come to hear me answer *hopefully* (please God) questions, and so, a question, please!

Julie Sexton: Joseph, you talk about evolution; I have had a couple of discussions with people who have said that souls don't evolve but it is merely a different experience each time. Would you say that there is a transcendence – an ascension – for the soul with each learning or is it merely trying different experiences?

Joseph: 'Ascension' is a word that is bandied about a lot today. Ascension seems to have been cheapened as a word, as I see it. Change is inevitable and change for each soul on Earth is inevitable, and the key to understanding evolution is the Fall. The key to understanding evolution is what went wrong *originally* – otherwise there is no need for evolution, there is no need for expansion.

Each soul evolves and expands to get away from the mistake it made in the first place, millennia ago. Each soul (we hope) expands to the point where it no longer wishes to be on Earth, and escapes and makes its transition through the spiritual cleansing realms into Infinity.

There is information at the moment saying that ascension will happen to certain souls and not to others... Ascension will happen at six minutes past seven on a certain day and a proportion of the population will move into another dimension, and a proportion of the population will stay where it is or – worse – will be pulled down into a lower state of being.

...Should I be forthright? Should I say: 'Nonsense'? Should I repeat the word: 'nonsense'?

Nonsense!

NONSENSE!

Each and every soul on this Earth has to progress out of the illusion that it has placed itself in. You could call this process 'the Great Escape' – you are going 'over the wall' **each** and **every** one **of you**. And we come back to make sure that *each and every one of you* does get over the wall. No one ...*no one* ...no one is ever left.

So, for 'evolution' substitute the word 'escape' ...'realisation' ...'remembrance' because evolution *spiritually* on this planet is nothing more than remembering who you are, remembering what went wrong and taking steps to put it right for yourself and for everyone else. Does that answer your question?

Julie: Err, yeah, thank you.

Joseph: That isn't the 'yes' I wanted.

[*Audience laughter*]

Why is it not the 'yes' I wanted?

Julie: Ooh, I'm trying to put my finger in it ... it's more like for the spirits on the other side of life rather than here – for their evolution rather than the soul's growth down here. Is that different?

Joseph: There is no difference.

Julie: Is it one and the same?

Joseph: It is part of the same process.

Julie: Yes, thank you.

Joseph: What is perhaps revolutionary in what I am saying to you – and what the group that I come from is saying to you – is that the spiritual realms are not 'heavens' as you understand the term. They are a continuance of the cleansing process that I have just been talking about with regard to souls on Earth. It is one great movement, and you can perhaps think of it as a series of 'trapdoors' or 'hatches'. And, in order to escape, you have to open one hatch ...go through it ...move up a set of stairs ...go through another hatch ...another set of stairs ...another hatch ...until eventually you are opening the final hatch into Infinity.

And at that point your evolution your cleansing is *complete* and you have total recall of who you are, what happened, how you got to this point. And you have a volition then to go onwards into pure creativity – pure projection of form through Love and through connection with the Divine. That is what you do now, but unfortunately the waters have become muddied, and so, as you try to create, the filter of your mind and the filter of the physical Field around you cramps your style!

Does that make more sense?

Julie: It does indeed.

Joseph: That's the 'it does indeed' I want!

[*Audience laughter*]

Another question, please!

[*Silence from the audience*]

Julie Sexton: Well, I've got another one [*laughing*] if nobody else has got anything they want to ask. I have heard (you know hearsay is a bit of a bad thing isn't it, or can be) that some souls don't come here through choice but there is a forcing to come down here.

Joseph: Ah, if only it were so!

Souls come here through *choice*. Souls come here through *forgetting*.

What have they forgotten? They have forgotten how wonderful it is on our side of life in the higher spheres of being. They have forgotten how wonderful it is to be pure creation, to project whatever you conceive to be true and to give it form around you. They have forgotten that so much *more* exists than this particular plane of being. They have, in forgetting, become attached to ...the next cigarette ...the next company merger ...the next house ...the next sexual encounter ...the next acquisition of earthly power.

And so, when they progress to the spiritual realms, as they must when their earthly projection terminates and comes to an end – they, instead of looking around them, never get past the 'customs house' that I was talking about earlier. And the customs officer says: 'There is a wonderful view from that door. There is a wonderful land. There is a wonderful existence. There is somewhere to live. There are people who love you. There are opportunities to grow.'

And the soul says: 'I want to go back *that* way. **I want to go back *that* way!** I cannot see any of this. I only think about the things that I haven't finished. I only think about the things of Earth that I want again and can't let go of, and I want to go in *that* direction.'

And the 'customs officer' asks his 'manager' to come in, and some other 'customs officers', more able to advise this soul than he is. And they do so; and they surround the soul; and they show the soul pictures of the next place; and they show the soul some of the objects from the next place; and they show the soul what the soul will look like as it goes through that door and progresses, and becomes more and more filled with Light.

And the soul says, 'I want to go back!'

And so the soul places itself, through its *own* volition and its *own* choice, in a holding area until the Lords of Karma decide where to place that soul in an earthly life, and what advantages or challenges (perhaps both words are the same thing... they *are*, actually) to attach to that soul's aura, so that at certain times in that soul's life it will come up against challenges (*advantages*) that will help it to progress if it tackles them in the right way. And then that soul is prepared again for an earthly life ...and is smacked on the bottom and off it goes again.

[*Audience laughter*]

Does that answer the question?

Julie: Partly... In that case, if it is such a hard job, then why is it that so many queue up to come down here?

Joseph: Can you expand on that?

Julie: If from spirit – if you do, when you come down here, kind of get stuck on a bit of a treadmill, and for those who do get stuck with an earthly mind, what on Earth would possess a spirit to want to come down to Earth in the first place?

Joseph: That is exactly the point.

We have to go back to what the Earth was. And the Earth was a learning sphere; the Earth was an agreed area of projection into which spiritual beings projected parts of themselves in order to experience, in order to add to what they were, in order to become more than what they were. That was the original intention and is *still* the original intention of this planet.

Unfortunately, souls have become stuck and we can't get them out because of two words ...God's two words ...Divinity's two words ...two very, very *important* words in everything that we do. ...What are they?

Julie: Free will.

Joseph: Free will!

Free will – if a soul believes *solely* in this area of matter, in this area of illusion, then it cuts off its memories of anything else. It cuts off, through its own creative ability as part of God, as part of Divinity, the ability to see anything other than the Earth. **What you want through free will, you create.** And so you create the *need* to come back, and no amount of argument will take you out of this situation until you have seen, with your own eyes, through your own experience, the need to move on, seeing this world as what it is at the moment: an illusion that is muddied by the effects of the human Field of consciousness that is set to negative. But until that time ...you come back ...and you come back ...and you come back.

I have come back in order to give you information that gives you a choice *before* you get there. **It is a choice** – you can throw away the information or you can look at it, you can take it in, and examine it, and see if it *feels* right. And at that stage, if it feels wrong, throw it out. But, if it feels right, then when you get to the spiritual side of life, *if* you are one of those souls that argues to go back, perhaps you will draw on that knowledge and say: 'Wait a minute – there's a different way. I see where I should be going; I see where I have been and I am making the choice to move on through my own *free will*.'

Does that answer the question?

Julie: It does, thank you.

Joseph: Another question, please!

Mike Sly: Can I just develop that theme? I am interested in the different reasons why spirits choose to return to the Earth plane, particularly spirits who have progressed through the spirit realms and are relatively 'advanced' in that sense. Is it your understanding that some advanced spirits actively choose to return to the Earth plane in an unselfish way in order to make some contribution – either to an individual's spiritual evolution or to mankind's collective development?

Joseph: We ...you ...I ...the millions of souls in my soul group ...the other soul groups ...the other expressions of life **are family.** What you see in a human family is a pale reflection of what the spiritual family is. The spiritual family is bound one to another with bonds that cannot be broken – **cannot be broken** – and are recognised from a spiritual point of view *instantly.*

Therefore, the fact that souls are suffering, the fact that souls are separating themselves from their greater spiritual family by returning ...and returning ...and returning to the Earth – upsets us (and 'upset' is such a tiny word), mortifies us (except we can't die), makes us restless, makes us beyond sad, beyond grieving because part of us is still there; part of us *literally* needs to 'see the Light'.

And so we do not abandon you – how could we? To abandon someone is a human concept – not a spiritual one, not a Divine one. So certain of us, with great reluctance, at times decide that we will enter this arena, this playhouse once again to try and bring Light through, and we are allowed to do that through *free will.*

Having said that, there are many who reincarnate with the express intention of advancing mankind through spiritual teaching, through being a vessel for bringing Light into the Earth, who then fall prey to the effects of the Field.

As soon as a soul comes back here, because of the Field of human consciousness, its physical mind has a dominant role to play in that soul's makeup. The physical mind takes over to a great extent. The physical mind says: 'This is *all* there is.' The physical mind says: 'There isn't a spirit world.' The physical mind says: '**I will bring to you all that I can see and touch and sense** and feel and hear, and there is *nothing* more.' And all those senses are bringing in negative images... So many fall, as it were, by the wayside.

But one or two points of Light, here and there, *do* get through.

When that soul returns to the spirit realms, it does not carry with it karma of the type that most souls on Earth do. It carries with it the *pollution* that it has picked up during its time on Earth, but that can quickly be dispensed with depending on how entrenched in Earth-thinking the soul has become during its time in physical life. Once that pollution has been dispensed with, then the soul returns to the point that it was at before it came to Earth, and *hopefully* will also have progressed the soul group that it is a part of because of its endeavours on Earth. Does that make sense?

Mike: It does. I suppose it connects with a concept of 'Divine intervention' where there are certain potentially catastrophic events that may lie ahead of us that would require some form of intervention from the spirit world.

Joseph: We are only allowed to intervene to the extent where we can *influence* people.

The chain of events is this: the souls on Earth through unrest, through anger, through the lust for power, *influence* the Earth. They influence it like an irritation, like a disease. It is just as easy to influence the Earth through the transmission of Light into the fabric of the planet, but mankind chooses instead to influence the Earth *negatively*.

So, the catastrophes that you are seeing at the moment have been created – not by God, not by the planet – **but, unfortunately, by you.** That sounds a terrible thing to say, but at some stage the souls on Earth have to take personal responsibility for what is happening to the Earth.

Your thoughts cut into the Earth like a knife; your thoughts invade the vibrations of the Earth like a virus. And the hatred, and the anger, and the lust for power that you see every night on your televisions builds up, and builds up to the point where the Earth cannot stand any more, and is cut to the point where it is ruptured. When that happens you have a release of energy: you have tidal waves; you have volcanic activity; you have the plates of the Earth's crust moving against each other. And people say, 'What a terrible thing has happened! How can God allow this to happen?'

God doesn't!

If you are waiting for a Divine 'hand' to come down and stop you from killing each other – **it won't happen.** Why won't it happen? Because of two words ...what are the two words?

Audience: Free will.

Joseph: God cannot prevent a part of Himself ...Itself ...Herself from doing what that part wants to do. That is not part of Creation. That is not part of projecting parts of Yourself out to gather information and then bring that information back to Yourself. If You impede Your Divine children then they are not experiencing and You, therefore, are not experiencing.

If You impede Your children they become puppets and not children.

And so God, Divinity, Creation, waits *patiently* to be recognised by those parts of Itself that are out within the Field of human consciousness.

And *if* the souls reach a point where they destroy the *physical* – not the Earth – but themselves and the buildings and the edifices that they think are so important, then they have to wait, if they do not *wish* to return through the cleansing realms into Infinity. They have to wait if they *cannot recognise* the cleansing realms that go back to Infinity. They have to wait until the planet has repaired itself, until the planet has grown again into the Eden that it once was, so that they can enter a physical form *once again* to make choices *once again* that will lead them out of that Eden and back through the cleansing spheres into Infinity ...or back to a repeat of what brought them to that point of stasis in the first place.

The intervention comes from us consciously (as we have just discussed) projecting ourselves back into physical matter to inform you so that you can make an informed choice. And the things that we want to inform you about are so simple – *so simple*:

Take personal responsibility.

Love what you are.

Love and respect the planet.

Love and respect each other.

Put Light into the Field so that you change it from a negatively charged area of consciousness into a positively charged area of consciousness, into a balanced area of consciousness.

Return the Earth to what it once was.

Return yourselves to what you once were.

That is all we come to teach. And I have stood in this room and people have said: 'But we've had this message before.' **Of course you have!** Of course you have – it's the basic, defining message. Don't look for complexity. Look to what those people who have come to teach you in the past have said ...love each other ...love yourself ...respect the planet ...send Light to the planet ...send Light to those around you.

That is it!

In doing that you recall, you remember, you change and you escape. And the planet becomes what it once was so that other souls, if they *wish* through free will, can visit it with the right intention and the right perspective.

Does that answer the question?

Mike: Yes, thank you very much.

Roy Bennett: I have a question, thank you, Joseph. I have studied spiritual writings for many years and one of the things I have noticed over time is that there tends to be *key words* in each generation around which the teachings gather. If you look back to the eighteen hundreds it was 'truth' – most of the spiritual movement gathered their teachings around the key word of 'truth'. Then we had the hook, which emerged through the sixties, seventies and eighties, where the key word tended to be 'Love' around most of the spiritual teachings. Now it has become the word 'Light'. Each one of these words, I understand, is encoded with a particular energy. My question is, as each generation passes on, these words become degraded and overused, and my curiosity is do you have any information on what the next phase will be?

Joseph: The next phase frightens me! The next phase *at present* frightens me – this is why there is such an urgency to what we are doing.

First of all let me talk about words, and let me talk about a time when you didn't need words – as I, in my state in one of the cleansing spheres (because I haven't emerged into Infinity yet) don't need words. Words are an example of the Field of humanity encapsulating, embedding and entrenching concepts.

When you originally visited this planet in your angelic form you simply communicated by heart-thought, by heart-intent, by heart-projection. And so, because there was no subterfuge, because the energies were *balanced* between positive and negative – the creative force that you wield as the angel that you really are – your intent in communicating with someone, in communicating with your God and in communicating with yourself **was always apparent and always pure.**

Following the Fall of mankind (or should I say the *second* Fall of mankind because this brink that you find yourself on has happened before) the encapsulation within the physical, the entrapment within the projection gave rise for a need to vibrate the air between yourselves in order to communicate.

And so you made sounds, you wrote down symbols and these became wholly your means of transmitting your thoughts and innermost feelings to someone else. But, as you know, because of the effects of the Field and because not everyone you meet is a Light-bringer or a Light-emitter, words can be meaningless at best and words can be a lie at worst.

Words can be a means of focussing the mind. **It is what lies *beneath* the words that is important, and what lies beneath the words *always* is the projection of Light.**

'Light' itself, as you said, is a word. 'Light' describes a wavelength, and behind the wavelength there is another wavelength that is you – or *appears* to be you. But behind *that* wavelength there is your pure being and that pure being is not a wavelength. You are *totally* apart from the wavelengths that allow you to communicate with someone else except in pure spiritual intent.

And so in your spiritual readings and spiritual teachings, the best way to deal with them and make the best use of them is to go within, to take the concept within. Not into the computer [*reference to the head-centre*] but into the heart – into the heart of the spirit, into the heart of what you really are **...and meditate on them.** Don't look at the words. How do you *feel* with the concept? What lies beyond the concept in terms of energy? And once you have determined that – **you *know*** whether the concept that you have in word-form is right ...is misleading ...is good for you and mankind ...or is to the detriment of you and mankind.

The phase that you are in unfortunately *at this point* (and it is always 'at this point' or I wouldn't come here) does not lead to another word – the phase that you are in leads to a fallow period during which the Earth can repair itself ...**if things do not change.**

If globally, if within this room, if within each of you, you became focussed tonight on the Light that you project – 'you' being the Divinity behind the Light that you project and your ability by wielding that Light, by sending that Light out into the Earth – if you became convinced and dwelled upon that Light as being **your being** the world would change.

It changes by every word that we put out – not because the people read the words, but because the people understand the energy behind the words. So, we have to condense (I am condensing now, through Michael) concepts into the words and then we have to condense words into books.

A book cannot change your life. The concept behind the words, and through the words, and under the words that you can take in – given out as a parcel of Light put into each book and into each word – *can* change your life, *can* change the world.

Truth ...Love ...Light.

Truth is a perspective ...Love is Oneness ...Light is what is needed for the Oneness to change the perspective.

Have I answered the question?

Roy: Yes, but that leads me on to another concept that I need to sit and give thought to but, yes, it answers the question.

Joseph: You're sure?

Roy: Oh, certainly, yes.

Sue: Joseph, could you tell us the significance of the date the 21st December, 2012 – what is the significance of that date?

Joseph: I have absolutely no idea.

[*Audience laughter*]

Absolutely no idea! Sometimes with my ability to project (which is an ability that you each have) I put myself into a bookshop – I create around myself a bookshop, and then I say to myself, 'Draw from the Earth all the books that are currently being written about spiritual matters.' ...And then I have to build a bigger bookshop.

[*Audience laughter*]

And I look at dates, and I look at worship of *this* concept or *that* concept, and do you know what I see? **I see deception by the Field in many cases** – in many cases, not in all cases but in *many* cases. I see people becoming entrenched in certain ways of thinking, and then projecting, through that way of thinking, their view of how the world should be. And thinking something is going to happen on this date, or this particular mineral has a certain meaning, or the low level of mediumship (that we see at times from our perspective) is what the spirit world is about: where people are very much like they are here, and all they are concerned about *really* is the next pint of beer and whether you have painted your back door or not.

[*Audience laughter*]

And so you have to question dates, you have to question concepts, and you have to say, 'Does this make sense?' and even more importantly, 'Does it help the world?'

Does it help everyone in the world? If I am concentrating on this date and thinking it is going to be some magnificent event or has some deep *mystery* behind it, does it benefit me progressing as a soul? Does it benefit the people around me and the way that I interact with them? Does it benefit the world in what I am able to give to the world to help it change?

And only you, *each* of you, can answer that question in each case. Do *my* books benefit the world? If they don't – throw them out. Throw them out! Burn them! Throw them away! But also, if anything else says to you: **this has no meaning – this is too complex** – throw it out!

If you are looking for an explanation of the meaning behind numbers – they are simply creative building blocks. They are simply as words are – as the gentleman said – a means of expressing concepts. Similarly numbers are a means of expressing concepts.

Are you moving into a different phase? ...Daily.

Were the ancient peoples able to see that you are moving into a different phase at this time or **around this time** – not *precisely* at this time? Yes, they were. But there has been misinterpretation, re-interpretation, examination by the physical mind – always by the *physical* mind – and layers and layers and layers of complexity have been added to the original simple statements of these things by ancient peoples.

Does that make any sense?

[*Pause*]

There is a silence.

Sue: No, I am sorry it doesn't.

Joseph: OK. Why doesn't it make sense?

Sue: It doesn't because to me you are using words, and you have seen a whole library of books and you are using all those words, and the words are superfluous to what you are saying. Your words create confusion for me and I don't understand why. I have read the books as well, and the thing that amazes me is that you are from the spiritual realms and the date of the 21st of December you know nothing about.

Joseph: Nothing at all.

Sue: Well, that amazes me.

Joseph: I can only ask that you look at these things from the point of view of the heart and not from the head.

Sue: I am looking at it from the heart.

Joseph: What is the heart saying to you?

Sue: Pardon?

Joseph: What is the heart saying to you?

Sue: The heart is making me very confused at the moment. I don't know. I don't know – there is something I am feeling that is uncomfortable.

Joseph: If you are confused, go away from this. If you are confused, go away and be silent, be by yourself, be with your God and throw out every complexity, every word, every thought...

Sue: But isn't this why I am here – to hear the word, to hear your spiritual voice talking to us, explaining these issues, explaining the Earth, explaining the spiritual world to us?

Joseph: May I suggest that the mind...

Sue: I'm not being awkward...

Joseph: May I suggest that the mind loves complexity and that many times what you think is coming from the heart is coming from the mind. With the heart the answer to any question is binary:

I understand it – I don't understand it.

Yes or no.

It feels right – it doesn't feel right.

Anything more complex than that is coming from the mind; and the mind, as I have said, loves complexity. The Field of human consciousness loves complexity because it masks the *true* state of things.

I, as I have said earlier, can only talk to you in words because I am using a human vehicle. If I was to stand in front of you and 'disrobe' – and I don't mean that in a rude way – I mean divest myself of the human projection that you are used to seeing, and you saw instead a swirl of Light. And if I said to you that that swirl of Light – but I can't '**say**' to you because we can't use words – if I impressed you with the fact that that swirl of Light is my expression and not me; if I then expressed to you that *behind* that swirl of Light there is another swirl of Light ...and then there is nothing but there *is* me, what could you latch onto from that?

I have to use the means of communicating in *your* sphere of projection in order to get across to you some *portion* of what I am attempting to do. I have to use words, I have to use concepts, but at no stage do I want those words and concepts to be upsetting to you.

Sue: Oh, they're not upsetting me at all. Well, they are ...I am trying to understand where you are coming from, from a spiritual point of view. I try to understand your words. I am trying to understand the words.

Joseph: I am coming from the heart. If you do not feel ready to accept the simplicity of the heart's point of view, then I would suggest you walk away from spiritual concepts that obviously, at this time, are weighing too heavily.

The truth ...the Love ...the Light.

It's simple.

Truth, Love, Light – as the gentleman said. There is nothing more to it than that. If you automatically, at that point, then wish to add complexity: 'Why is it truth? Why is it Love? Why is it Light?' Then it is the mind that is influencing you and not the heart.

Can I *suggest* that you spend time silently with yourself? Can I suggest that at each point you switch off each thought, and attempt to move your consciousness – the real you – from here [*pointing to the head-centre*] to here [*pointing to the heart-centre*] and to listen in silence – not in complexity. **And there you will find your answers.**

There is nowhere else I can lead you to for answers because nowhere else exists for answers except there. Be still. Be quiet. Listen to yourself. And if what comes to you from the heart-centre throws out everything I have said – that is fine, that is wonderful! But listen *there.* Become reconnected to your Divinity and you will find that the answers are simple – not complex. Yes?

Sue: Well, I thought I did that anyway – I don't know.

Joseph: The mind is complex. The mind throws up smokescreens. The mind will tell you that black is white and white is black.

The heart is *knowing* – the mind is wondering.

Get to the point of *knowing*. Become silent ...throw out the books ...throw out the concepts ...become silent ...listen to the *real* you ...ask to connect to God ...and see what the heart tells you. That is the starting point.

Another question, please!

Roy Bennett: Can I ask very quickly, Joseph? You said earlier, when I asked the question I asked, that the next phase frightened you. One of the things that has been running around within my heart has been the idea of God's free will being paired with human free will, and the concept of the 'un-thought thought'. Have you any information on that at all?

Joseph: Each of you creates minute by minute. You create whatever you believe to be true; whatever the dominant situations are that you give power to in your life you create minute by minute. So, in that sense, you always use God-power. You always use God-power because there is no other power. If the truth is that you are part of God, that you are an expression of God, then you use those God-powers to exist and to create and to have your being, so you are always using God-power.

I hope that this, therefore, signals the need to be *very careful* in what you wish for because you are able to use God-power for great destruction.

Actually you should be using the tools of creation and of destruction to put around yourselves scenarios to investigate and then to be able to tear them down. But you cannot do this at the present time, because of the effects of the Fall where the vibrations became skewed towards the negative, where the vibrations became an investment in taking power from others, an investment in the negative. What you have do is to have a *balanced* view of your own life...

[*Interruption as the mobile phone of the previous questioner starts ringing*]

...a balanced view of the world and a balanced view of society, and – as you see society perfected, as you see your own life perfected, as you see the world perfected – you give God-power to those concepts.

Unfortunately, at the moment, most people – not knowing that they are part of God, not knowing that they create the situations around them by investing in them – are using God-power to destroy, to tear down. But, because of the effects of the Fall, you can never completely tear down. **You are trapped between creation and destruction with an emphasis towards destruction.**

So, God-power can never be harnessed to the extent that it can destroy beyond the sphere and immediate region of space just outside this planet ...can *never* be used because outside of that region the effects of the Fall have not been felt, and God-power is used for creation, experience and progress.

But within this area God-power at the moment, because each of you is God, is being used destructively. But you cannot destroy yourselves – you can destroy the 'vehicle' you are in, you can destroy your buildings, your cars, your society, your edifices, but you can't destroy yourselves.

What we hope to do is restore the balance by saying ...use God-power in a balanced way ...see the world as being balanced ...don't believe in the news stories ...don't believe in somebody saying it's a terrible day today ...don't believe in somebody saying you are ill.

Instead say: 'My view of life is that societies get on with each other. My view of life is that I am in perfect health and so is everyone else. My view of life is that the Earth is healed and the pollution of the Earth has stopped.' And you are wielding God-power, as you *always* do, but you are wielding it to create the world that you want, the world that we want for you. Does that make sense?

Roy: Yes.

Joseph: Are you sure?

Roy: Yes, but I was taking it a step further than that.

Joseph: Please explain.

Roy: The question I have is: there is always the belief that God, of Its own free will, will not intervene in man's free will. Man's free will and God's free will are separate, and yet, by logical deduction, there has to be a point at which man's free will consciously states to God: 'I am asking You to use Your free will in whatever way You see fit to break this eternal cycle that we have of being unable to collectively surmount the filter that we have collectively created.' Now in my world, I term that 'the un-thought thought' and I have *huge* difficulty trying to explain to people what I am trying to communicate.

Joseph: Thank you, I understand.

Roy: Thank you.

Joseph: Your free will is always God's free will.

It may be your free will to say to God: 'Father, this world is insane. I wish to place into this world – Light. I wish to place into this world – Love. I want *You* to do something.' That is your standpoint as part of God, but what is your brother's standpoint next to you? What is your brother's free will saying? Your brother's free will can be saying: 'I don't believe in God – You don't exist.' And so God is distanced through that expression of free will: 'I don't believe in a better world. I don't want a better world. I want a better *me*, and I want more of *this* and more of *that* and more of the *other*.'

And so you have to, in order to change the world, bring Light into the world *en masse*. You have to gather together, and at the point where there are enough souls saying: 'God, I want You to change the world' – **they have *already* changed the world by using God-power** because there are enough of them to make the difference, to tip the balance, to disperse the illusion. And so when you say to God, 'I want You to change things,' what you are really saying at soul-level is, 'I want *me* to change things. *I* want to change things.' But you also have to connect with *enough* people so that the 'projection' – the Field of illusion, the Field of human kind, the energy given out by the souls on this planet – changes ...changes over to Light, changes to be malleable enough to let the God within you – and everybody else who thinks the same way as you – *in*. Does that help?

Roy: Sort of.

[Audience laughter]

Roy: Sorry Joseph, it's just that with this particular concept, I am trying to take it one step *beyond* the free will of the souls that I heal. What I am looking at is: when will souls (separate to whatever any collective being wishes to choose) choose in partnership an *entirely* different thought that completely changes everything for everybody?

Joseph: In order to answer that we have to go back to the Fall, and 'the Fall' is a vast subject.

Roy: Yes, I know.

Joseph: What actually happened in the Fall in a nutshell – but not really in a nutshell because it needs to be explained further, and we are bringing through this information in 'instalments' as it were [*reference to the Fall book*] – is that by free will the souls, at that point of the original Fall, decided that they would move away from God in consciousness because they knew better ...they knew a better way *collectively*.

The rest of Creation – universe and universes – is not like this.

This is a splinter group but still a part of God. Until that splinter group comes back in harmony with God, God says: 'Have your adventure! Take yourselves off. Take big sticks and hit each other for a million years, and one day you will think, "Maybe this isn't the thing to do." Build your missiles, build your weapons, blow each other to pieces ...and you'll still be there and I'll still be here.'

And then one day you will say, 'We've had enough! There must be a different way.' This is what we are hoping for now – the different way.

God is never going to force on the people – who are alienated by themselves through free will via the Fall – He is never going to force His will on them. His will exists in here [*pointing to heart-centre*]. If you want to have God's free will flowing through you, you connect here and you listen. And then you align your free will with God's free will ...**and you work miracles.**

It is a quiet change. It is an internal change. God will never grab you by the lapels and shake you. God will always say: 'When you are ready, when you are quiet, when all this cacophony is silenced for you, I am ready to listen and I am ready to act.' Does that answer the question?

Roy: Yes, thank you.

Joseph: Another question, please!

Pamela: I have got a question. My understanding is that God created everything and everything is full of God-energy, so who created God and where did He come from?

Joseph: Ooh, the big question!

[*Audience laughter*]

Not the little questions tonight – the big questions. How long have we got?

The answer to that is first of all I have to take you outside of the perspective of the Earth and outside of the perspective of a life that begins with a physical birth and ends with a physical death. Because you are living in a finite Field of energy, you expect and see around you everything as having a cycle of birth, progression and then a dwindling away to a death, and change. That is only the Earth.

It is difficult to imagine, with your earthly mind, a state where beginning, middle and end have no meaning. As I have often said to Michael, when I deliver the chapters of Joseph information, I am visiting him *once*. I am allowing parts of my consciousness to tune in with his timescale, but really I am visiting him and talking to him *once*.

If you are asking me to explain the nature of God, I can't. The people who visit *us* can't.

If you are asking me: do I understand God? Yes, but in order to understand God I have to plug in via the heart. And, in plugging in via the heart, I become part of everything consciously, and I know consciously that there is no beginning and no end.

There is simply experience ...ever-changing experience.

There is simply growth ...continuous, continuous, continuous growth.

And I know from the spirits who come to visit us in our realm, the spirits who have gone on into Infinity and choose to come back and advise us *as they can*. ...and 'as they can' means that they *struggle* putting their concepts – not into words – but into thoughts that we can understand ...just as I struggle putting my concepts into thoughts and words that you can understand, but they come back and they impress us with the glory of the journey

404

that they are on. They will say to us – or the *equivalent* of saying to us: 'We can only illustrate *part* of that journey to you and you can only understand a portion of what we are saying, because our vibrational rates are different, and you cannot fully pick up what we are saying to you.'

God is the eternal mystery, and the highest beings that we have encountered and spoken to always like to reserve a little mystery about God because God is constantly changing. And when you reach the point where you feel that you have discovered all you know about God ...there is *more* to discover, because His children – us and the other expressions of angelic life throughout the universes – are constantly bringing back to Him *experience*, which changes the Base, which changes the Source.

I have used in the books the analogy of God being, through the ancient symbol, the 'dot-within-the-circle' and you feel that you travel in a straight line from birth to death but you don't. You go round in a circle. You orbit God and, when you divest yourself of physical matter, you find yourself drawn, not outwards, but *inwards* ...a little closer to the bright Light in the centre that is God.

God has no beginning and has no end because those are earthly terms, and those were not originally earthly terms. The terms 'beginning' and 'end' simply, in their original form, applied to the length of experience of the angelic beings who chose to visit this planet, in order to grow – not through birth and death – but through a change of consciousness into a beautiful sphere of possibilities created for them to enjoy and experience.

High stuff, isn't it?

[*Audience laughter*]

I would suppose that hasn't brought you any closer. What I am trying to illustrate is the human concept versus the bigger concept, and unfortunately, from the point of view of your physical senses, you can only view things from birth to death, and you can only look at *other* things and gauge them as having a birth and a middle and a death. But that is a concept that only applies to the Earth – not beyond it; only applies to this particular expression of *heavy* matter – not beyond it. We never think of a beginning, a middle and an end for ourselves. We are beyond that point and, therefore, God is beyond *our* point in terms of not having a beginning and a middle and an end.

We have to talk about the ETERNAL NOW but that would take too much time. Suffice is it to say that we can experience different aspects of our lives at the same time, and 'time' is a concept that is a misnomer and only applies to the Earth. You see how complex it is and how difficult it is for me to translate something that I see in pictures into something that I have to transmit into words.

GOD IS.

To simplify everything, to crush it down to its core: **GOD IS** – and that is *all* you need to know.

Will God end?

No!

Will God begin?

No!

GOD IS!

If you want to know about God, if you want to understand Him better – again there is the need for silence; there is the need to go within; there is the need to understand from the point of view of the heart, because that cuts off the mind, that cuts off the input from this world.

People say, 'I believe'. I love people to say, 'I *know*'... 'I believe' is another trap of the mind. You have to fuel belief; you have to shore it up; you have to put fuel into it each day to say: 'I believe! I'm holding up this wall of belief.' Once you know with the heart – you *know*. It doesn't matter what anybody says – you *know*. It is beyond the mind **and to know God you have to get beyond the mind.**

I don't want to ask if you understand the question.

[*Audience laughter*]

Have I answered the question in *some* way?

Pamela: Yes.

Joseph: Are you sure?

Pamela: Absolutely, yes.

Joseph: Thank you.

Jane: Joseph, could we make this the last question please so that we don't over tire Michael?

Joseph: Another question, please!

Shirley Hayhurst: I'd like to ask you, Joseph, how many lives you can remember experiencing here, and did you experience lives *before* you came to the Earth?

Joseph [*laughing*]: That's a very personal question!

Shirley [*laughing*]: I feel that I know you, Joseph.

Joseph [*smiling*]: We don't delve into other people's lives unless we are asked – and, of course, you have asked.

I can remember five lives that were important to me. If I put my mind to it I can remember many more, but I choose these five lives because they are, for me, turning points. And you know how I view them? I view them as 'suits of clothes' in a 'wardrobe' and every so often, in relative terms, I go to the wardrobe, open it, look at the suits of clothes, and I think, 'That suit taught me something.' And there are other suits in there – quite a few, actually, and they are a bit tatty, but I leave them in there because they are part of me.

The life that I felt necessary to recall in order to give some weight to the first book was, of course, the life in Atlantis. And that is very dear to me because of the religious aspects – and I don't mean 'religion' in the way that you view it now, but in that life I was very *attuned* to creation. We were very attuned to creation, and we were able to create very close to the way that we were *supposed to* create as angelic beings and we used to create as angelic beings.

My religion was a blend of God-knowledge and earthly science – but again, not the earthly science that you would understand. We had machines that moved without moving parts; we had energy that would give out light but that did not harm the planet. We did not have hospitals as such – we had places where people could go to talk and, in talking and talking and talking, we would eventually get to the seat of the problem, release the problem and the person would be whole again. So that life is very important to me.

If you are asking – and you *are* – about lives before the Earth, all I get when I look in that direction and try to look further than my experiences as a spirit evolving through the plane of the Earth ...is the image of a seed. That is all I get. At times that seed seems to have Light within it. I don't see the Light, but I see the seed and know that one day it will open.

And I know that the day it will open is the day that I walk through that last 'hatch' – open it up, walk through the hole that it produces – and get back into the realm of Infinity. Because *that* 'suit of clothes', that seed – my angelic persona of course is what I am now, but is ready to be worn again when I have gone through the cleansing spheres.

You have to remember, in everything that I say that I, too, am progressing through spheres of cleansing. And so, just as to many people on Earth their spiritual life seems to be locked away and they are blind to it, I have an *inkling* of what I was before, but I am waiting for the Light within that seed to burst open again for me. Does that answer the question?

Shirley: Yes, thank you for sharing that, Joseph.

I would, at the end of this session, ask you – whatever you have taken from this session – to do one thing that will be *key* in your understanding of God, your understanding of each other and your understanding of the Earth ...**GIVE AWAY.**

Give away your time ...give away your Light ...give away your Love ...give away the truth that the gentleman was speaking about. Give it away!

If you want peace – work to find peace in others.

If you want a lack of confusion – work to enlighten others.

If you want a happy life for yourself – see that happy life in others.

Work always for others, and you will find at the end of a tired day working for others ...that you have found yourself.

Chapter Fourteen

Band of Light Closed Circles

Spiritual topics discussed:

Will mankind destroy the planet?

The reason for differing information in channelled material.

Are some spirits more intelligent than others?

How do we evolve into a group soul?

Why has the true meaning of life been hidden for so long?

Can there ever be an end to the soul's journey?

Why does evil exist?

Can we reincarnate backwards in time?

How to get souls to realise that they are co-creators.

Releasing past-life trauma.

Sacred Geometry.

The DNA myth.

Michael's preface: In the course of delivering his third and fourth books Joseph would, as each communications session was drawing to a close, invite questions from the group on the spiritual information he had just delivered or on other spiritual topics that group members desired further insight into. Many of those questions feature at the end of the chapters of *Your Life After Death* and *The Fall*. The ones included below did not directly relate to the categories created by Joseph's chapters in those two books, but are nevertheless worthy of inclusion here as they touch on spiritual subjects many readers will have considered in the course of their personal journeys.

For the first eight questions, however, we travel back in time to 2006 – the time of completing *Revelation* – when, as a Christmas 'treat', Joseph allowed us a special, 'bonus' circle communication during which he invited questions from Jane and David. It should be noted that these questions from early in our connection were answered at a time when my link with Joseph was a clairvoyant, rather than a trance one. Also interesting are the hints in Joseph's answers alluding to the Fall information, something he slowly prepared us for and introduced over a number of years.

Band of Light Closed Circle – December, 2006

Jane: I was just wondering whether mankind could or would destroy the planet completely and, if it does so, where we will all go then? [*Note – this question was asked prior to us receiving information from Joseph regarding the presently uncertain future of this planet*]

Joseph: You are looking at this from the point of view of complete global destruction by explosives and weapons. However, mankind has 'destroyed' the planet many times in the past. On a metaphysical level mankind destroys the planet daily. It depends on what you mean by 'destruction'.

Half the world destroys what it has created *on a daily basis*, while the other half is awake. When that first half awakens from destroying its version of today, the other half sleeps and begins to destroy its version. Each day is destroyed when you go to sleep. The daily illusion is destroyed when mankind goes to sleep. Were it not so there would be such a great pressure of thoughts and concepts and mental rubbish in the Field that you would not be able to function as human beings.

The illusion, the Earth plane, should this daily destruction not take place, would be like a computer hard drive that has become clogged with its own information. You are destroyers as well as creators – it is your nature and I have talked of this principle in the book [*reference to* **Revelation**].

Construction and destruction are opposite sides of the same mirror, so you need to destroy as well as to create, but the concept of mankind destroying itself by destroying its 'backdrop' – the illusion, the Field – is only a dream as yet, as are most things in your lives.

You are the masters of your own destiny. Your question cannot really be answered until it is an absolute, and it is not an absolute. It is not written, it is not *intended* that mankind should destroy itself, and part of our spiritual work together is to guide people away from the brink – not through teaching them a new way to deal with others, but through teaching them a new way to master the illusion. We are working to get them to step back from the precipice in thought.

Everything that needs to be changed in your world has to be changed from within the soul outwards because your world *does not exist*.

Your world is a 'stage' and it is futile to try to alter the stage – you have to alter the 'players'. If you alter the minds of the players *then* you automatically alter the stage, because you equip the players with new 'paintbrushes and materials' so they can deck the stage in a different way. But you have to give them those materials, that new way of thinking *from within* by changing their perception of the nature of reality. This is where mankind goes wrong: it tries to alter the stage and not the players.

'We need to change the world,' people say.

No, you don't – you need to change the *people* in your world, the *thinking* in your world, the *belief* in your world – not the world itself.

The world is neutral. The world is changeable via new thought, via those people who need, instead of putting a plaster on the wound, to think in a *new* way that stops the wound from being constantly recreated in the first place. To do this you have to alter the players.

Doomsday? ...No, not if we, and *you*, can help it.

A further question, please!

David: Whilst you are channelling information through Michael, obviously other spirits and souls are channelling information through other mediums. Some of that information overlaps whilst other channelled information doesn't. Are we, in fact, just seeing different facets of reality as perceived by guides in channelled information? People will expect, when they read material such as yours, absolute answers, and I'm guessing that there are no absolutes other than God?

Joseph: Yes, Creation – God – is the only absolute.

The life-path of a medium colours the spirit information that is brought through to a greater or lesser extent.

The ideal situation for a guide is to have their 'instrument' – their medium – under the complete control of trance (of which there are different levels). This is difficult to achieve regularly because we are dealing with the degree of volition of a soul – the medium – to be used by their guides minute to minute on behalf of mankind. Because we work from a perspective of Love – *everything* we do is in the name of Love – we cannot risk harm coming to the channels we use, and there are only certain times when conditions are right for trance and only certain mediums who are able to be taken into trance.

It is inevitable in mediumship that every message be coloured to some extent by the life experiences of the medium. As I am speaking through Michael now, he, at a certain level of awareness, is aware of me. He hears his own voice; he also hears my voice. I have to use his voice, I have to use his imagination, I have to use his biases to *some* degree, although he has learned enough over the years to subdue his ego to a great extent during times of communication.

You also have to understand that we have our own biases. So, I talk through Michael as the end product of a soul memory. I have had many lives: I have been a female; I was once a brutal man, long ago; I have suffered disease; I have suffered from setbacks; I have had triumphs; I have lived in certain parts of the world; I have found my God in my own way. So, any communication I bring to you is coloured by Michael, is coloured by *my* experiences of having lived through various lives, and is also coloured, to a lesser extent, by the thoughts of the other spirits who aid me in establishing and maintaining communication.

Further, my soul group has a group-soul memory, which is a complex construct as you might expect, because it draws on the soul memories of thousands of individuals. We are united in purpose, but we began as different people and each one of us, therefore, brings a slightly different note or flavour to the proceedings.

What we are seeking to offer, what I am seeking to offer through Michael, is an insight into the mechanics of creation.

And the mechanics of creation exist *despite* soul memories, *despite* the illusion of individualisation. They are the building blocks of creation; they are the symbols you can see in action everywhere on Earth and in the heavens, and say, 'There is God at work.'

So, in describing the mechanics of creation (which I pray I have always sought to do in our times together) I am divorcing from the communications, as much as I am able to, the biases of the medium and of myself.

Much mediumship is about ego; much mediumship is based upon the seeking of wealth. And we find that many mediums, if they are confronted with something they do not like as part of a communication, cut it out, 'That's not part of me. I won't have that!' Their own minds *resist* us. The mind of the medium resists the communication because that mind has been programmed for years to think in a certain way. Even within the medium there is the mind that at times says, 'This *cannot* be taking place.' We have to bypass the physical mind; the medium has to bypass the physical mind, in order that accurate communication can be brought through.

The purest mediums are those who bring through information and say: 'This is what I have been given. I may not agree with it but there it is.' Where you find that spiritual information matches and overlaps and harmonises you find mediums who are able to do this. You will also find suddenly harmonious passages within communications brought through by mediums, that otherwise do not match, at points when they have been able to let go more fully of their ego's point of view and allow us to talk freely.

What you should find, as the world progresses, is that spiritual communication from various mediums matches and harmonises more and more. Each passage will have its own flavour, yes, because it is being brought through different channels by different guides, **but essentially it will be the same information.**

You have not yet reached that peak – mediumship is still in its infancy. You have materialisation mediums, you have trance mediums, but you have yet to understand the *mechanism* of mediumship, and that that mechanism can be useful to mankind from the medium's birth and early age through to death if it is used effectively, if you nurture it.

We seek out the scientific medium, the one who understands the mechanics of his or her craft – for those are the ones we can use most *effectively*. Michael does an excellent job of blotting out his emotions so, although it is not in his nature to be scientific, his mediumship is meticulously scientific, and that is why we can use him. Certain other mediums colour and cloud the information with their own emotional biases, and very often what you see in books is not the start-point; it is not how we actually spoke to the medium …it is the result of the medium or an editor going through the material and changing what we have said.

A further question, please!

Jane: Are there different levels of intelligence in the spirit world and are some spirits more intelligent than others?

Joseph: Intelligence is the ability to assimilate and act upon data and nothing more. However, there is a universal intelligence – a universal knowing – that is divorced from the physical intellect each of us possesses.

We each possess this intelligence deep within our souls.

If you were to gather ten people in a room, their ability to assimilate and act upon data would be different in each case. But if you were to look at the universal understanding those ten people actually possess, and which is hidden within their souls, you would see that they are *completely equal*.

Intelligence should not be confused with *knowing*. Knowing does not need data. Knowing *knows*. Knowing expresses. Intelligence is a dead factor; intelligence assimilates and offers nothing more. Intelligence shepherds people towards brick walls and dead ends, because intelligence is arrogant. Intelligence says, 'I understand this, therefore it exists,' or, 'I cannot understand this, it therefore cannot exist.'

Intelligence is stupid – knowing is *all*.

I spoke of knowing when I spoke about the heart [*reference to a chapter in **Revelation***]. The physical mind deals with problems and offers its own solutions which it pours into the consciousness of the soul as it constantly tries to steer the soul it belongs to through and into different situations. That is intelligence at work; that is the physical mind at work. Note I say 'tries' to steer the soul – from the perspective of spiritual growth the soul *should* be steering the physical mind, but that is another story.

The spirit mind is a refined version of the physical mind, with an ability to make sense of its surroundings on a spiritual level. There are many layers to the spiritual mind, many skins that are gradually shed as the soul climbs the 'stairs' into other existences …until what is eventually shed is all need for data – this being replaced from within by a love of knowing. And at that point the equality of all souls is apparent, because God – as a blanket of intelligence, a field of knowing – cannot know more in one area than in another. **God is all-knowing through all souls.** They have simply forgotten this.

The higher we climb up those stairs to God, the less intelligent we become and the more *knowing* we become …and in knowing we become creative, loving, God-like and fulfil our potential.

Another question, please!

David: Michael mentioned the other day something about group souls and group members. How do we originally start out... do we start out as part of a group soul or are we 'out there' on our own, so to speak? How do we evolve into a group soul?

Joseph: I will draw on Michael's love of science fiction in order to answer the question.

You mentioned a programme you watched recently [*reference to a Doctor Who Christmas Special*] and was there not a sequence in it where there was a single rock to which other rocks were then attracted through gravity? When souls are first flung out into the physical universe from the heart of God-spirit into the heart of matter there is, at first, a benefit in those young souls being 'alone' physically, because there is so much for them to discover through existing in that illusory state.

So, the first part of the soul's journey is concerned with the discovery of the self. Having discovered itself, however, the soul begins at soul-level to long for the joy of *interacting* with other souls physically. It begins to long for more than itself, or for more of the same as itself; for a mirror in which to look and to appreciate itself; for a review of all aspects of itself, to see if its thinking is unique. And at that point, when it has absorbed and contemplated all of the experiences of being single, of being alone, it begins, by invisible threads, to pull itself towards other souls who have reached a similar point of development.

Suddenly it finds that it is no longer alone and there are two souls interacting with each other and enjoying 'the dance' ...then the two attract two more and so there are four ...then the four attract four more and there are eight ..and so on, with the colours, the ideals, the beliefs of those attracted souls being fairly identical. I believe you say: 'They are singing from the same hymn sheet.' So this process is going on all the time. You have souls who are discovering themselves in a unique way, in a singular way, then slowly discovering that it is not a unique way.

If you were to watch an explosion in reverse, those particles that have been thrown out would be pulled back into the whole;

and that is the process that is going on with God. It is like a beating heart that throws out a pulse of energy – it expands then it contracts, then it gives out again, different colours, different notes. And it brings back to itself constantly – from a distance in the case of souls on Earth or more closely in the case of souls in the spirit realms – observations about its own creation that make it more than it was before those sparks had been sent out.

You have always existed, because 'always' is a concept that doesn't exist. There is only *now*, so all your existence is *now*. And if you exist *now* how could you never have existed? How can you cease to exist? There is no past, there is no present – there is only *now* and you exist *now*.

It is not in the nature of the soul to be alone. It is not in the nature of God to be alone; that is why God created you. **'One' cannot share – millions can.** 'One' can create, but to what end? There have to be other aspects of the 'One' to create for.

Another question, please!

Jane: Why has the *true* meaning of life been hidden for so long?

Joseph: You make dresses. If I bring you a box and I open the box, and there is a dress in the box, and I give it to you and say you may have it... where is the adventure in that for you? Where is the discovery? Where is the time spent in creation? Where is the pride? Where is the joy? Where is the expansion of your soul?

The human soul is at first in a 'box'. The soul grows and matures by opening that box. If God sends you out and presents you with the full story at that moment – *he has brought you back.* So you have no journey, no adventure, no experience. You come straight back.

You are Proto-Gods in everything you do ...in learning to sew ...in making a model ...in reading a book. Once that experience is with you it remains in your heart *forever*. If it is given to you

420

like that dress – fully formed – there is no flavour, there is no joy ...there is simply the object and all has been revealed.

For us, there always has to be something else to discover. There have to be new horizons. We do not want the 'dress' presented to us fully made – we want to make it ourselves; and when we have made the 'dress' we will go on and make something else.

Experience... Being...These things are the reason mankind is not given the full story. I know you refer in part to the ending of the violence of mankind; I know you refer to what seem to be the pitfalls of mankind, but are they really pitfalls? If, as you said before, mankind destroys the world, and one soul learns from that experience [*reference to that 'one soul' escaping from the effects of the Fall*] has it not been worth it from a God point of view? God works through Love. God builds through Love, and through Love we slowly discover who we are.

Do not be too anxious for the journey to end, because when you understand everything, there is no journey.

Another question, please!

David: Just following on from that, can there ever really *be* an end to the soul's journey? If there was an end to the journey, and we then set off again, would that mean repeating experiences, or would it mean us going off in a totally different direction?

Joseph: The soul has to move on. The soul by its nature cannot be still; it has to have energies moving through it and to it. It has to experience, that is its nature, because the soul is created in God's image and God's wish is to experience His universe, His limitless limits, so the journey cannot end.

If you are obsessed by something, can you ever have enough of it? No, because there is not enough of that substance in the *whole* universe to satisfy your thirst for it. The soul is obsessed with experience, so there always has to be experience.

From your point of view you look at things with time limits. In soul-reality there is all the time you will ever need to have all the experience you could ever wish for. And everything is a stage. My existence is a stage in an ever-growing experience. Your existence is a stage in an ever-growing experience.

It is as if you are a slide-projector and you can only see one of the slides that is in your carousel at a time. You can only see the slide that is projected in front of you at any one time; and you think that that slide is permanent, that it is your world ...and then along comes *another* slide and changes everything, and you benefit and you grow, but you then think that that new slide is your whole world ...and then the slide changes again ...and so on ...and so on ...and so on.

That is Love. That is life. That is existence. That is being. It has to be so ...experience and worlds without end.

A further question, please!

Jane: Why does evil have to exist?

Joseph: In the darkness there is a light, but how do you know it is a light unless it is surrounded by the darkness? How do you make choices? 'This water is cold. This water is hot. This water hurts me – it is *too* hot. I like hot water. I like cold water, but the one that is too hot I do not like.' ...So many choices.

Even the mime artist pushes against an invisible wall to express himself – there has to be something to push against. There has to be 'something' so you are able to distinguish, to say: 'This *is* me, however, that is *not* me. *This* is what I want to be, but *that* is what I do not want to be.'

Evil is simply the 'room' that has not acknowledged the Light in its midst.

If you bring light into a darkened room is the room at fault, is the darkness at fault? It does not know the light until it can measure itself against it.

As you hold up the darkness as a mirror to yourself and say, 'I do not want this,' so the light is held up as a mirror to the darkness, so that the darkness can say, 'This is a different way of life I have discovered. I want this.' ...But it has to be made *aware* of the choice.

The manifestations of evil on your level – for they do not exist on ours – are simply the death cries of certain ways of thinking, the cries for help of certain souls that are in darkness, and indications that society – souls – need to look at things in a different way. If you regard evil thus, then you have a useful tool, because in observing evil you know what needs to be changed in your world.

We look at the darkness in your world and see it as an indication of souls who need to be educated. Each area of evil is an indication of what is wrong.

Michael is tiring, so one further question...

Jane: Can we reincarnate backwards in life?

Joseph: Existence is a map. It does not move backwards, it does not move forwards, it is like a map spread out on this table. The map can take you to places in your mind or the map can take you to different countries. You live your lives consecutively from *your* perspective as a soul, but you live your lives **at the same time** as a truth of the soul. So, guidance comes to you – not just with regard to this lifetime – but with regard to a number of lifetimes you are living at the same time.

You can't go backwards. The nature of creation is forwards, but your experiences are *nested* within each other, are dependent upon each other, influence each other – until you escape and release yourselves from the... 'real' is the wrong word... *cyclic* nature of reincarnation. And then there is another story regarding how the soul experiences itself from that point onwards.

So, instead of seeing 'past' and 'future' in three dimensions – try to see your life as a map. You are visiting certain places, and each destination, each life, can be seen as a pin in the map marking the route you are taking. As a soul, and as guides, you and we can see all those pins at the same time because we – we and you as souls – are looking down on the map. Each of those pins is representative of one existence, a single life's perspective existing as part of a number of incarnations taking place at the same time.

I have tried to answer a very complex question – one that really needs answering by bringing you greater insight into the nature of the soul and of life and incarnations, and I promise you I will attempt to answer it, but it is a subject that will take at least an hour to fully cover and I do not have that much time here.

Band of Light Closed Circle – April, 2009

Joseph: I am finding it difficult to maintain the communication because Michael is very tired but I would like you to have the opportunity to ask me something.

Mark: Yes, Joseph, thank you. I am intrigued to know the work I do... I try to encourage people to realise their creative ability. Like you say, they are part of God and can create their own reality around them. Part of that is lifting the awareness of who and what they are, and I believe that if they can demonstrate to their conscious physical minds that they are co-creators then they will become more empowered and start 'awakening' and moving on the journey that you have talked about [*reference to chapter three of* **Your Life After Death**, *which Joseph had just delivered*].

Have you any advice or guidance in respect of how we can get souls to realise that they are co-creators?

Joseph: It is a slow process. You have the weight of thousands of years behind you in your 'reality' telling you that this is not so. And your society is geared to make the majority dependent on the minority in *all* circumstances – in politics, in health, in religion. The Field is geared to making the majority dependent on the minority, and the minority enjoys that perceived power and control.

What we wish to do – what *you* have to do – is touch the soul; you cannot appeal to the physical mind. Beyond the words that we give to you there is a message that touches the soul. This is why people say, 'This is such a wonderful book!' It is a collection of words but *beneath* that collection of words there is a vibration. The book contains a vibration and it is this vibration that sings and speaks to the soul.

In all things – with all groups of people, in all situations – take in the Love of God. Ask that God feed the people that you are about to talk to and communicate with. Ask for the words always and, as with the book, it will not always be the words that you say – it will be the vibration that goes out with those words that touches their soul.

You have to bring 'food' to the masses – this is how you change people by making them aware that they *need*. Most people realise that they are not happy but don't know why. You have to make them aware of that spiritual need. You have to say to them: 'It's not your car that will make you happy ...or your house ...or your holiday ...or your career. It is only the simple knowledge that you are God.'

You are God.

And it is the most *difficult* thing for you to get across to people. They still see God as separate, reachable through religion or

425

prayer and 'someone' to be revered, yes – which is right – but they do not see themselves as a part of that God …a complete and whole part of the Complete and Whole. In order to be completed they need to acknowledge *only that* then everything else is added.

So whatever you do, whatever you say to people, however you motivate them, the one thing that you are doing is the simplest thing – and the *hardest* thing – to say to them: 'You are God. Believe it – *know* it and your destiny is in your hands.'

That is also something very difficult for people to understand and appreciate. They do not want their destiny to be in their own hands – they want their destiny to be in the hands of someone else: 'Take it away! Make it better! Tell me what to do!'

Be humble as we all have to be humble – *we* have to be humble. And before you try to influence any group, spend some time asking that God – the God that you are and the God that is within you – supply you with the words to touch people's spiritual hearts. Know that God is always with you, will never let you down in this work and then you can move forwards.

Do not analyse too much what you have done by speaking words to people because you will *here* have touched a heart, *there* have touched a chord, *here* have set someone on a different path – not necessarily by the words but by the *volition*.

You must be a rock, you must be a beacon, you must be a comforter and you must exude all of these qualities when you are speaking to people and when you are in their presence. And you do not do that *consciously* – you do that by connecting to God. There is a path for you to take; there is a path for *each* of you to take. And all that is required from you is acceptance of that path and the very *selfless* act of making yourself available for this work – so many do not.

So God bless you in what you do. Be encouraged and enlightened by the knowledge that we are always with you, that you cannot escape from God because you *are* God, and that you are *right* in doing what you are doing.

The illusion has to be *shattered* – the future has to be different for this planet.

Band of Light Closed Circle – July, 2009

Tony: Can I ask a question? Everything you have described today about the journey from anguish to joy in the spirit dimensions [*reference to* chapter six of **Your Life After Death**, *which Joseph had just given*] seems like something we are trying to achieve as therapists at the Sanctuary of Healing. It almost felt as if the talk today was describing *exactly* what we are trying to achieve – in a very *small* way, I might add.

There are things that I notice as a therapist which stop people moving towards joy. And one of the questions I would like to ask is: can people in the present physical existence carry forward things from previous existences – like pain, like an abrupt death and like anger – that affect them in the current life to the point where, as therapists, the past life needs addressing as much as the symptom in the present life arising from that past life?

Joseph: Always!

Always the source needs addressing. Always the symptom is a symbol, reflection and indicator of what is *really* wrong because each person that you deal with is a spirit. The experiences that they have gone through in their present life and in their past lives are simply 'energy flows' that have been there to enable them to learn. Many of those energy flows have been put in place by *themselves*, by their soul saying: 'I need to learn about this area of emotion, this area of how to treat people, this area of disease.' But then they become trapped by making 'friends' with the very aspects of life that they are supposed to evolve from travelling through.

So your task, in many cases, is to gently make people aware that they are clinging onto or sticking to their illnesses. Your battle is not so much with the symptoms but with the *belief* in the symptoms. And you must pray (as you do) for enlightenment when you are sitting with people for the right words, because often two or three *key words* will release that spirit from the suffering that *they* are putting *themselves* through.

Remember that, through free will, those souls (the souls that the people you treat *really* are) can choose to associate themselves with disharmony and with 'dis-ease' for whatever reason – either because they have made a friend of it, are used to it and it is something they would feel bereft without – or because there is an *advantage* in the illness. **An advantage in the illness!** Does the illness bring them sympathy? Does the illness bring them attention from loved ones that they are desperately trying to influence? Does the illness allow them to escape from responsibility? Does the illness put them under the spotlight so that they have a moment of attention that they have not had thus far in their lives?

It seems contradictory to earthly beliefs to say that there is 'an advantage' for a spirit in an illness but there is. There is, at soul-level, in that illness teaching the soul something karmically, and liberating that soul *if* the soul listens to the instructions that the illness is relaying to that soul.

There is an advantage in that illness often excuses souls from certain tasks and responsibilities. There is an advantage in that often illness can *control* the people who are involved in that illness: 'This person will not leave me today – I am ill. This person will not ignore me because I am ill. Surely this person cannot upset me any further because I am ill and they must be sympathetic towards me.' This is not criticism – this is simply saying how things are …that illness can be used in so many ways

but at its *best* it is a tool to enable the soul to evolve. And, once the soul has evolved from the lesson the illness is trying to teach it, that illness disappears.

Your task is twofold. Your task is the task of the magician or the illusionist to say: 'I am healing you by bringing into play ... this substance ...this machinery ...this method ...this massage ... this manipulation ... this process,' to give the patient on a *physical* level something that it can anchor on to as a cure being effected physically.

But your *real* task whilst you are appearing to heal the physical is to reach in and heal *the source*. And you do that through the simple task of loving your patients, and by asking God if He feels it appropriate during any particular session to allow you to stimulate the patient by something that you say or by the Love that you are sending out so that they will give you an indication of what is wrong; so that you will feel in your solar plexus: 'Ah, that is what is wrong! That is the key. That is the source.' And then you can talk to them and then you can heal through Light, through Love, through absent healing.

And you will know when you are succeeding because the people will open up to you; they will talk to you and reveal what is wrong even if they don't know what is wrong physically or mentally ...they know what is wrong on a soul-level and will find themselves talking about something that will be your key as to how to treat them.

What you are doing is not in a 'small way' – anything that challenges the darkness of the world with Light is in a 'vast way' and is *essential* treatment and essential work.

Pray always! We pray constantly that God advises us in all our dealings with every soul we meet or have to uplift. And prayer must be your 'washing of the hands' – prayer gets rid of the mental equivalent of physical germs so that you are in a pure state to treat the souls who come to you.

And make no mistake... the souls who come to you are sent to you – either by their own guidance or by intuition via their guides and by God saying, 'Try this!' God is always working to illuminate souls, to elevate souls. It is not His wish that they be in pain; it is not His wish that they be in darkness, but He can only influence them in those moments when they let Him in, when they acknowledge Him, when they acknowledge inspiration.

So, the people that you are dealing with you are *supposed to* deal with and you will come across different ways to deal with them as the future (as you see it) unfolds itself. Always be flexible, always be open to new ideas and always challenge those ideas until they sit correctly with you here [*pointing* to *heart-centre*]. And if everything sits correctly with you here then you are doing God's work and you proceed – no matter how outrageous or odd the instructions that you receive appear to be. Have I given you sufficient information?

Tony: Beautifully, thank you.

Band of Light Closed Circle – August, 2009

Mark: For a human in physical form is it possible to enhance or 'entrain' the soul vibration by means of places, artefacts or things like sacred geometry that enhance vibration in terms of light and sound? Would that help entrain the soul vibration to a higher level through exposure to those artefacts and environments?

Joseph: Your Earth has within it a history that you cannot see. You live life on the surface. Were you to delve into the history of the Earth, you would find that it has been enhanced and degraded dependent on the civilisations that have lived on it and the understanding that they have had.

This civilisation that you find yourself a part of is quite dense and, because of the effects of the Fall, has chosen not to investigate the mechanics of spiritual power in the name of God. But certain civilisations *did* do that, and there are echoes through the layered history of the planet of these points of power, of symbols of power and of means of using power.

But you are not ready for these things; you are not ready to rediscover this knowledge. **Far from it!** As a civilisation, as a whole, you are *barely* ready to accept the spiritual truth of what you are, which is why we are working so hard and in so many different areas to raise your vibrations.

So, my answer to that is that usually, unless you have full spiritual knowledge that links you to one of those civilisations, unless you have access to a soul-memory that gives you a full explanation of the power that you have and how to use it ...the *only* way to enhance your soul is by going *within* and bringing out the truths of *within* to share with those *without*. **This is safe.**

The access of power and the access of the Earth's power – which also exists and can also be channelled (and *was* channelled both correctly and incorrectly by past civilisations various) – is not for you at this time. As a species, as a civilisation, you would be pulled by the Field to corrupt the power that you would find. And remember that that power is not 'power' as you would understand earthly power – political power or material power. It is the power of Creation that is inherent in every molecule that is around you. And that power is there to be tapped and shaped *only* by those who have **the highest spiritual intent at heart**, as was the case before the Fall.

When the Earth 'Christs' itself that power will be a part of the change, will be a part of the transformation. Until that time that power, those artefacts, those places are best left alone – except for a handful of souls, who have enough inherent knowledge to handle that power correctly, and to use it as it was originally intended to be used in line with *God's wishes* for this area and this part of His Creation.

Do you see that?

Mark: Yes, that was most helpful, thank you.

Band of Light Closed Circle – October, 2009

Mark: Joseph, there is a lot of talk on the Earth at this time about DNA, and how it affects consciousness and our ability to evolve. Have you any views on that you can share with us?

Joseph: I have, within this circle of friends and of like-minded spirits, something to say that I will *not* say when making a public demonstration.

Many points of view that are recorded as books, discs or visual presentations are *skewed* and they are skewed for a variety of reasons. They are skewed because it is so difficult to translate non-corporeal concepts into terms that make sense within a physical matrix. So it is dependent on the ability on the communicator on Earth – the medium – and the communicator from the spiritual realms – the guide or the personality on that side. It is dependent on how those two fit together as to what the finished result is.

And you have many books that say **this is happening ...*that* is happening ...the human race was altered.** Well, the human race *was* altered but not by other intelligences *physically*. The human race was altered by *itself*. The human race was altered, at the time of the Fall, by encapsulating itself in the illusion of physical matter.

What I will not say at a demonstration is that a lot of the 'perceived' communication that you have in your hands as books, etc is *wrong*, is tainted and corrupted by the Field, is corrupted by sometimes, unfortunately, the *perceived* need by the writer to make a living, to sensationalise.

As I try *constantly* to get across, the answer to your problems is simple: **the answer to your problems is connecting with God and changing the world through Light.**

Many of the things that you read that seem plausible within the concepts of a physical realm are smokescreens, are the Field creeping up on you, saying: 'Believe in this! How about *this* for a concept? How about *that* for a concept?'

And I also have to tell you that there are certain spirits on my side of life from lower spheres, who have learnt how to communicate effectively with people on the Earth plane and present a point of view – either because they want to deceive or because they want to lift themselves up in the view of people on Earth. So, not all communication is authentic – either in terms of who is delivering it or in terms of what it is saying.

And it matters not what you read about DNA ...about alien communication with Earth ...about goblins ...and pixies ...and fairies! **It matters that you connect to God and attempt to change this world.**

Many of the books that you are presented with are a *deception* and are designed to be a deception by a Field that inputs into the undisciplined medium's mind something of itself in order to hold a portion of its servants enrapt and misguided – because, whilst they are misguided, whilst they are thinking of alien infiltration and DNA and other subjects, they are not concentrating on what matters.

And what matters is very, very simple ...**you are God ...connect to that God ...bring Light out into the world ...change the Field ...you save the world ...you change humanity ...you *Christ* the world.** It is so simple!

It is so simple – the core of my message, and the message that links to all the people who communicate through me, is *that*. That is it!

If I could communicate that to every person around this globe, and they believed it and acted upon it *now* – your world would change *now*. And I would be redundant because, apart from that core message, all I am giving you is information. It allows you to understand how you work, yes, and how the spirit worlds work, yes, **but the core mission is the changing of consciousness through Light.**

That is it!

And I will never put down or decry another book in a demonstration because, in doing so, it appears that I and the group that are working with me are saying, 'Believe us and no one else,' or to the untrained mind, 'Joseph wants to seem *better* than these people.' That is not the case so I will not put those things down, *but in private* I have to say to you that there is much nonsense written. **Nonsense!**

And with any book or presentation that purports to bring to you spiritual knowledge, become quiet with that book and react to that book from your heart and not from your head. The head will say, 'This is interesting. This can involve me in something that I can invest time into.' But what does the heart say? If the heart says that something rings true by all means absorb it. If the heart says, 'Wait – there is a note here that is not being played correctly.' ...*Listen* to that.

Listen to that!

I want at demonstrations so badly to say: 'Throw away your concepts of aliens and altered humanity – you are wasting time!'

You are wasting time. There is only time to go within and change things. Then you will know, as you change things, you will automatically know whether Joseph is speaking nonsense; whether the book that you have, on some view of the past or how you came here or what you are, is speaking nonsense. You will *know* that.

God first! Light first! *Change things first* ...and then all else will present itself as either something that is worthy of you, or something that is not worthy of you and should be discarded. Is that OK?

Mark: It's better than OK, Joseph. Thank you for that expanded perception. You have helped me greatly and many others.

Acknowledgements

Jane – thank you for being my partner, for working longer and harder transcribing *Trance Mission* than anyone could reasonably expect you to, and for having the drive and determination to see this project through.

David – thank you for being there to film the sessions, format the words, design the cover, organise the print and be a constant source of tea and crumpets.

Tony – thank you for providing the venues, for keeping the faith, for championing the cause and for tempting me back into my body with the promise of chocolate cake.

Joan – thank you for being the touchstone for all this and a safe harbour and sage teacher for so many precious years. We miss you.

Maria Luisa – thank you for tirelessly and selflessly translating *the Joseph Communications* into Spanish.

Joseph and the soul group – thank you for taking on this mission and for caring enough about humanity and the planet to head back to this troubled Earth when you could so easily have headed away from it and into bliss.

This book would have been impossible to produce without you.

Michael G. Reccia

Jane's Spirit Contacting Society

At the age of ten, inspired by a recent Halloween party, Jane decided to form a ghost club with some friends from her junior school.

'We called it the *Spirit Contacting Society* which was ironic considering it was actually *forbidden* in the rules to contact the dead. The meetings, held in the cellar of my parent's house, were in fact just a glorified excuse for a group of little girls to play with candles, tell ghost stories, and eat sweets and biscuits.

'Influenced by the formalities of the Women's Institute meetings that my mother took me along to as a child, the activities of our club were meticulously documented in a special little book – complete with rules, minutes, agendas, attendance records and even a mission statement. That book, with its juvenile command of the English language, survives to this day and below are selected excerpts from it.'

SCS
Of course you know that SCS stands for Spirit Contacting Society But we are not going to contact the Dead. It is realy [*really*] just a Society were [*where*] you tell ghost stories and sing ghostly songs.

Its for no good corse [*cause*] or to raise moeny [*money*] for something. Its for our own benefit and injoyment [*enjoyment*].

Most of them will wunt [*want*] to contact the spirits and play weger [*Ouija*] But you don't realize how dangerous this could [*be*]. It could kill one of us or all or us. So is it worth it?

There could be no better place to meat [*meet*] than in the celar [*cellar*] of an old house.

A new member is al-ways welcome and I always hope she enjoys it. We started out with four then five then six. You can always come even if you are not a member to begin with. We have temporary members too like people who dont [*don't*] go to are [*our*] school. By Jane.

RULES
It is very important that you should never ever come to a meating [*meeting*] with a cross on.

If you panic and run upstairs you will be made to stay in the celar [*cellar*] for two minutes without a candle.

You must not be silly or play about with candles.

You have to pay atention [*attention*] to all meatings [*meetings*] and you must be nice to new members.

SCS MEMBERS
Miss Jane Kneen - is the business talker (and gets the celar [*cellar*] ready beforehand).

Miss Janet Dumsky - she writes the number of people down.

Miss Fiona Taylor - rights [*writes*] the meeting down and looks after any moeny [*money*].

Miss Ann Stringer – in charge of refreshments and sweats [*sweets*].

Miss Susan Castledine – in charge of tipe-writing [*type-writing*].

Miss Linda Lovage – in charge of singing and candles.

MINUTES EXCERPTS
3rd May, 1971
'Our meeting began quite unexpectedly when Janet and Jane were having tea and Fiona and Ann came to play. It was Jane's decision that we should have the meeting and we all agreed. First we started in candlelight and we talked over the last meeting. We decided to clean

the cellar. After this we sat down to discuss the meeting and then we began to do the written work. Soon after this the meeting ended.' Writter [*writer*] F. Taylor.

6th May, 1971

'The meeting began at half-past five. Everybody brought refreshments. Ann very kindly supplied us with candles. Fiona brought lots of ghost stories which we all enjoyed. In the first half of the meeting we ate some sweets. In the middle we had some biscuits and some orange pop. Michael [*reference to Jane's brother*] let some bangers off (smelly ones too) [*reference to fireworks*]. This was while we were having refreshments. Shortly after I wrote this we ended our meeting.'

10th May 1971

'Half past five was the time when our meeting began. We discussed what we should do at the next meeting which was to be a party. We practised some actions to "a woman in a grave yard sat" [*reference to a song*]. Fiona, Jane and Ann were to be corpses and Janet was to be the woman sitting in the graveyard. Jane and Ann then brought down the refreshments and then after this we put the things away and went out to play.'

30th October 1971

'Just before dinner we made paper decorations which we decorated the cellar with. At about half past two we began the party. First we did some apple bobbing but kept cheating. Mrs Kneen brought the food which Jane asked her for. We had a glass of orange, two brandy snaps and a chocolate biscuit each. When we had finished eating Mrs Kneen shook a cloth on the end of a mop and we screamed. After this the board over the window fell down and we all screamed and ran away. The lights were then turned on and the turnips were blown out and we sang a ghostly song.'

'Our little ghost club was tremendous fun, and little did I know *then* as a child that in years to come I would be involved in the 'contacting of spirits' for a more serious purpose and that it would play such a major role in my life.

'My mother, somewhat bemused by my continued interest in spiritual matters into adulthood would sometimes blame herself, saying: *You know, I should never have let Jane play in the cellar.*

'Ironically too, Susan, my best friend and founder-member, died tragically in her early forties, and soon after I first got together with Michael, she came through on several occasions with messages for me. What would Susan and I have thought if we had known as little girls that one day we would be doing it *for real* with one of us contacting the other from the spirit realms?'

Revelation

who you are, why you're here

...a book to change your world.

In this first book of the series, Joseph invites you to understand who and what you really are, where you came from, why you are here and the miraculous things you are capable of, revealing the amazing potential of the human spirit and presenting a plan to change the future of this planet before it's too late.

Intelligent, thought-provoking, non-religious. In direct, concise language, **Revelation** will revolutionise your views about life and the nature of reality, empowering you through a new awareness of the active part you play in creation and inspiring you to look at your world in a whole new light.

'I've read every metaphysical book I could get my hands on for years but there is information in this book I've not come across anywhere before. I would wholeheartedly recommend this series to anyone seeking answers and the inspiration to finding wisdom within.' *jmj4 (Amazon).*

'Whatever your religion Revelation will inspire and help you to understand why we are here on this planet and make you think about the way you are living your life.' *Joy (Amazon).*

'The most direct and compelling book on spirituality I have ever read.' *G. R. Munro-Hall (Amazon).*

ISBN: 978-1-906625-07-8

Available from good bookshops, Amazon or direct from thejosephcommunications.us

Also available as an e-Book and audiobook.

Illumination

change yourself, change the world

...A powerful manual for personal and global transformation.

Time is running out; Earth is heading for cataclysm! **Illumination** reveals how we can literally save this world ...before it's too late.

We need to change and accept personal responsibility now – or Joseph warns there are only three generations left. The Field is so polluted by mankind's negative energy that the planet cannot sustain itself much longer unless radical changes are made to the way we think.

Illumination provides all the 'tools' needed to achieve personal and global enlightenment, empowering readers to direct Light and transmute negativity into harmony, joy, love, peace and spiritual progression.

There is great urgency to Joseph's words – we do not have an infinite number of tomorrows in which to put things right.

'Read the book, adopt its practices, discover a new life of spiritual harmony and lasting fulfilment.' *Jan Quigley.*

'A masterpiece of spiritual work! What is very clever is the way Joseph builds up his case throughout this book with possibilities to test his meditations as you go – this is not dry theory! I will certainly continue the daily Light-work which I now regard as essential.' *Tony Cross.*

'If you wish to bring peace, joy and abundance to yourself and those you love this book gives you the means.' *Mr. C. Fraser-Malcolm (Amazon).*

ISBN: 978-1-906625-09-2

Available from good bookshops, Amazon or direct from thejosephcommunications.us

Also available as an e-Book and audiobook.

Your Life After Death

...your final destination is anything but final!

Countless opportunities and wonders await beyond physical death.

In **Your Life After Death** Joseph delivers arguably the most comprehensive account ever written of what lies ahead when you leave this world behind.

An essential source of comfort and inspiration, **Your Life After Death** is the definitive guide to the afterlife...

... read it and you'll never look at the next life, or, indeed, this one, in quite the same way again.

'Packed with very important information, which should have been made available many, many years ago.' *David Feuerstein.*

'The book is outstanding and one of immense value to humanity, particularly in contrast to the mumbo-jumbo we are exposed to in various religions and philosophies.' *Scott Rabalais.*

'Over the years I have read many books on this subject but none have been more informative and in-depth.' *Peggy Sivyer.*

'I have never sat up nearly all night and read a book from cover to cover in one go before and it has had a major impact on me.' *Valerie Ann Riddell.*

ISBN: 978-1-906625-03-0

Available from good bookshops, Amazon or direct from thejosephcommunications.us

Also available as an e-Book and audiobook.

the Fall___

you were there,
it's why you're here

...aeons ago everything changed – AND YOU WERE THERE!

You have forgotten the cataclysm that created today's dysfunctional societies and wounded planet...

In **the Fall**, Joseph reactivates that astonishing inner knowledge of your spiritual origins.

By the last page, many, if not *all*, of those elusive answers regarding existence and the great mysteries will be elusive no longer.

From the Big Bang to your role in creation... if you seek meaning to life in general, and your life in particular, you *absolutely, definitely* should read **the Fall**.

...Your views of spirituality, science, and reality are about to change forever.

'If I had to be on a desert island with only one book, this would be it.' *James D'Angelo.*

'The Fall is the most important spiritual book ever written.' *Jean Whittle.*

'I have been on this journey for more than 40 years and this book just joins all the dots for me. It is astonishing. It is of vital importance, please read it.' *Katydr (Amazon).*

'Here are the answers to life's impossible contradictions, and what we can do for ourselves and others – brilliant!' *Jan (Amazon).*

'One of the most powerful and influential books in my entire life, completely altering my world view.' *Peter De Ruyter.*

ISBN: 978-1-906625-05-4

Available from good bookshops, Amazon or direct from thejosephcommunications.us
Also available as an e-Book and audiobook.

From Here to Infinity

...In his sixth book Joseph clarifies, demystifies and redefines earthly concepts we take for granted and find ourselves immersed in, including: Time, Space, Energy, Perception, Memory and Infinity.

He also offers further insights into the nature of the Divine and reveals advanced ways of transforming and elevating our inner and outer worlds and infusing our lives and this planet with the highest expression of Light.

This 288-page volume is set to expand your ability to live in and give out the Light, empowering you to make a real difference by – literally – illuminating yourself, those around you, and the physical landscape you are a part of.

'Joseph REALLY gets into the nuts and bolts of what's NEEDED for us Warriors of the Light! I'm so humbled by this information.' *Jorge Castaneda.*

'I don't mind admitting the last chapter moved me to tears. This book has made me more determined than ever to meditate daily to send Light out to the world.' *Tracy Dewick.*

'I wish it were required reading in every school, library and institution, so important is the message.' *Jeannie Judd.*

ISBN: 978-1-906625-08-5

Available from good bookshops, Amazon or direct from thejosephcommunications.us
Also available as an e-Book and audiobook.

Many Voices, One Mission

Group Soul wisdom from the Joseph perspective

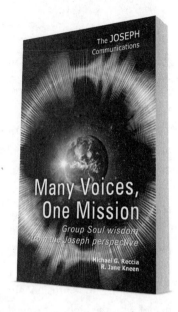

The new Joseph Communications title Many Voices, One Mission, giving voice to key members of Joseph's soul group through powerful lectures delivered over many years to medium Michael G. Reccia and life partner Jane, is now available.

Themed sections Life's Journey, Aspects of the Afterlife, The Sacred Earth, Spiritual Science, Connections, Co-Creation and Health and Healing feature wisdom from Joseph's co-workers, and transcripts of Michael's first two public trance demonstrations are also included, plus fascinating insights into how Michael and Jane's lives have been affected by regular interaction with spirit messengers.

ISBN: 978-1-906625-15-3

Available from good bookshops, Amazon or direct from thejosephcommunications.us

Also available as an e-Book.